D1175668

Madeleine Henrey, though born in
Montmartre, came to London as a
young girl, married an English
journalist and, for a time, worked on a
London evening paper.

But autobiography, the painstaking
diagnosis of every phase of her life, was
to prove her constant concern.
'Author, story, language are
absolutely one,' wrote a critic. 'We
expect a book and find a human being.'

THE GOLDEN VISIT

THE GOLDEN VISIT

by

Mrs Robert Henrey

J.M. DENT & SONS LTD

LONDON   TORONTO   MELBOURNE

WILLIAM WOODS COLLEGE LIBRARY

First published 1979

© Mrs Robert Henrey 1979

All rights reserved. No part of this publication may be
reproduced, stored in a retrieval system, or transmitted,
in any form or by any means, electronic, mechanical,
photocopying, recording or otherwise, without the
prior permission of J.M. Dent & Sons Ltd.

Printed in Great Britain by Biddles Ltd, Guildford, Surrey
and bound at The Aldine Press, Letchworth, Herts.
for
J.M. DENT & SONS LTD
Aldine House, Welbeck Street, London

BRITISH LIBRARY CATALOGUING IN PUBLICATION DATA

Henrey, *Mrs* Robert
 The golden visit.
 1. Normandy – Social life and customs
 I. Title
 944'.2'0830924   DC611.N851

 ISBN 0-460-04433-8

PR
6015
E46
Z517

FROM THE AUTHORESS TO THE READER

This is the story of the farm in Normandy in 1977–8, forty years after I bought it, and of myself, *The Little Madeleine*, by then a grandmother, who received a visit lasting many golden months from my eight-year-old grand-daughter, Dominique.

This volume forms part of my autobiographical sequence and is written with the same scrupulous attention to accuracy as were *The Little Madeleine* and the subsequent books in my life story.

65040

MADELEINE HENREY

For Dominique
the little girl of the Golden Visit

Give me, great God! said I, a little farm,
In summer shady, and in winter warm.

Lady Mary Wortley Montagu. 1718.

1

THIS SEPTEMBER the grass in the orchard was once more fresh and tender with occasional fallen cider apples half hidden in it. The cows, some with their young, would towards midday slowly fold their long legs under them and sink down contentedly round the gnarled trunk of a very old pear tree, fairylike and half hollow, which faced the sixteenth-century house and its flower garden. The lavender was still pungent and heavy with bees.

In appearance everything was peaceful, just as it had always been, just as it was when war was declared in 1939. Only the murmur of occasional traffic, rather distant, and just now and again the whirr of a helicopter manned by police patrolling the coastline, on the look-out for foolhardy bathers or inexperienced yachtsmen on weekends from the cities. A warm sun picked out in its rays the delicate Louis XIII château perched on a hill above sloping woods and pasture land as yet unspoilt. The sky was blue, the breeze gentle and at the bottom of the orchard trickled the water where the cattle drank, water running lazily over boulders and fallen tree trunks.

The house with its Caen stone and half-timbering hidden in a hollow in the middle of the orchard was not visible from the lane to which it was connected by an ancient winding cart rut in the middle of which grew thick grass. This rut climbed so steeply up to the lane that if one negotiated it in a car one had either to drive fast or very slowly in low gear.

The day was Sunday. As I climbed thoughtfully towards the gate, nature made it clear to me that at a pinch one could live without money — mushrooms hiding in the long grass, apple trees laden with oncoming fruit, hedges (though badly tended) full of hazel nuts and blackberries, and the dozen or more walnut trees (the last trees to break into bud each spring) now full of oily walnuts ready to be stolen by passers-by.

Ahead of me on the white track walked Tiggy, a long-legged American street cat which my son, before going to Singapore, brought me over by air from New York, leaving me to look after all the complications it brought into a house where there were already four cats of native extraction. Tiggy, after six years in Normandy, still answered only to English, and had the peculiarity of accompanying me on my walks to distant hay-fields and orchards, leading the way, purring with content, inspecting trees and grass, hedge and trickling stream with a knowledge gained by repeated nocturnal wanderings. One felt that nothing would have induced her to return to Greenwich Village.

It was now forty years earlier that as a young married woman, at Whitsun in 1938, I had walked along this lane in the hope of buying a small farm. The elms and wild cherry trees were so numerous and stately on either side that their topmost branches met overhead making a leafy roof through which sunshine filtered — for which reason I had dubbed it Cathedral Lane. The carefully trimmed hedges, some five hundred years old, were in those days garlanded at appropriate times with honeysuckle and wild rose. Amongst the damp moss grew wild strawberries which in Paris restaurants were served with fresh cream. No trippers then sauntered along these lanes, against whose moss-covered sides a drunken farmhand in the hay season would sleep off libations under a hot sun.

Did it seem such a very long time ago? Here at the end of the lane was a red brick farmhouse, the first when one had walked up from the village. A good, solid, square Victorian house with stables, outhouses and a cobbled courtyard. In this house, when I first knew it, lived the Poulins. M. Poulin, the father, must have died about a year earlier. I was only to know him by reputation. The farm was then run by his three daughters Madeleine, Nenette and Louise, and two sons, Peter and Ernest. Comprising some fifty acres, it was in many ways a model for the efficiency with which it was run and for the cleanliness of the buildings. Before the Poulins the estate had been farmed by a man called Anger who one day was found hanging from a beam

10

in his cider press. His widow, who inherited nearly a hundred acres, later moved to her own property some three miles away which she kept until her death, running the place herself, a strong-willed woman, taking her produce down to the village every day in her buggy.

Madeleine, the oldest of the three Poulin girls, married Montague, her father's farmhand, and had a baby called Michael. Nenette, in turn, married Riquet Roginsky whose parents owned a shop in the village. Shortly after the birth of my own baby on the eve of the Second World War, as soon as I was strong enough to go out, I paid a promised visit to these neighbours. I found little Michael Montague in his cot in a corner of the big cool kitchen, where splendid brass polished pans hung from the wall. Madeleine Montague was delivering the milk in her covered cart and I was welcomed by a brunette I had never seen before. She was Yvonne, wife of Ernest, the younger of the two Poulin boys. The marriage had taken place in May. Ernest was still doing his military service and was not due for release until October so that his young wife had seen practically nothing of him since the wedding. She came from a neighbouring village called Formentin where her parents, M. and Mme Castel, owned a small inn and six acres of land on which they kept a few cows and some chickens.

The Poulins did not own the farmhouse or their orchards and hayfields. These belonged to a country notary called Maître Bompain. Nevertheless at the death of farmer Poulin there was some division of livestock and farm implements that was to result in a realignment of interests. Nenette Roginsky and her young husband bought a farm of their own, a low Norman house, all bathed in sunshine as I first saw it with green shutters and smart white doors. The windows had bright chintz curtains with red squares and they were gathered with a bow in the centre. Meanwhile at the Poulin's red brick house Yvonne, after minding Madeleine Montague's baby all day, announced to her sister-in-law that she herself was expecting a baby. This news produced a reaction that Yvonne could not have guessed. The Montagues decided to take a farm of their own. This left Yvonne, who had been without news of her soldier husband for thirty-two days, almost alone on a large farm with insufficient cattle to stock it, and not enough people to work it. Her parents, M. and Mme Castel, came to her help. M. Castel put his little café at Formentin up for sale and eventually he and his wife moved in to the brick house having negotiated a new lease for the farm from Maître Bompain.

But now as I stood in the lane, the tragedy of the German Occupation and the long story of Ernest, Yvonne and the Castels had dimmed into half forgotten history. They also in turn had sold their stock and disappeared. A young couple from the Eure took their place. Levannier was the man's name, bronzed, good looking and modern in his farming ways, proud of his pretty young wife whom he would haul up beside him on his brand new tractor. After fifteen years their lease came to an end and they also left to join their parents in the Eure.

So now gone were the Angers, gone were the Poulins, gone the Levanniers so that the square red brick house was deserted, the window shutters torn, several wrenched from their hinges and flapping in the breeze. Slates had fallen from the roof of the stables. The outhouses were deserted. The rose garden was overgrown with weeds. The bell that for so many years called workers in from the fields for evening soup had been removed. The courtyard gates were padlocked and rusty. The low stone wall was quite broken down in places where it had been hit by a reversing milk-truck and not mended, but everywhere covered with convolvulus. The farm had become a neglected ruin.

I had vaguely thought of going as far as some of our more distant hayfields but having passed my seventieth birthday these routine inspections on foot often tired me and I ended by sitting on a mound at the foot of a holly tree from which I had a very good view of an orchard of perhaps eight or nine acres which I had for long coveted because it belonged to the Bompains and separated my home field from all the rest of my farmland. The grass was lush, the cider apple trees numerous and the same little stream that lapped lazily over boulders at the bottom of my home field watered the far end of it dancing

12

merrily between oak and ash. When one loves the countryside one is apt to covet one's neighbour's most desirable plots, reflecting like a miser how nice it would be to add this piece or that to what one already owns. At one time it was possible without being very rich to satisfy just now and again this legitimate desire. There were dozens of small farms in this part of Normandy, and if one waited long enough, and was kept well informed by the village notary, there ws a reasonable chance for the orchard one wanted to come on the market. But that was long, long ago, before the age of the speculator when orchards were bought to bring forth fruit, and grass to feed cattle.

When this particular orchard was part of the Poulin farm, Ernest had tended and grafted the apple trees with love and almost a touch of sorcery. But then his two great interests were cider and laying traps for rabbits and hares in the hedges. The cider apple trees were of carefully chosen varieties so that the fruit matured at different periods — some early, some in November, some later. Mixed in correct proportions the result was nectar to the knowledgeable peasant.

Seated on my tuft of grass I now saw two women emerge from a bend in the lane and, as they talked, they came slowly towards me. Was I growing fanciful with age or was I seeing a ghost from the past?

The smaller of the two women, whose dark hair was flecked with grey, whose sharp eyes looked up with swift recognition into mine, could only be the once youthful Yvonne Poulin whom Ernest had brought from Formentin as his bride during those fateful months before the German Occupation, and who with the help of her parents, the Castels, had for so long been mistress of the red brick house.

I recalled her in the radiance of her youth, I recalled her a certain evening in April, before I fled with my own baby back to England, lying on a massive peasant bed of shining walnut which stood high because of the number of downy mattresses piled upon it. Mme Castel, her mother, a short, trim woman, stood motionless beside her daughter, Yvonne's head esconced in the bend of her arm. Yvonne wore a nightgown embroidered

13

in red wool which made her look like a young lady in a boarding school. 'Oh, mother,' moaned Yvonne. 'Don't it hurt?' 'Offer your suffering to the Virgin,' said Mme Castel. An hour later the doctor, hurriedly summoned, using me as an assistant in a Picaresque drama, delivered the tiny heir to the Poulin dynasty, saying: 'Hi! Dress that for me, will you?' Thus her son, André was born.

'Admiring the countryside, Mme Henrey?' came the now well-remembered voice full of laughter.

'I was not sure. I could hardly believe it!' I cried.

Yes, her dark hair was the same and yet streaked with grey. She looked smaller and plumper but her eyes still had the old gaiety. I sprang up and embraced her. At the age I had reached it was good to meet again somebody who had played such an important role in one's life. Ernest Poulin had brought her to the red brick house in his buggy after the wedding at Formentin.

We did not quite know what to say to each other. She had the advantage of surprise over me. She had doubtless expected to see me whereas for me she had materialized out of a dream. Both of us now turned our gaze upon the former Poulin orchard.

'What a change!' she said softly. 'What a change has come over what was once Ernest's favourite orchard! See how the cattle having cropped down the sweet grass have left tall thistles and stinging nettles in seed. Some of those weeds would reach up to my shoulder. Has nobody had time to clean up the orchard after the cattle left? With the tractor — or even by a man with a scythe? As for the cider apple trees some are dead, others are garlanded with mistletoe. In my time it was against the law to allow mistletoe to grow unchecked.'

'In December it goes to England for Christmas decorations,' I said. 'Young men kiss the girls under it.'

'They would never think of doing that here,' said Yvonne. 'Times have changed since the Druids.'

'As for cutting down the thistles and the nettles,' I objected. 'One would have to know whose work that ought to be. With

14

the land momentarily without a farmer, and this rumour that Mme. Bompain, who since her husband's death is presumably the owner, intends to take advantage of the Levanniers' departure to sell as much of her land as she can to speculators.'

'Nevertheless,' said Yvonne nostalgically, 'It was in this very orchard that I learnt to milk my first cow — I who had been brought up as a young lady, the daughter of a prosperous innkeeper in Formentin! It is a miracle, Mme Henrey, what love can do to a girl! I should add, however, that milking cows and making cider was Ernest's business more than mine. I was always for being mistress in my home.'

'Young women won't stay on farms any longer,' I declared, quoting from those experts on television who were continually urging the rural populations to migrate into the towns and cities where they could earn a union wage and be sure of a month's holiday every year. 'Helping a young husband on a farm is hard work for a girl. She loses her beauty.'

'At eighteen I knew nothing,' said Yvonne. 'But we women are adaptable creatures. I thought nothing of washing the linen summer like winter in the stream, rinsing the sheets in the clear water as it ran over the little stones and broken boughs. We would pack it wet into a wheelbarrow and trundle it back to the farm.'

'And hang it up in the sun to dry,' I added to this evocation of the pre-washing machine age. Personally I had no regrets. My mother and I half killed ourselves washing linen.

'Of course,' agreed Yvonne, 'but first love transforms a girl, and I was in love. Do you remember crossing your orchard every evening with your milk can at milking time. Helen and I would be sitting on our three legged stools milking the cows in this very field, and you would lean over the hedge that divided your property from ours — and we would all laugh together?'

Yes, indeed, I remembered Helen, a girl from Yvonne's village of Formentin with whom she had been at school. A lovely girl with the bearing of a princess and pink cheeks like the apples in the orchard. They had celebrated their First Communion together and Helen had followed Yvonne as a sort of companion-maid when she came here after her marriage.

Then the war came and Helen disappeared.

'I knew nothing when I first came here,' said Yvonne. 'But soon I found myself at the head of a big farm, all the men away. But how gay we were before the Occupation, Mme Henrey. You with your baby and I with mine. I can still hear our laughter as if the world had given us everything it had to offer, and the sun would never stop shining. And that was only a few weeks before the German tanks began rolling across the countryside, and all hell broke loose.'

Her voice trembled slightly. She said:

'But we were young and I had my mother to guide me. As you had yours.'

'I no longer have her,' I said. 'What happened to Mme Castel?'

'Mme Castel,' said Yvonne, 'is about to celebrate her ninety-fifth birthday. She complains of a weak heart but her mind is as active as ever. I should not really have come to revisit my past. One should let one's memories sleep, says my mother. Fifteen years have gone by since I left the red brick house but it seems an age. Just now when I saw the shutters of my dairy torn from their hinges and creaking in the wind, and weeds all over the garden, I nearly wept. Is it true what they say — that the bulldozers will be coming before long to pull it all down? And what will happen to the lily pond where the ducks used to swim and the little half-timbered structure beside it, no larger than a doll's house, into which they would waddle in the heat of the day?'

'Did you expect to find me?' I asked. 'Did you somehow hope to see me walking towards you along this lane?'

'I suppose I did,' she conceded. 'We have lived our lives in reverse. You left the city to live in the country. I have left the country to make a living in the town. I have exchanged a red brick house with servants and livestock for a small apartment in a modern city block. My world is of petrol fumes and cement. Instead of picking my vegetables in the kitchen garden and milking the cows, I sell canned milk and frozen peas in a supermarket. I no longer wash my linen in the limpid waters of a stream. I own the newest, most expensive washing machine.

16

What sometimes surprises me is the ease with which one can completely reverse one's way of life.'

'What happened to Ernest?'

'As soon as the children were grown up, I divorced him and married again. I am happy. I have a car of my own.'

I pictured her at the wheel of one of those small French cars threading her way through traffic, taking home the tinned meat and frozen vegetables she doubtless bought at her supermarket. But this fantasy melted into the remembered enchantment of sitting beside her in her buggy, the hard seat very high, the spirited horse trotting ahead, Yvonne expertly tickling his mane with the long whip of lacquered, shiny rosewood. How exciting it was to drive with the warm wind rushing through one's hair at this elevation, so highly perched that one could look over the top of the hedges at what was happening in other people's orchards! I recalled picturesque drives to market but also an occasion when we had gone together in her buggy, her *carriole* as it was called, to the funeral of a young woman who had died in childbirth, a girl we were all fond of who had married the most eligible young man in the village. She was far too young and pretty to die and we were all broken-hearted. The coffin was lowered into the ground, the family in black dispersed, we gave a last pitying handshake to the red-eyed husband, and then up into the buggy and away down the road — back into life, back into the heady joys of the countryside on a sunlit day. How gay we were, Yvonne and I.

We started walking down the lane, and it was at this moment that I noticed that she wore those tight fitting leather boots that for some absurd reason townswomen wore in crowded streets or in centrally heated buildings. Even the girl announcers on television wore them in the studios. Yes, she had really become a supermarket townswoman.

'I left my husband at the beginning of the lane,' she said. 'I did not want him to come with me. I wanted to be alone while I was looking at that orchard. It gave us the best apples on the farm. Ernest loved every tree, and it took the entire family hours kneeling on the damp grass to pick up the apples in late

17

autumn. They nearly all went to the cider firms in England.'

Now we were in sight of the white gates leading into my home orchard. White painted oak gates could no longer be kept fresh and clean. The paint peeled off and the heavy rains rotted the wood. I was rather ashamed of mine but to replace the gates on the estate would have cost as much as to build a small house and, like everybody else, I kept on putting off the evil day.

'Were our successors at the red brick house happy here?' asked Yvonne, perhaps with a tinge of jealousy.

'Differently. Their happiness was of a more modern kind. Ernest brought you here in a buggy, a white ribbon tied to the top of his whip. Levannier came with his bride in a sleek new car. You and your husband kept horses and a farmhand to look after them. . .'

'. . . two farmhands,' she corrected. 'Emile whose birthday fell on the same day as your mother's, and Pierre. Old Pierre we used to call him, to differentiate him from my brother in law. They not only looked after the horses. They harnessed them to the farmcarts and to the buggy. I could not have done that myself.' She laughed. 'My arms are too short!'

'I remember how on hot days after binding the newly cut hay Emile would disappear with a bottle and curl himself up under an oak tree,' I said. 'What a lot of cider they could drink!'

'I don't think either of them ever slept in a bed,' said Yvonne. 'They were happier sleeping on straw in a hayloft. We paid them very little money but they ate and drank their fill and they lived closer to nature than anybody does today. There was so much to do but such a lot of time to do it in, passing over the orchards with a scythe after the cattle had been there, making bundles of faggots and piles of logs. The art of faggot-making had already quite died out when we left the farm. And then there were the gates to keep in order and the hedges to trim but neither Emile nor Old Pierre ever hurried. They delighted in taking their time.'

'I wonder what happened to them?' I mused.

'They and all their like have disappeared,' she said. 'Did the Levanniers have any help?'

18

'None,' I said. 'They claimed that it would have been uneconomic — what with union wages and social security. Of course, they were mechanized. They also had a positive mania for insecticides and chemical manures. They couldn't resist trying out every new invention advertised by the chemical firms.'

'Did she make a pretty bride?' asked Yvonne nostalgically.

'Yes, indeed,' I said. 'He used to arrive on top of his tractor and as soon as he saw her he would haul her up beside him and then with an arm round her slim waist, off they would go! They were the new generation, talking like slick city folk, none of those picturesque Norman words or expressions that dated from peasant times. And, of course, they thought they knew better. In order to increase the acreage for grazing they cut down hedges that had stood there for over five hundred years, perhaps even from the time of William the Conqueror. The hedges with the hazel, the honeysuckle, the wild rose and the forest trees. And what took the place of the hedge? Brambles and stinging nettles. At least there would have been black-berries to gather in September — but no, they came along with chemicals to kill the blackberry bushes which eventually withered, leaving an unsightly graveyard of prickly dead branches that no longer even gave forth their fruit.'

'They should have made them tidy,' said Yvonne.

'They were too busy doing something else,' I said. 'The government was just then offering farmers the equivalent of one pound for every cider apple tree they cut down. The Levanniers cut down hundreds of your husband's most beautiful trees. Later the same government offered them money to replant their orchards but it was too late. The farmers lacked the necessary labour and the price of cider apples had slumped. It would not have been economic.'

'Governments invariably do the wrong thing,' said Yvonne. 'Originally the idea was to diminish drunkenness. The men drank deeply in my day.'

'Perhaps, but the cider apple tree is disappearing from the Norman countryside just as, because of insemination, the Norman cow, the sort one sees on the coloured boxes of

Camembert cheese, has been replaced by all sorts of breeds. You have only to look at my own cows.'

'Yes,' agreed Yvonne. 'I noticed.'

'In spite of all this the red brick house was to know the laughter of little children again,' I said. 'but it was no longer the fashion for a woman to have her baby at home as you had yours and I had mine. Mme Levannier went to a smart clinic in Deauville to have first her daughter Pascaline, then her son, Bruno. After you left we continued to take our milk from them. Occasionally one of the Levannier children would bring it as far as the hedge by my kitchen garden. By then the Levanniers brought in their cows every evening and did their milking by electricity. I remember Bruno, when telling me one evening about the coming wedding of an aunt, exclaimed in a confidential whisper: "Yes, she's getting married but she's not yet in the family way!"'

'And to think that people consider it necessary to teach sex to children in the schools!' said Yvonne.

'The Levannier children are charming,' I said, 'The boy intelligent, the girl already slim and elegant but there is little to distinguish them from young people brought up in the cities. Their parents are not the sort of people to dream about the beauties of the countryside, to listen to the cooing of a dove or to admire a sunset. They were brought up with a knowledge of the law, the legal rights of farmers, the maximum yield to be got out of an acre of land, the best way to kill poppies and cornflowers in a cornfield, or daisies in a hayfield, and the very latest in pesticides and chemical manures. The land they farm is merely a vehicle to allow them to make as much money as possible in the shortest time. The countryside is no longer a treasure to be tended lovingly and carefully passed on.'

I checked myself. The Levanniers were excellent farmers. The trouble about modern farming techniques was that they were invariably deadly to something. We wept to see clouds of chemicals sprayed from a tractor killing not only the weed it was meant to kill but also the blossoms, the butterflies and the bees over the tops of the hedges and far away. These were the first signs of the disintegration of the sweet scented meadow.

Under the walnut trees at the top of my home orchard stood my husband and two strange men. What were they talking about? I supposed that the two strangers, attracted by the walnuts falling down from the trees into the damp long grass, had passed through the white gates to fill their pockets with the plunder. The trees when young had been planted far too near the lane. They were now so tall and stately that the walnuts were not only a temptation to grown-ups tolerably certain they would never be seen but also to youths in the lane armed with sticks. The walnut trees had been meant to replace the age-old elms that we had known here forty years ago. One of these beside the entrance gate had probably stood there for some two hundred years. This one was cut down during the German occupation. The others followed on the entirely erroneous belief that they had elm disease. None of them had. Too late when felled their great trunks were found to be intact. They were carted off to the saw mills for a pittance. Nobody worried about leaving the lane without shade. Like those miniature half-timbered sixteenth-century buildings so often to be found in the middle of hayfields and orchards – when they fell, they fell. Nobody troubled to replace them. The clay turned to dust and was carried away by the wind. The hand-sawn oak rafters were burnt.

'My husband must have found those two men stealing his walnuts,' I said. 'He gets furious. Though heaven knows why. We don't even trouble to pick them up. But we are always afraid that strangers will damage the trees.'

'Those are not two strange men!' exclaimed Yvonne. 'One of them is my new husband. The other belongs to my friend who is from Lisieux. We left the men here before we came along the lane.'

'But why?' I asked.

'I have told you already,' she said. 'I wanted to be alone.'

My own husband was puzzled. He had not yet understood. 'Look who is here!' I called out.

'Yvonne Poulin!' he cried in sudden recognition. 'To think that I was on the point of scolding these two gentlemen for trespassing. How could I have guessed? Won't you all come down to the house?'

21

'No,' said Yvonne gently. 'I have seen what I wanted to see. Now we must go back to town.'

2

WALKING SLOWLY BACK to the house on the grass between the cart ruts, I felt miserable. It seemed only a few years ago that everything was serene, the countryside almost unchanged in four hundred years. Was this sudden disintegration typical of what was happening all over the world?

The village we had come upon on that Whitsun bank holiday before the war was still unspoilt. Some five hundred inhabitants and a few white villas overlooking the sea between Deauville and Cabourg – miles of golden sands in which one found strange coloured seashells, clear water in which shrimps and small fish darted when one went in to paddle, hardly anybody in sight to destroy the illusion of a deserted beach.

Small farms on the plateau above the village had farmhouses and cider presses almost all dating from the sixteenth century, more picturesque than comfortable, with mud floors or ancient tiles and stone fireplaces. Few had running water and none electricity. The women washed their linen in the streams. Trees were hewn down with the axe or with hand saws. Every farm had its horse and buggy. Milking was done by hand, the churns being taken to whatever orchard the cows happened to be in, on the back of a donkey. The farmer and his wife, seated on three-legged stools, would milk their cows, softly talking to them, calling them by name.

These were all dairy farms where the cows grazed in small orchards, seldom more than eight or nine acres in size, divided one from the other by century-old hedges in which grew oak, elm, ash, wild cherry and a great deal of hazel, so valuable not only for the nuts in autumn but for its excellent wood. These hedges were a sanctuary for birds, rabbits, hares – and a joy in September when the blackberries were ripe. Sometimes a wild boar would come down from St Gatien.

The secret of having cows in a cider orchard is not to have too many. Even so, when the apples start to form, cows will stretch up their necks and tear at the branches which is both damaging to the tree and a danger to the animals who, greedily eating too much fruit, can choke. The farmers of those days accordingly put chains on their cows which kept their heads down. In this manner the animals grazed but without harming the trees. In summer they would congregate under the oak and the wild cherry for shade. Every farmer kept a kitchen garden in which he grew his soft fruit and vegetables, and as in many Scottish gardens, flowers bordered the vegetables.

Most of the farmers came from adjacent villages inland. The farms were family affairs, not always owned by those who farmed them. Land was jealously guarded but was apt to come on the market at the death of its possessor because of the Napoleonic law which called for a division of the property in equal parts between the widow and the children. One had to bide one's time but a friendly notary would often advise one by letter when a piece one coveted came on the market. The price would be reasonable. People liked to own land but they did not gamble with it. They tended to collect it as they collected sovereigns and the Louis d'or hidden away in an old stocking – because it made them feel good to have a bit of land and a bit of gold. They were still, to a great extent, of that breed known as 'peasants' because of their language which was distinctively Norman, full of words and expressions that dated from the time of the French kings and which were no longer in use in towns or cities or in other parts of France – though to be discovered amongst French Canadians in rural Quebec, who in Montcalm's time brought that way of talking with them when they crossed the seas to settle on the new continent.

The Norman peasant, when I came here first, was as Guy de Maupassant described him in a previous century – suspicious, crafty, never committing himself, a lover of devious ways and ghostly secrets, a firm believer in sorcery and an imbiber and worshipper of his own brew of cider and applejack. That he was seldom sober and that when on the eve of tragedy he was apt to

24

hang himself from a rafter in his cider press was undeniable. But as a grafter of apple trees, as a woodcutter, as a fashioner of faggots and six-foot tall walls of logs, as an artist with the scythe and as a lover of woods and pasturage and country lore he was a joy to watch and to emulate. That his cunning with his hands and that his very language should have so totally disappeared – nay, more than that, his very breed, between the time of my having my baby and the present time is almost unbelievable. It is as if an entire race had been wiped off the face of the earth. There is no longer an actor on television who knows how a character from Guy de Maupassant or Lucie Delarue-Mardrus should speak.

At what stage then did things begin to change? When did we fail to see the warning signal?

Did it start during my absence in London during the German Occupation? Assuredly not. In Normandy, at least before the Allied Landings, the Occupation had the effect for farmers of putting the hands of the clock back. There was no petrol, no possibility of change. The horse, however old and decrepit, replaced the tractor – or perhaps one should say, continued to be the chief motive force on the farm. Because of the smallness of the orchards and the unevenness of the ground there were hardly any tractors in this part of Normandy before the war. The Occupation merely prolonged the ancient way of life.

At this time mine was one of about six farms on the plateau – all more or less of the same size, very small in comparison to farms elsewhere but considered quite large in the Pays d'Auge where land, like the Niagara fruit belt in Ontario, was considered to be of special goodness.

You will remember that Mme Anger, at the death of her husband, had left the red brick house to go on a farm of her own. She developed into a stately matriarch and lived in a large, rather ghostly farmhouse bordering my land on the west. She owned her sixty-odd acres, was rumoured to be wealthy and was somewhat of a recluse though driving down to market twice a week in her buggy to sell her produce – especially her cream and butter. She once accused my husband of trespassing on her land and two of her henchmen marched him back to her farmhouse before he had time to explain who he was and what he was doing. She apologized, sitting very upright in her chair like Queen Victoria, dressed in black, authoritative and regal in a huge, half-empty room without a fire. The trouble had arisen because we owned a wood (with a river running through it) to which we only had access by crossing a narrow tongue of her domain.

To the south of our land was the original Déliquaire farm where the crafty old man lived with his wife, Madeleine, and their two sons, Roger and Jacques. We were neighbours with only a stream to cross between us and I loved him for his crooked scheming and picturesque parlance. For a short time after the war I leased my orchards to him.

To the north of our land between ourselves and the road to Caen, the mayor, Toto Duprez, lived like a gentleman farmer with a modern house, a kitchen garden and some fine orchards managed by a bailiff. His farm was admirably run and his first wife had built upon his land a small model farmhouse with outhouses, stables and a cider press. This was called Berlequet. It had a kitchen garden and a very picturesque old bakery which had been turned into a wash-house.

To the east of our land was the Poulin farm where at that time Yvonne reigned under the loving guidance of her mother, Mme Castel, and her husband Ernest just back from a prison camp in Germany. Beyond them, on the way down to the village and the sea, two wealthy farms lay on either side of the most picturesque country lane I have ever seen, a bower of sweet scented foliage and tall forest trees up which squirrels ran in summer and which in winter formed on occasion weird patterns of snow and ice of unbelievable beauty. This, the continuation of our own lane, had the same peculiarity of making a high roof over one's head so that one had the impression of walking through the nave of some celestial church. It was the main portion of what we called Cathedral Lane.

The first realignment of property took place when Toto Duprez, the mayor, decided in 1951 to sell both his house and the model farm which he administered under a bailiff. Though he was to remain mayor of the village, he intended to take an apartment in Paris to which his business called him. We were sorry to lose a pleasant neighbour whose dinner parties were apt to be fun. He was a man of great culture who was equally at home with rich and poor. Those who were erudite found in him a man of great learning; the peasants loved him greatly because he sought out their company, delighting in old manners and picturesque customs. Also he had a ribald side to his nature that gave his conversation a Scarronesque character.

Though there was nothing remarkable about his own house which was mostly of wood and rather ugly, it was sad to see his eighteenth- and nineteenth-century books with their leather bindings being removed in packing cases and his pictures and portraits of Napoleonic times (on which he was an expert) taken away. He had visited every château and peasant's cottage within driving distance, and probably knew more about the history of the Pays d'Auge than any other person. Subsequently he was killed in a busy street while getting out of his car on the wrong side.

I was in London when his property came on to the market. This was the year in which *The Little Madeleine* was first published, and I had less time than usual to come over to Normandy, though my mother was living on the farm and wrote regularly. A telephone call from Maître Vincent, the notary, informed me that as Berlequet, Toto Duprez' model farmhouse, and a number of his orchards cut across my property it might be important for me to make a bid for them. By obtaining possession of them I would find myself with a much more valuable estate comprising some fifty acres, and having two farmhouses – my own and Berlequet which would be ideal for a tenant farmer, self contained and distant by about a quarter of a mile from my own house.

Because I am going to try to trace the slow but inevitable drama that was to bring steel and cement encircling the countryside with its deathlike jaws, it is important that I should give some idea of the nefarious role which money – money in terms of inflation panic – played from this moment forward. But we were as yet unready for it. Nobody on the day that the notary phoned me thought of rushing in to buy where Toto Duprez sold. The countryside was still the countryside. Birds sang in the hedges, bats circled over our heads of an evening, owls hooted in trees at night – and the little white villas blinked along the seafront at the unpolluted sea.

At the rate of exchange the notary was asking the equivalent of some £4,000 for Berlequet, the farmhouse, its dependencies and some fifteen acres of lush orchard land stretching all the way from my own house up to the road to St Vaast. As usual in this sort of transaction, the farmhouse was thrown in with the pasture land. This had happened in exactly the same way when before the war I had bought my own house and the orchards surrounding it. The price was reached by computing the current value of farmland. The value of the house was not counted. In my own case it was considerable.

My own acquisition coincided with old man Déliquaire's decision to retire. He divided his stock amongst his two sons and abandoned his lease in favour of a former farmhand called Rémy. His son Roger became a truck driver in the village; his other son, Jacques, was just back from military service in Indo-China, and was looking for a farm. I offered a nine-year lease of Berlequet and all my pasture land. A few months later he set up house with his young bride, Georgette, and in due course they had a daughter – Brigitte.

The sale of the mayor's farming land accordingly made no significant change in the aspect of the plateau. What was farming land remained farming land, though under different ownership. But it did perhaps make one subtle difference. One of the six farms had disappeared, its land being merged with my own. There were six farms before the mayor's departure; only five remained.

Jacques Déliquaire had not been a soldier for nothing. The days of the buggy were over. He bought a big shiny car on credit and then a great tractor which thundered down Cathedral Lane while Yvonne Poulin continued to wash her linen in the stream. But when Georgette bought her first washing machine, all the wives followed suit until eventually, against my better judgment, I did the same. Today what puzzles me is that I put it off for so long.

The farms on our plateau overlooked the sea which was distant by about one mile. The coast line made a beautiful sweep past the broad estuary of the river Seine, its right arm (as you gazed towards England) curving round the port and oil refineries of Le Havre, and the promontory of Sainte Adresse.

One could run down to the village in no time. It was like careering down the side of a mountain. The main road from Deauville to Caen was right on the sands and often in summer the sea was so blue that it might have been the Mediterranean.

Returning home with the shopping (unless by car) was quite a different matter. One almost needed an alpine stick. We generally used the Rue Pasteur at the corner of which Maitre Vincent, the notary, lived and had his fine office. He was right in the middle of the village, almost facing the Post Office.

The Rue Pasteur ran straight up the steep hill like a white arrow – an aristocratic street of late nineteenth-century villas whose ornate façades and comfortable gardens gave them a fine air. At the top of the street was Bois Lurette, Andrée Pradeau's estate whose white gates gave entry into her majestic park with its forest trees, its lawns and gardens, and its self-contained farm. Here great French painters like Claude Monet, Pierre Bonnard and Toulouse-Lautrec did much of their best work. Vuillard painted his portrait *The Two Sisters* on the terrace, the same terrace on which Andrée and her family lunch on hot days.

At the time of which I write, Andrée Pradeau's domain was separated from another of about the same size, Les Pelouses, by Cathedral Lane. The trees bordering each of these two estates nodded their heads over this narrow lane which was just wide enough for a horse and buggy. On the mossy banks grew the primrose and the violet.

But whereas Bois Lurette remained a living home full of children's laughter and the barking of dogs, Les Pelouses, deserted by its original owners, became for a time a summer holiday home for children from a Paris suburb, and then left empty. But the small farm which was once part of it had been

29

sold off to a widow, Mme Bellay, who lived in its picturesque sixteenth-century farmhouse, not so very unlike my own.

Once at the top of the Rue Pasteur, therefore, one passed into Cathedral Lane which, skirting Andrée Pradeau's estate, brought one, after twenty minutes' walk, to a crossroads. On one's left another white gate led into Andrée's farm; to one's right, a lane led off to the main road to Caen, while straight ahead was the red brick house of the Levannier family which in turn faced a property once owned by Mme Michelin, later by the Wolfs.

At this point the dwindling lane split into two, encircling an island site of about five acres which rose up so high that it dominated all the country round. From its plateau one could look down on my house and see smoke curling up from the chimney. This breathtaking view was seldom enjoyed by anybody. Only our cows stood amongst gorse and wild rose in silent contemplation.

At the far end of this island site stood Berlequet.

During the years immediately following the purchase, though my mother was on the farm, I remained mostly with my husband in London. The countryside changed very little.

At the bottom of my home orchard, however, down by the stream, I was obliged to allow a very fine sixteenth-century cider press and hay barn to deteriorate until at last it fell to pieces. This was sad. It had been a museum piece with its huge solid wood wheel for the squashing of cider apples, its immense kegs, its outer staircase, a marvel of design, and hand hewn rafters. The massive oak doors had wooden pins and iron locks. The building had suffered considerably from neglect during the German Occupation. Originally it was owned jointly by my estate and by that of Mme Bompain, my neighbour. When it became clear that it needed urgent repairs, Mme Bompain sold me her share in it for a few thousand francs, and I received a many-paged legal document dating back from medieval times.

I would have much liked on my return to Normandy after the Occupation to have this beautiful building repaired. Was it not, after all, a thing of beauty – a heritage for future generations – but the Bank of England, extremely strict at this moment, only allowed me to send sufficient money over to make my own house habitable so that I was forced to allow what was, after all, a picturesque luxury to fall into ruins.

Unhappily, similar sixteenth-century gems were being allowed all over the Pays d'Auge to crumble away. Nobody was willing to spend money on them. It never struck people that they might all suddenly disappear. Owners of small farms who were often notaries or modest business men living in some small sleepy town, generally retired, received too little in rent to allow them to spend money on keeping in good repair half-timbered museum pieces which their tenant farmers had no respect for. Hay was too often over-stacked under their delicately fashioned roofs; the walls were kicked by donkeys or heifers. If the roof caved in the rain would be kept out by a sheet of corrugated iron. Who could have foreseen that within the next fifteen years, millions of French people in towns and cities would join in a frenzied rush to own a secondary residence – a little place in the country which would increase their social standing and hopefully prove a hedge against uncontrolled inflation.

The age of the developer was still just around the corner.

In May 1962 my mother, Matilda, died on the farm and my husband and I buried her in the churchyard of the tiny twelfth-century church at Auberville where she sleeps at the foot of a simple white tombstone copied from those that mark the graves of British and American soldiers who are buried on French soil. In September of that same year Mme Anger died in her large, lonely farmhouse and was buried in the same churchyard – very near to my mother's grave. The church is built on the top of high, rugged cliffs known as the *Vaches Noires*, from which one has a wild, sweeping view of the Channel and the distant English coast.

At that time it was a lonely, deserted spot with only the roughest road leading to it. Today the cliffs are studded with small white huts allocated to the employees of a great industrial concern for their summer vacation.

Early in November when we were back in London, Maître Vincent, the notary, phoned us to say that Mme Anger's estate was up for sale. Would we be interested in acquiring any of her orchards? Once again there arose a question of foreign exchange. Though this was not the only problem to be taken into account.

The farm in Normandy was never intended to be more than a place where we could all go to for work and rest. But because it was a farm I was determined that it should pay its way, that the rent roll should be sufficient to cover the taxes and the rates, and that quite apart from living rent free, we should derive from it our dairy produce, our vegetables and all the incidental advantages such as apples, pears, cherries, mushrooms, blackberries, chestnuts, hazel nuts, wood, and so forth. As nearly as possible I continued to believe that it should house us, feed us and heat us. This was the challenge I had set myself from the first – that unlike a town house or an apartment one might purchase, I must never run the risk of being swamped by fiscal charges which could force me to sell. I wanted to be like the woman with the cottage and the one cow who provided her with milk, butter and cream! She imagined that she would never starve.

In return it seemed to me that as the country was lending me for an indefinite period the orchards, streams and woods under my control, I must try to keep them as beautiful as I could.

After careful discussion, my son decided to buy one small orchard from the Mme Anger estate. It was the one in which my husband had been pounced upon by two of her henchmen who found him one Sunday morning on the wrong side of a pretty wood which I had acquired at the beginning of the war for a trifling sum. This orchard, about four acres in size, was some fifty yards beyond Berlequet and would therefore merge into our land. There was a slate-covered, half-timbered building in the centre for hay and animals and the orchard ran down to the stream which watered the wood but which was quite a different one from that which ran at the bottom of my home field.

Adjacent to this orchard, at no additional price, was a small cottage with its own garden. A couple called Bessel lived here. The man had been a labourer on Mme Anger's estate but he was now old and suffered from a painful hip, so that he spent most of the day seated on a kitchen chair in front of his cottage, leaning on a stick. Mme Bessel was expert at milking cows. We leased the new orchard to Jacques Déliquaire and Mme Bessel helped Georgette henceforth to milk her herd.

The remaining orchards in Mme Anger's estate were eventually absorbed, and leased out to various farmers. The house in which she had lived was modernized by new owners and turned into a typically flamboyant secondary residence with trim lawns, garages for cars and sailing boats and impressive gates. The old farmhand therefore ceased as an entity to exist – just as Toto Duprez' farm was no more. The rural community on the plateau was thinning out.

Though London was my home, I continued during the next few years to come over as often as possible, especially in the summer. That Christmas the Poulins had left the red brick house and the Levanniers moved in. Because both the Déliquaires and the Levanniers were young and newly married, they immediately became friendly and always ready to give one another a helping hand. Soon also the children became friends.

Both families were of farming stock. Jacques Déliquaire was born in his father's house on the other side of the stream and I had known him always. The Levanniers had come here in the hope of building up a little fortune before going back to the parents' farm in the Eure.

The young Levannier especially understood that times had changed and that it was no longer possible to adhere to the old customs that had remained constant in the Pays d'Auge for five centuries. The Poulins had respected them. So had Jacques' father. Many of these customs were unwritten laws handed down from generation to generation. Such and such a portion of your hedge belonged to your neighbour, the other part was yours. Where was the dividing line? Originally there had been a carved stone to show it but this had long disappeared. But what did it matter? Everybody was aware of it. If a tree fell down in that part of the hedge which belonged to the neighbour it was his and he must come and cut it into logs, and carry them away. The owner of the hedge technically owned a yard of soil on his neighbour's land. It was all very complicated but in the old days non-observance of the rules would lead to family feuds.

If a cider apple tree died or ceased to give forth fruit in an orchard the trunk belonged to the tenant farmer. He would use it for firewood. The owner was responsible for providing at his own expense a new apple tree. But the farmer was expected to plant it and surround the tender trunk with a steel corset so that the cows would not sharpen their teeth on it or pull down the young branches. Because the cider apple crops were as important to the old Norman farmer as the milk from his cows, usage demanded immense care to see that the trees were not harmed. But in those days the tenant farmer and the owner shared a common interest in the land. The tenant farmer had every reason to fuss over his trees in order that his cider should be his pride and the delight of his friends.

The grass of an orchard was so highly thought of that there was a clause in most contracts that disallowed geese, for instance, which were supposed to soil the grazing – and, of course, sheep were not tolerated. These small enclosed orchards were never made for tractors that barged into them rather like the proverbial bull in the china shop. It had never struck me when I first bought the farm that the day might come when the entire aspect of the province might change – that almost everything I loved about it might become nothing but a memory. We took so much for granted. In my girlhood we had been so poor. I had so often dreamt of the little half-timbered house, the garden, the cow, the hens. Surely there was not anything strange in such delights being the dream of a little city girl? I dreamt of being a princess at the ball, like Cinderella, of being a film star, I dreamt of designing beautiful dresses – of being a radiant young farmer's wife.

What frightened me about Levannier, so youthful, so good-looking, so ready with his smile – was that he descended upon this quiet countryside with all the terrifying adjuncts of the modern experimenter. When, with goggles and a cylinder fastened to his back, he sprayed the stinging nettles he gave me impression of a Nazi soldier manipulating a deadly flame thrower. Nature in the form of bees and butterflies, of wild flowers and tender blossom, was being exterminated.

I am ashamed at feeling so badly about chemical manures,

pesticides and what became known as 'rentability'. About one hundred yards of the hedge that divided our home orchard up by the white entrance gates from the adjoining orchard, belonged by tradition to Mme Bompain, just as the rest of it, that part running down to the stream, belonged to me. One spring morning the new farmer sent a man to cut the whole of this hedge down, oak, ash, cherry, hazel, wild rose and honeysuckle – everything, on the astounding excuse that this would give him a yard more grazing space on his side. I was left with the stump of a hedge that would never grow again – except to give forth brambles that would be later sprayed with weed killer.

Time passed and little Brigitte was beginning to grow up. I would often in summer go down to the sands. In the village there was not yet any violent sign of change. Just here and there a new house would go up. An hotel would close. The era of the small French hotel was coming to an end. Guests could no longer afford to pay for the salaries of the staff and the unrealistic imposition of social security. Caravan sites on the other hand multiplied on the marshy ground overlooking the sea between Blonville and our own village. Rumour had it that all this land would one day become a vast new town. Holiday makers on the caravan sites tended to use the beaches facing them, and they even had their own shops and traffic police so that small coastal resorts such as ourselves, which were formerly divided one from the other by long stretches of golden sand, were now joining up with no open country between them.

Just above the main street of the village a property called San Carlo, which had once belonged to the Countess of Béarn, was being divided up into small lots. Prospective buyers were offered lots of a fifth of an acre on which they would build houses to their own design. They would have tiny gardens, a garage and a rockery. The former mansion was being turned into apartments and the avenue of chestnut trees leading up to it was already robbed of its stately beauty, but though we felt a little aggrieved at this passing of the Edwardian age, it was to be expected. The village shopkeepers looked forward to doing a

35

little more trade.

For a time no more orchards came up for sale. Because of this it was difficult to gauge their value, though it was commonly rumoured that the agricultural land on the plateau might fetch as much as £1,500 an acre. Just now there were no sellers and one might be tempted to wonder if there would be any buyers.

A tiny cloud had begun to appear on the horizon, in the form of a French law which, like many laws, sprang from noble intent, but threatened to achieve the exact opposite of what it was intended to do. It was to the effect that though a tenant farmer could break his lease at whatever moment he chose, the owner of the land was virtually saddled with his tenant, or even with his tenant's descendants, for ever!

This law which was supposed to protect the small farmer was proving suicidal to the countryside which because of it was disintegrating. Many owners saw themselves virtually dispossessed. Who would buy their land if the sitting tenant could never be expelled? Originally leases were made for three, six and nine years. But now such a clause no longer meant anything – except that in certain cases an owner, giving due notice before the end of the ninth year, could regain control of his property if he were himself intending to farm it. Such an eventuality was extremely rare. Land was something that people had owned for generations – not for greed but because it was a nice thing to feel that one possessed a green field, a woodland glade or a few acres watered by a clear stream. French people for hundreds of years past had learnt that land over the years is apt to rise in value. They felt more sure of it than paper money or shares in a bank. It was real and enjoyable. They could visit the tenant farmer and drink a friendly glass of his new cider. It was warming to their sense of importance.

Besides, even those owners who normally would have had no intention of selling, disliked the idea that they were being told that they could not. Because nobody in his senses would have bought a farm of which he could scarcely be called the master.

Indeed he no longer was the master. Young tenant farmers were well acquainted with their legal rights and as soon as they discovered that they could not be expelled they treated the land, not with traditional love, but as an expendable commodity which they could discard like an old coat as soon as they were tired of it. So inevitably enmity began to arise between owner and tenant.

In due course the tenant farmer discovered something else. Down in the Landes where natural gas was being drilled, local tenant farmers, attracted by the high wages offered by the petroleum companies, without abandoning the farms they rented, signed on to work eight hours a day extracting gas. As the owners were unable to expel them from the farms, these men earned what surprised even themselves – the union wage of an oilman and the normal profits of a tenant farmer.

Anybody running a dairy farm would have been unable to inspire himself with this example. There would be the cows to milk, possibly by hand, morning and evening. But the French government chose this very moment to offer dairy farm owners a bonus for every cow they killed – on the grounds that such a surplus of butter had been accumulated that much of it would have to be sold to the Soviet Union at a loss!

Some farmers replaced their cows with meat cattle which could be left in the fields for days on end with only an occasional visit to make sure that none had strayed out on to a motor road. This wonderful new-found freedom allowed them to work from 8 a.m. to 4 p.m. as truck drivers, mostly for the cheese firms, at the usual rates. In the evening they would return home for supper and then make a quick tour of the orchards which they were supposed to farm and from which no owner could dismiss them. As they had a tied farmhouse, they also lived virtually rent-free.

3

I T WAS NOT UNTIL the spring of 1968, famous for the May student revolution, that we suddenly became aware that our green fields were being menaced from every side. Until now most of the danger had come from within – farmers who, at the government's advice, cut down cider apple trees one year only to be told the next to replant new ones – but of course nobody did replant. It was too much trouble. Farmers, again on the government's request, sold their milk cows for butchers' meat, allegedly because there was too much milk, only to discover that our grazing land was not at all suitable for fattening meat cattle. So, too late, they were advised to go back to dairy herds. But now the enemy came from outside – an enemy backed by the wealthiest banks in the land-astute, determined, and planning its campaigns with the strategy of army corps commanders. We had no arms to oppose them. This enemy with its ammunition of millions in fast-devalued currency was already at our gates in the hope of transplanting the town into the country, of running motor roads through babbling brooks, of building six-storey apartment houses where once the owl had hooted in the night.

For some weeks there had been talk of the Pelouses being sold to a developer. This was the once noble mansion in its fourteen acres of parkland that was separated from Andrée Pradeau's Bois Lurette by the moss-covered, leafy-domed path known as Cathedral Lane. The socialist town council of a Paris suburb had been using it as a summer holiday home for workers' children. News that they intended to abandon it in favour of a site in Brittany was revealed in the Paris *Figaro* where it was advertised for sale, the asking price being in the neighbourhood of seventy-five thousand pounds. This at the time had seemed a fabulous price to ask. We had not yet become accustomed to the vast sums that such speculations were to assume. Later a figure nearer one hundred thousand pounds was mentioned. Then suddenly it transpired that a man who was making a name for himself for swooping on sites all along the coast and building thereon modern apartment blocks, had struck again – this time on the Pelouses. He planned to pull down the mansion, cut down the trees and put up some six or seven five-storey apartment buildings for about three hundred and fifty families. Already plans had been drawn up and the projected apartments, some of them very small and known as studios, were being offered for sale for a modest cash-down payment and long, easy credit. Soon they were being advertised on full page spreads in the newspapers as secondary residences at low prices with a distant view over the English Channel.

Almost at the same time the widow Bellay, at the request of her children, announced that she was anxious to sell the farm which had originally been attached to the Pelouses but which was now her property. Like the Pelouses itself, the farm was bordered by Cathedral Lane. At the far end of it, just before one came upon the Levannier farm, a transversal lane, known as the *Chemin aux Loups*, ran down to the Deauville-Caen highway.

A charming family called the Poirots decided to buy the Bellay farmhouse and its very lovely sixteenth-century out-buildings which they would convert into homes for their children, but as they had no intention to run a dairy farm they agreed that Mme Bellay could dispose of the orchards which ran down to the *Chemin aux Loups*. She sold them to a speculator who divided the land up into small lots which he sold to prospective house buyers.

Thus yet another farm was to disappear from the plateau.

This was not all. The bulldozer and the mechanical saw, the sound of whose high-pitched wail I was beginning to dread, would make short work of Cathedral Lane which for so long had allowed the countryside, in all its rich splendour, to reach down almost to the sea. Now conversely the town would stretch up and bite deeply into the woods and meadows of the plateau. The red brick house and Levannier's fifteen-acre home orchard would alone separate us from the lights and clamour of holiday crowds.

All this time there had been rumours about a new road whose function was to by-pass the village, and allow motorists to drive more swiftly along the coast. First news of it came to me during Easter week. Later when seized by panic I bent over the blueprint in the Town Hall, I saw that it would pass right over my house. I nearly fainted with emotion. Would it be a secondary road? A major road? A four-lane highway? Nobody seemed quite certain. It might, said some people, never be built. But the mere possibility gave me the feeling that my home had virtually ceased to exist.

The village notables, when meeting me, invariably brought the matter up, as if it were a matter of joy to them, and pointed out that with such a blueprint in existence my sixteenth-century house and the orchard in which it stood had ceased to have any practical value. I had not sufficiently realized that with the lightning town-planning which reached up to the Levannier farm, the village was madly speculating on the vertiginous rise in the price of land. Everybody wanted to sell. Jealous looks were doubtless cast upon my acres. Had there not been this question of a new road, how valuable, people must have reflected with bitterness, my small farm was bound to become. But now great was their satisfaction at the discovery that my hopes, had I entertained any, were crushed.

My old friend the notary, Maitre Vincent, nearing eighty, also brought the matter of the road up when we met one day in the village street. 'Supposing I wished to sell?' I asked. He smiled the way he did when explaining patiently the details of the law to a woman. 'No, no,' he said, 'you couldn't sell with a thing like that hanging over the house. Not at any price worth taking.'

Surveyors from the Prefecture at Caen came to view the land and measure it up. In due course a new map was issued. This time the road, instead of passing over my house, was scheduled to sweep across the little stream at the bottom of my home orchard and then go right through the field that I found Yvonne Poulin looking at so nostalgically that Sunday morning when

40

she came back like a ghost to haunt the scenes of her youth. The new course was very clear. There were two minute sixteenth-century barns at the top of what had been, in Yvonne's time, the Poulin orchard. The road would pass between them so that they would stand like sentinels on either side. After this, it would cross the lane in which we had been talking and cut its way between Berlequet and the hedge that divided my magnificent island site in two. At least I would be left with that prodigious view above my own field. What happened to the projected road after that was no concern of mine.

I got a little comfort out of this. I tried to live with the constant thought that the road would lop off a piece of my home field and go thundering across Mme Bompain's orchard, then past Berlequet, where my farmer Jacques Déliquaire lived, to its unknown destination. After all it was not scheduled until the early eighties and I would certainly be dead by then.

Nevertheless it did very actively concern me and already I was forced to witness the savage destruction of all the forest trees bordering Cathedral Lane on the opposite side of Bois Lurette, Andrée Pradeau's estate. Though her property would remain intact, the noise would become constant and because this part of Cathedral Lane was to become a wide, busy road to accomodate all the people who would live in the apartments, each presumably with his own car, racing up and down the hill which led to the sea, the local council wanted her to cede part of her land near her entrance gates. She agreed and they said they would build her a nice fence. Meanwhile lorries groaned their way up the hill and the cement mixers worked all day and far into the night.

As long as my farm continued to function, as long as the Levanniers remained to bring in their hay and to milk their cows, I could pretend that all was still well with the world. Of course if the new road were to be built, my house and the home orchard would be caught in a pincer movement that would encircle us. On the assumption that pedestrians would not be allowed to cross the new road, how would I reach all the rest of my orchards which would be on the other side of it – some fifty acres of woods, stream, pasture land and apple trees? It was as if

41

65040

WILLIAM WOODS COLLEGE LIBRARY

the farm were to be decapitated – the head on one side, the body on the other.

My meeting with Yvonne in the lane brought the memories of these past years hurrying back into mind. So much was to happen on our plateau after the Levanniers replaced the Poulins – so much to frighten me, to make me increasingly aware of the vexation of no longer being young and aggressive at such an historic moment. I wondered how I would have seen things if I were once again a little girl.

What I was to find curious was the comparative peace of my domain with so much happening around me. When I first abandoned my London apartment to spend more time on the farm, my mother being dead, nobody was at the door waiting for me when I arrived. Georgette had lit the Aga stove, and the house was tidy and clean, but how empty it seemed! It was in March. The lawns were full of multi-coloured crocusses, and the smell of violets came up from the damp beds. The lowing of cattle reached us from distant meadows, and the bells of the village church were being tolled for Dr Leherissey, our village doctor, who had delivered me of my son before the war, and who had just died during retirement at Nice. Now they had brought his body back to Normandy where he had helped to bring all the children for ten miles around into the world during these last fifty years. Accouchements took place in the homes. It was rare for women to go into hospital. They gave birth to their children in their half-timbered farmhouses which were often as primitive as the stables in which they kept their cattle. The French farmhouse never reached that peculiar warmth and cosiness that distinguished those in England since Georgian times.

But both Dr Leherissey and the local midwife knew every farm and cottage in the Pays d'Auge, and the doctor, during most of his life, had driven in a horse and buggy to his patients, even harnessing the mare himself in the middle of the night, and lifting in the messenger beside him who had come to make the urgent call.

Yvonne – I kept on coming back to Yvonne – had yelled the house down when she gave birth to André just before the

42

Germans arrived to occupy the land. Her bedroom had been far from comfortable but when I came back after the Liberation the big Norman cupboard was full of family linens which her mother, Mme Castel, had just inherited from various relations in Le Havre. The old lady's family hailed from that city, and at one time they owned several small hotels facing the busy quays at which liners from all over the world tied up. It was then cosmopolitan and very picturesque, but towards the end of the war, air raids had obliged the population to spend most of its nights underground. The streets and houses all about the quays were wiped out; many of Mme Castel's family were killed, and she inherited great piles of sheets, napkins and tableware from the houses they had owned. She now took pride in handling this fine linen and appeared to know the history of every piece. Her weekly wash was impressive. When a sheet showed signs of wear, she would pick up her scissors and cut a dress out of it, or a pinafore for one of the girls. She was also well stocked with the German army sheets of blue and white check gingham which the retreating enemy had left behind. All the village children were dressed in this distinctive material. Unfortunately none came my way. The only thing that remained to me from the German Occupation was their vicious barbed wire, much more effective than the French kind, which farmers used to prevent the cattle from straying out of pasturage. As time went on it became increasingly dangerous.

The Levanniers brought a measure of modernity to the red brick house. Mme Levannier as a young bride was radiant with youth, strength and the joy of possessing a place of her own. Her good-looking husband gave her first a boy, then a girl. This modern farmer's wife wore jeans and her hair in a pony tail. Later she rolled it up in a bun on top of her fresh, sunburnt features. The money they made went into mechanization for the farm rather than in comfort for the house, where only the large kitchen with its huge windows and high ceiling was heated – and that with a log-burning stove. Remnants of the last meal often remained untidily on the table, especially when Mme Levannier was called out by her young husband to help with the tractor in the fields. Soon new cowsheds were modernized for electrical milking.

I also had no help of any kind in the house. The Aga stove needed to be filled morning and night. Our central heating in winter was coal-fired. I had the shopping, cooking, washing and mending to do – not to mention the housework and two kitchen gardens and a farmyard of some forty birds. Nostalgic yearning for London was in part compensated for by the delight of the first spring flowers, the scent of honeysuckle, the gathering of soft fruit, the digging up of potatoes. There were moments, however, of loneliness, of reflecting that for all of us, there is a time to be and a time not to be. But how agreeable were those evenings in winter by a log fire which burned three-foot logs from our own trees, knitting, embroidering napkins I would never use. At these moments I told myself that here in the peace of my house, forgotten in the middle of my orchard, time continued to stand still. Nothing had changed.

During the summer of 1972 rumours reached me that Jacques and Georgette Déliquaire were planning to leave the farm at the end of the year.

Georgette herself was soon to confirm this. On bringing me the milk one morning she announced that she and her husband had bought one of the building plots on what had once been the orchards of the Bellay farm and that they were to have a house, facing the newly widened *Chemin aux Loups,* built to their design.

She said: 'We want a newly built house, a modern house, a clean house!' There was defiance in her voice. She wanted me to know that she considered Berlequet fit only for a peasant, and that its loneliness was beginning to tell on her. 'We shall leave your farm just as soon as our house is built,' she said. 'Perhaps before Christmas. We are already selling our milking herd. The government is offering us a bonus for doing so – and this money will prove sufficient to put down what money is needed for the purchase of the land. There may even be a bit over to give to the bank which is financing the building of the house. We ought to redeem the debt within a very few years.'

'What will Jacques do?' I asked.

'What he's doing already,' she said. 'Driving a lorry for a Camembert factory at Touques. They pay union wages. A fat cheque at the end of every month. As for me I can earn nearly as much as he can charring in the village. What a relief it will be for us no longer to live in the mud and the dung. To be free to take holidays like everybody else. Those people on television are right to say that one must be crazy to stay on the land. Well, I thought I'd better tell you. Though I expect you were aware of it already. This will be the last time I shall bring you milk. Most of the cows have already been sold!'

For some time past small houses had been going up on what had been the Bellay orchards. Not in a row as used to be the fashion in England but every one different from the other and no two facing in the same direction so that they looked as if they had been dropped into place by some giant hand. A few were thatched with false half-timbering; others had red tiles or plastic slates. They had trim little lawns, an occasional border of flowers and here and there an exterior barbecue. Building was still not outrageously expensive. A plot cost the equivalent of some £2,000. A comfortable little house could be built for ten to twelve thousand pounds.

Cathedral Lane was now a wide motor road with proper lighting and was named the Chemin de Bois Lurette, perhaps as a compliment to poor Andrée Pradeau who was faced across her single line of trees with six or seven immense apartment blocks, re-christened Les Marines, and which looked cold and functional with their gleaming white façades and narrow balconies, rather like hospital blocks. Just before reaching the Levannier farm, the road swept round into the newly built Chemin aux Loups so that the inhabitants of Les Marines could drive quickly into the road to Caen.

M. Poirot and his sons meanwhile had modernized the Bellay farmhouse, mostly by themselves and the three big half-timbered farm buildings that faced the house in the same field had been cleaned out, renovated and made to look like show places. They kept the name Bellay Farm, though there was only one field and no cattle or livestock.

This sudden decision of Jacques and Georgette to leave me gave me a disagreeable feeling of being left in the lurch. It was not a question of money. One seldom heard young farmers complaining about the money they were able to earn. They did very well for themselves and paid hardly any income tax. What they complained about was the hours of work. They were being taught by the media to make damaging comparisons between themselves and factory workers whose wages went up with the cost of living, whose working hours were being continually cut and who often had both their Saturdays and Sundays – not to mention three to four weeks paid holiday every year. They were beginning to think of themselves as an inferior class of society. The fact that they were their own masters and could, if they wished, obtain wonderful facilities to purchase land of their own did not compensate for the disrepute into which the old peasant class was falling. Much of the trouble came from the fact that it had become uneconomical for them to hire a farmhand, even if there had been any to hire. They had some reason by modern standards to consider themselves overworked. It was not the fault of the land but of a social system that insisted on such high wages for farmhands that no farm of our size could economically pay them. In Yvonne's day when she, Ernest and the Castels had a maid and two farmhands to look after the horses and help bring in the hay, nobody complained about being overworked. Ernest was accustomed quietly to graft his apple trees, make his cider and like a poet wander nocturnally dreaming over his pasture land.

Though I was puzzled and hurt by Georgette's attitude – so very different from that day, many years earlier, when she had pleaded so pathetically with me for the farm which she now claimed to despise, she was, of course, rendering me the sort of service that many other owners would have jumped at – the unexpected freedom to do what I liked with my land.

I was no longer tied for ever to a disillusioned tenant! I was free to sell the land, to keep it, to put a bailiff in, to do just what I pleased. This gave me an almost heady feeling, as if somebody had made me a priceless gift.

Berlequet, for which I had been paid merely a nominal rent,

46

had been costing me a lot of money in upkeep. I was continually being asked to have the tiles replaced, the electric light system overhauled, the water system modernized. Empty, it would become the target for vandals. I could not effectively watch over a set of buildings a quarter of a mile away from me. But inhabited, I could not hope ever again to do what I wished with it. I must either take advantage of this opportunity or forgo it for ever.

But if I disposed of it I would not have the model, self-contained little farm I had worked so hard to build up. There would be no problem, of course, in selling every year my pasturage and apple crop but it would cease to be a farm with a farmer. The orchards would have to be let out as had happened to most of Mme Anger's land after her death. They would temporarily lose their personality. Technically I would be helping to rob the plateau of one more going concern.

I spent far too much time with my poultry in which, against my better judgment and even more my purse, I engaged both my heart and my soul. I doubt if anybody else kept cocks and hens which as in the past ran happily over the orchards, running between the feet of the cows. The simplest things of yesterday have become the most difficult today. Whoever would have believed that there was anything remarkable in keeping a few chickens? Generations of children in England were brought up in such scenes, the farmer's wife throwing corn to her poultry, so brightly portrayed in picture books. The troubles on my farm were proving a minute reflection of a world changed, or in the course of changing, out of recognition. Not only had corn become too expensive to allow such dilettantism, but nature was taking revenge upon us by robbing many hens of their normal female desire to sit on their eggs. A broody hen was almost a phenomenon. Housewives who still kept a poultry yard bought their chicks raised from incubators at Dozulé market on a Tuesday morning and then fed them with industrial feed until the hens were ready to lay, or the cocks big enough to be killed, scalded and put in the oven – or the deep freeze. Quite disappeared from the countryside was the endearing scene of a

47

hen surrounded by her own brood, a dozen or so downy little objects darting here or there or sleeping cosily under her wing. Too many chicks left to run about with their mothers were eaten by rooks or drowned in a pond. Hardly a week passed when I was not obliged to bring one or more into the kitchen, wrap them up in a blanket in a basket next to the Aga, and nurse them back to health with a devotion that no farmer's wife would ever have had time for. Afterwards they followed me wherever I went. It was unbelievably touching but it was not farming. And most of all it cost a lot of money. But as Théophile Gautier once pointed out, the superfluous and the unnecessary tend to be the only really important things in life. Who today stops to look at a rainbow or listen to the chirruping of a bird in the hedge? Was it not Browning who wrote:

How good is man's life, the mere living! how fit to employ
All the heart and soul and the senses for ever in joy!

A turkey will sit on a dozen hens' eggs of which only one will produce a chick and then the bird, like a great ship in full sail, will steer the tiny living thing which is not even of her kind, all over the orchard, believing her mission to be God-sent. That has nothing in common with an industrialized chicken farm which is in no way different from an extermination camp.

As Christmas approached Jacques and Georgette went through all the delightful tortures of watching their first house going up. From time to time I would see their tractor passing slowly along the lane with various pieces of furniture being conveyed from Berlequet to the brand–new abode where the paint was at last beginning to dry. Their features, red at all times from the elements, now beamed with joy and their expression was of triumph because they would never experience the need of me again. I had the impression of being taunted by newly freed serfs as might have happened during the Russian Revolution. What I gazed upon underlined the inescapable fact that the era of the tenant farmer was over for ever. Land would either have to be worked by its owner or by fully unionized workers employed by a State co-operative. The feudal system, on however small a scale, was finished.

From time to time I would walk over to Berlequet. I know of no sadder sight than that of a home being abandoned. Doors and windows thrown open, dead ashes in the fireplace, a broken toy kicked into a corner, the rubbish of fifteen years in the same house heaped over the gigantic worn tyres of the much-overworked tractor to make a monster bonfire at the back of the house. Bonfires of this kind, because of the burning rubber, send columns of acrid black smoke into the air, and when after many hours it dies down one sees strewn over the blackened, poisoned earth the twisted wires and metal which go into the making of a modern tyre. But who would have the patience to kindle a fire with only paper and wood?

Nevertheless what a lovely place this was! Oh, not the interior judged by what was expected today. The rooms were old-fashioned, there was no central heating, town water had only just arrived in what not so long ago had been the depths of the country. Though my own house was served by a deep well, I had some months earlier arranged for town water to be laid on both in my house, as an alternative to the well, and at Berlequet. An underground pipe carried it over the whole length of the home orchard and the island site which overlooked it. It could accordingly be tapped for the castle if ever the streams ran dry. An orchard without water is no good for a dairy herd.

What was pleasant about Berlequet was the disposition of the house and buildings. The house itself was long and low with a tiled roof and honeysuckle growing up over the doors. To one side of it was the kitchen garden and the old bakehouse; to the other side of it, the cartsheds, the garages, the stables, the rabbit hutches, over all of which ran the immense, airy haylofts. At right angles to house and stables was the slate-covered complex of cider press, vat room, and spare living accommodation. The courtyard was separated from the lane by a holly hedge with a pretty little white gate and much bigger ones for carts or trucks, next to which was another small building for heifers or pigs.

Finally against the back of the cider press complex was an

immense shed for the storage of wood, farm implements and other material, the whole facing its own small piece of orchard in which grew a dozen or more apple trees.

This was the small domain that Jacques and Georgette were so delighted to exchange for a small modern house in a built-up area. But what new experience does not set a youthful mind afire? And though I was being providentially given back my acres there was a streak of cunning in the arrangement as so obviously pondered over by my departing tenants. They sprang it on me laconically at the last moment as though to savour any possible discomfiture on my part. They were giving me back my farmhouse and my land but they had decided to keep the two-acre orchard that my son had purchased from Mme Anger's estate just after my mother's death.

It would allow him, explained Jacques, to retain legally his status as farmer so that he would have the right to go on making cider, to brew applejack and to keep cattle. The small farm building in the middle of the former Anger orchard would be quite large enough to store his hay and to house a heifer or two if the occasion arose. Georgette might keep chickens, and if the two acres were not sufficient for his needs, it would be comparatively easy for him, he thought, to lease one of the other orchards that had been sold at the time of Mme Anger's death. He would thus, he added smiling, professionally have the advantages of the town worker and the country farmer. Yes, he stressed, for just so long as he pleased.

'But what right . . . !' I blurted unthinkingly.

For, of course, he had every right. The two contracts were separate. Besides which, strictly speaking, it had nothing to do with me, and Jacques was perfectly aware that my son, who was in America, or perhaps in Singapore, was in no position to prevent him keeping the land, whether the contract came to an end, or not.

How childish I had been to let him see that I was vexed. He had wanted to surprise me, to show me that of the two of us he was the clever one. The happy glint in his blue eyes reminded me of his father, old Déliquaire, when hiding a keg of undeclared Calvados under a bundle of straw in the cider press. He would diddle the Excise men. They would never guess it was there! Jacques had shaken off most of his peasant ancestry while fighting a war in Indo-China while learning from young Levannier how to make use of modern chemicals and sophisticated machinery. But there was still resurgent at times this touch of crafty peasant stock.

I was stupid because the orchard in question would have to be farmed by somebody. Grass must be cropped and cider apples gathered up in autumn. Hedges must be trimmed. Nevertheless I had been fooled. Led to believe that I was rid of him, he now showed me that by the law he could remain in possession of this one field for ever.

I was more than ever anxious to safeguard my peace of mind. I had never really wanted to buy Berlequet. Financially the idea was sound but owning farm buildings in these days brings rates, repair bills, taxes – and endless squabbles. I foresaw that over the next few years Berlequet was bound to become a symbol of the past being speedily, violently transformed not only into the present but also into the future. What had once been a pretty woodman's hut in the depths of the country would change, and change again until it became a snobbish status symbol for sophisticated men and women from the city. The speculator would hover over its honeysuckle-covered walls waiting for the kill.

Forty years had now passed since I first saw Berlequet in its primitive state. Goguet and his wife, the Goguette, then lived in my future house, the house I had fallen in love with. While waiting to buy it, I found him one day sharpening his scythe under a pear tree. 'Tell me,' I asked, 'how many acres do you farm altogether?'

'Fourteen,' he answered. 'The six-acre orchard in which the house stands, and which we call the home orchard, three acres opposite the gate you have just come in by, known as the Point because of its triangular shape . . . '

The Point was the pointed end of that island site round which the lane runs. The half of it as far as the dividing hedge, that

51

table mountain overlooking the farm in which Goguet lived would be comprised in my initial purchase. But the other end of the island site, the blunt end, was owned by a Mme Paul and it was here that the future Berlequet stood.

'I will take you up there now, if you like,' said Goguet, 'but the ground is hard and the cattle ponds are dry. This one under the poplar trees is different. There is a natural spring underneath.'

We went to the gate and passed left for about 500 yards along the lane. The two younger children had followed us, and seeing that we raised no objection their voices soon rose above ours.

'You see this orchard next to the one on which our house stands,' cried Robert. 'It belongs to the Poulins who live in the farm just before you come to ours. On the other side of the land is the Point, on the far end of which lives M. Groscol.'

Groscol (Thick-neck) was a farm labourer who hired out his services either by the job or by the day. He paid rather less than £10 a year rent for the house and the kitchen garden, but the fruit in the orchard and the cider press were retained by the owner. The house and the orchard in which he lived were known as Berlequet. Groscol had a wife, whose hair was the colour of dried straw cut straight as barley on a thatched roof, and four children – all young girls. This was almost a dishonour in a Norman, for the race prided itself in producing a preponderance of males. Groscol was a good farmer, being of farming stock. Physically he was a giant with ingenuous blue eyes, and he had a slight stutter, which he lost when he was drunk. His bouts of inebriety were longest at certain seasons and coincided with the completion of such jobs as the cutting of logs in winter, the distillation of applejack in April, haymaking in July, apple picking in October, and cider making in December.

As the liquor mounted to his head, Groscol, armed with a hedge-bill, strode in his tall rubber boots across his orchard to a favourite cherry tree at the top of the lane. There was a fork in this tree providing him with a commanding view over the adjoining lanes and fields. He sat there for hours, his legs dangling over the side, as he smote the air with his hedge-bill, convinced that each blow into space was cutting a neighbour's head off. Before beheading a victim, Groscol passed judgement in a voice so loud that on a still night it was known to carry half a mile.

His vociferations provided the most appalling scandal and made him bitter enemies, not the least of whom was the Goguette, who did not dare pass the gate to milk her cows when Groscol was seated drunk in his cherry tree.

'Keep away from here!' he cried. 'Only honest women are allowed on this path. It's no good trying to impress me with your four cows. I'd like to know where they came from. Don't you think I remember the day when you first came here dragging your three brats behind you like a gipsy? It's not I who would drink the milk from your cows.'

Some time after I had bought the farmhouse in which the Goguet lived I was passing along the lane when I saw the car of Mlle Lefranc, the midwife, drawn up outside Berlequet. It was just after seven, and night was falling. There could only be one explanation of her presence – Mme Groscol was having another baby. With four girls already, would her fifth child be a boy? We pushed on to the gate leading to the house when the midwife caught us up. She told us that everything was well and that it was a girl. 'But would you believe it,' she asked, 'Bichette, the Shetland mare, is in the kitchen with Groscol?'

Bichette and Groscol had for some time past been inseparable friends. The mare, who was very wild with everybody else, followed him like a dog and rested her head on his shoulder, and in the evening when the door of the shack was open, Bichette thought nothing of walking straight into the kitchen, and it never entered Groscol's head to shoo her away.

When the new baby was to be born, Mme Groscol cleaned out her house from floor to ceiling. The cracked tiles were scrubbed until they shone. From time to time during the travail, Groscol opened the door of the bedroom where Mlle Lefranc was looking after the patient and asked: 'Well, how goes it?'. Mme Groscol, looking up from her pillow, would then catch a glimpse of Bichette's shaggy mane and thinking of her clean floor, she would cry out between her pains: 'Will you get out of here and mind your business!' An oil lamp, suspended from the ceiling, threw a warm glow over the table, at which two people were sitting with tears rolling down their cheeks in front of a bottle of applejack. One of these was Groscol, the other a neighbour called Mme Kettel, who had looked in on the excuse of helping with the accouchement. Between these two people Bichette was quietly munching the sugar that remained in the bowl on the table.

A few days later I made up a parcel of baby clothes and some biscuits for the older girls and took it to Groscol's house, but I left the packet hanging from the door handle so that Groscol would find it when he came in from the fields. Although there was nothing to show who had sent it, Mme Groscol guessed that it was I, and she told her husband to go across 'and thank the lady who lived opposite'. He walked resolutely down the hill with the long, rhythmical stride of a giant, and opened the gate that led into our field. He was carrying a stout whip and he had drunk just sufficient to give him confidence in case he met his enemies, the Goguette or her husband. The visit passed off successfully and Groscol invited me to come and see his wife any time I was passing. Then turning round he walked majestically up the field, looking neither to the right nor to the left.

The remembrance of this scene took me back to the years when Berlequet was a shack in which peasants behaved almost as in the fairy tales of our youth. By the time Mme Duprez acquired the orchard, Groscol and his family had disappeared. The mayor's wife, who had similar dreams to those of Marie Antoinette, turned the place into a model farm and installed a new tenant. But already Mme Duprez' ideas were in advance of her time. The Norman farmer was not yet ready to live in a picture-book ambience with romantic nooks and honeysuckle growing up the front. When after buying it I turned it over to Jacques and Georgette Déliquaire, both house and stables were subjected to the harsh treatment of a busy farm. Theirs was a world of hard work and profitability. The place would need considerable sums spent on it before being fit for a new tenant.

Was I disposed to spend several thousand pounds on Berlequet to modernize it? And when I had done so, what would I do with it? Let it to another farmer of whom I could never rid myself? Who, by law, need only pay me a nominal rent – not much more than Groscol had paid Mme Paul for the shack in which he had lived with his wife, five little girls and Bichette, the mare? No! it was unthinkable.

Sell it?

This might not prove easy with the threat of a major road scheduled to pass within a few yards of it. I recalled what Maître Vincent, the wise old notary, had told me about my own house.

What had happened to Groscol?

Strangely enough, this hot-headed, gentle giant had in the end done rather well for himself. When, after the Second World War, I returned to Normandy to find my own house empty and pillaged (not by the Germans!) I was obliged to bring almost everything I needed from England in small packages. As we had not yet bought a car, my husband and I, every time we came over to France, mostly by sea by way of Le Havre, carried these heavy parcels up from the bus stop to the house. On one such occasion, as we were walking slowly and painfully up the main road to Caen, we were passed by a tall, powerfully built, greying man driving a pony and trap. Because of the steepness of the hill, he passed us very slowly and my husband, who had very long sight, read on the side of the trap:

GROSCOL – FARMER

We shouted at him and he drew up at the side of the road. Yes, it was my genial giant who remembered the parcel of baby clothes that I had hung on the door-handle of his shack before the war.

'You were so disappointed,' I said, 'because of all those girls. But I recall that when Mlle Lefranc, the midwife, broke the news to you, instead of being angry, you exclaimed: "Never mind. Depend on me, Miss. I'll be good!"'

'Oh, and I was good!' exclaimed Groscol leaning over the side of his trap. 'I was as good as gold. And see how heaven rewarded me. I have a son at last!'

This was truly wonderful news and by the time he left us at the corner of the old Chemin aux Loups (in those days very narrow and full of ruts) we had become the best of friends.

But he had never entirely reconciled himself with his old enemies. Indeed he vituperated deliciously about the Goguette and poor old Goguet who had finished up, thanks to a son, in a Nazi extermination camp in Austria. For, as you will remember, Goguet's son sold his father to the Germans for the price of a motor cycle, revealing where Goguet kept his shot gun.

Well, not long before my mother's death we again had news of Groscol. Mlle Lefranc, besides being a midwife, also travelled round the countryside giving injections to Dr Leherissey's patients. Or to those of any other doctor who prescribed them. One day when she was in the house giving my mother her weekly injection for arthritis, she exclaimed:

'Do you remember that strange giant who used to live at Berlequet before you bought it and who quite terrified me when on that evening before the war I helped bring into the world Mme Groscol's fifth little girl?'

'Yes, indeed,' I said. 'We met him driving his pony cart up the steep hill on the main road to Caen some time ago, and he told us that he had finally become the father of a fine boy.'

'Well, believe it or not,' said Mlle Lefranc, preparing her instruments, 'this past night I brought into the world that little girl's first baby! But this time there was no Bichette to put his shaggy head into the bedroom. Only a reformed Giant Groscol, beaming with pleasure at having become a grandfather.'

She laughed:

'But, my goodness,' she said, 'how terrified we all were of him in the old days when he would put his thick neck through the gap in the five-barred gate, imitating the roar of a savage beast!'

So, faced with this dilemma of what I should do with Berlequet, I finally decided to sell. That is, if I could find a buyer. But at first, the notary did not seem very hopeful. He kept on talking about the threat of the road.

'But if the road were never to be built?'

'Of course. Of course. But the threat remains. It hangs over your head like the proverbial sword. An intending purchaser will require the usual document to show that the land, or building, he proposes to buy has no impediment attached to it.'

'Who issues such a document?'

'The council on whose territory it figures. In this particular case – the mayor of Gonneville. He has a blueprint showing exactly how the proposed road affects his part of the world. Of course, if the prospective buyer doesn't mind about having a road passing through his back door, if he is willing to take the risk – that's his business.'

'But it would affect the price?'

'Naturally. Would *you* buy in such circumstances?'

'I don't know,' I said. 'I suppose not.'

4

IT WAS NOT UNTIL well into the New Year that Jacques and Georgette were able to move into their new house overlooking the Chemin aux Loups. By this time what had been the Pelouses and the Bellay Farm was in the process of becoming a modern garden suburb. Cathedral Lane, rechristened the Chemin de Bois-Lurette, was a wide avenue flanked on either side by a line of newly planted young trees – a mixture of chestnut, ash, rowan, poplar and so forth. There were grass borders and up against the boundary of Andrée Pradeau's property, Bois-Lurette, occasional vestiges of the old lane. It was at first intended to turn this into a row for horse riders, but it had by now degenerated into a path where the residents from the huge complexes in the old Pelouses, rechristened Les Marines, (to give them a seaside appellation) could take their dogs for a walk in the morning or before retiring at night. The Déliquares could watch other houses, similar to their own, going up all round them. They would not lack company. Georgette had found herself work looking after the premises of a local real estate agent near the Town Hall whose plate glass windows and front steps she could be seen cleaning and polishing in the morning. Her daughter, Brigitte, in spite of having done well at college, was to find herself a temporary job at the cash desk of a butcher's shop. Money would soon be flowing into the new home. Jacques was employed collecting milk from surrounding farms, lifting the heavy churns on to his truck and then driving off with them to a Camembert factory a few miles away on the country road to Touques. In the evening when he was not busy moving his last possessions from Berlequet he would go to my son's orchard where he had already installed some young animals and a chicken run adjoining the small farm building in the centre of the field.

Berlequet looked more and more abandoned and the little wicker gate into the garden was in such a sorry state that I commissioned Longuet, the carpenter, to make a new one in spite of the fact that it cost me a great deal of money. All the animals had gone. Not only the cattle but the geese, the ducks, the poultry and the rabbits of which there had once been quite a number of different kinds in beautiful modern hutches. The former bakery, or wash house, next to which there had been pens for dogs and tame pheasants was equally empty. The only live animal in this ghost farm was a large black and white cat which had belonged to Brigitte and which she kept on removing to the new house, but every time she closed him in there, he managed to get out and the next day he would be found back at his old home. Once or twice when I went to Berlequet surveying the scene with sadness in my heart, I called to him and after a while he would come, but not near enough for me to stroke him. Then at the slightest noise he would rush back to the empty house and I would see him crouching high up over an attic window.

I took advantage of my occasional walks to Berlequet to collect faggots from the sides of the lane. This is something that I have never been able to resist. Just as I am unable to remain in the house with my hands idle, sewing or knitting when other women are perfectly happy to sit still, a walk through the countryside without a purpose would trouble me. Thus in spite of having spent nearly all my life in London I rediscover instincts of witchery latent both in my mother and in my grandmother, their love of collecting tender plants and sweet herbs for rabbits, for instance, their lonely wandering through pasturage and woodland, communing with themselves, awake to every sound and smell in the countryside. On these expeditions I often regretted not owning a donkey. Most of the farmers on the plateau at one time or another went through a phase of owning donkeys on which to fasten the milk churns before electric milking was introduced. But milking electrically was another of those modern inventions to which our method of farming never succeeded in adapting itself. With small herds of cows constantly changing from one orchard to another in country so hilly that it was justly called Norman Switzerland – every orchard separated from the other by tall hedges, it was much easier to take the churns to the cows on the back of a donkey at milking time than to bring the cows slowly back to the home field, which especially in muddy weather was an exasperating operation.

Nevertheless the donkey has mostly disappeared. Perhaps this is a good thing. Our last donkey on the farm was left out in the open one winter's night, doubtless because he had ceased to be very useful. The next day he was discovered with his hooves imprisoned in ice, dead in the bitter cold.

On my return to the farm, I found two men waiting for me. One of them was Pierre Maignier from Douville. He had brought his friend Michel Robert who had a farm at Gonneville, a picturesque village some five miles inland.

Pierre Maignier.

Many years earlier, before Georgette had a car of her own, she asked me to drive her to Caen where she was anxious to consult a specialist about her back which was painful. We set off, Georgette, Brigitte and I, on one of those hot summer mornings that leave an unforgettable picture in one's mind – of golden corn iridescent under a quivering heat haze, poppies and cornflowers, and sleepy cottage gardens alive with butterflies and bees. On the way back, Georgette was anxious to call on her old school friend, Mme Maignier, who lived in a farmhouse at Douville, a picturesque village quite lost to the world which would require us to make a detour of some ten or fifteen miles. 'She keeps hens,' Georgette explained, 'but as the village is so small she has difficulty in selling them, whereas we on the coast at the height of the summer season never have sufficient to meet the demand. So whenever I can, I collect her eggs and sell them for her to our summer residents.'

We drove along narrow country roads whose hedges were garlanded with honeysuckle and when we arrived at the lovely old-world farm we found a dark, pretty little woman washing some light woollies in her kitchen. This was Mme Maignier.

Georgette and her former school friend kissed each other on

the cheek three times which is Norman custom. First on one cheek, then on the other and once again on the first cheek. Brigitte meanwhile had gone off with Mme Maignier's little girl, Annie, to pick strawberries in the garden.

It was a Monday and Mme Maignier began telling us how she and her family had spent Sunday. She had bought a new car and had driven her husband and Annie to a river, or a lake, I'm not sure which, where there had been some sort of fête, after which they watched Karting, then a new sport. She was happy with the new car, happy to have driven the family herself, happy to have had this change from the monotony of daily existence. She showed us her house, which was charming, and very old, took us out into the courtyard where there was a small building in which, she said, lodged her dairy maid – an unmarried mother with two children. She's pleased to have the job,' said Mme Maignier, 'and I'm delighted to have her. If I didn't have a woman to milk the cows in the evening, I could never get away.'

I looked at Mme Maignier in the sunlight of the courtyard and I found her even prettier than in the semi-obscurity of the shaded house. She was slim and had beautiful eyes. I remember thinking that her daughter Annie would assuredly grow up like her mother into a beautiful woman.

Georgette was suddenly anxious to be home. 'I'm never easy when I'm away from the farm too long,' she said. 'One never knows with animals. Something so often goes wrong as soon as one leaves the house. It's as if they knew that one's back was turned.'

The two friends bade one another farewell, with a renewal of the three kisses. The two little girls came back with their mouths stained with strawberry juice and we carried the big basket of new laid eggs back to the car.

I drove back very slowly because the slightest jolt was painful to Georgette. On leaving her friend, she said: 'I'm almost jealous of her. She has everything in the world – beauty, an adoring husband who does exactly what she wants, a woman to help her in the house and a sweet little girl'. I might have answered that this applied equally to Georgette but we always covet another woman's advantages without sufficiently appre-

61

ciating our own.

On our way back to Berlequet, we passed the red brick house. Mme Levannier was watering the roses in her front garden. She was passionately fond of flowers and this year they made a fine show.

'Well,' she cried out, as we stopped to bid her good evening, 'How goes your poor back after the visit to the "bone-setter"?'

'Painfully,' said Georgette dramatically. 'The bones in my spine cracked like a gun going off. He says it should do me good.'

'I'm glad for you!' said Mme Levannier. 'A man always gets sympathy when he's ill. A woman never.'

The next time I saw Mme Maignier and her little girl was at the rejoicings for Brigitte's First Communion. M. Maignier was there, of course, and there was that wonderful supper party in the marquee tent at Berlequet – a memorable occasion in the history of the farm. Perhaps the last of its kind.

Some months later I learnt from Georgette that her former schoolfriend had killed herself.

We all went to the funeral in the tiny twelfth-century church at Douville. The village was called Douceville – gentle-village. The poor husband was utterly unable to understand what had happened to his young wife whom he had so loved and so spoilt. How could she have done it? How could such happiness end in tragedy? She, so pretty, so young – mother of such an adorable little girl.

Why indeed had she done it – she in her cottage set in the almost unbelievable beauty of the Norman countryside? Could it have been loneliness? Could it be that if farmers all over the land were deserting the farms, it was fundamentally because young women could no longer stand the utter loneliness (quite apart from the hardship) of the lives they were expected to live? The men were much less recalcitrant. They drove their tractors, they tended their beasts, they brought in the hay, they went off to shoot rabbits in the copses and woods of a Sunday. They were not likely to experience the loneliness of a young, pretty woman without friends.

Because in the old days women on farms were not lonely. The young farmers' wives at Marais when I was a little girl were always visiting or being visited by neighbours or relations. They met at Mass on Sundays, drove to christenings in their pony carts, quarrelled, made it up, dressed on Sundays in their finery, presided at meal times at a long table at which there were perhaps a dozen farmhands, and when a son or a daughter got married the rejoicings lasted for at least four days and four nights. The villages themselves were fun. The church functioned. The priest made his rounds. There was a school with a schoolmaster, an inn with an innkeeper, a café with little tables outside and a baker who for a few sous would cook a goose or a turkey in his ovens. But today our villages in the Pays d'Auge were totally deserted. Take Gonneville, for instance, one of the prettiest villages that the mind can picture. There is no school, the church is mostly closed, no innkeeper smiles at passers-by from his welcoming hostelry, farmers no longer meet there of an evening. Who own the majority of these cottages which were once so bright with hung-out washing and smoke curling up from chimneys? Why, they have been bought by city folk as secondary residences or speculations and are shuttered and closed for ten months in the year. The village is dead. The men have gone. Where would a girl find a husband, or a young married woman the companionship that would lighten her appalling sense of loneliness? Now that Georgette had left Berlequet to seek the comparative gregariousness of village suburbia, who would bring me my milk and recount me the gossip of the day?

All this had taken place some years before. Little Annie was grown up. I had not seen her since the funeral, a poor little thing convulsed in tears. Then two or three summers later I went to the baker's in our village square. As soon as the holiday crowds arrive the local shopkeepers take on hands to deal with the sudden rush. At one time Brigitte, for instance, had worked for a season at the paper shop. But the baker fills her shop with young village girls to help sell her bread, her *croissants*, her *brioches* and her delicious home-made cakes. So into the bakery I went to be faced by three or four young girls. But one of them stood out by her beauty from her youthful companions. She was the image of that bright-eyed, slim, dark young woman whom Georgette and I had surprised when she was washing her woollies in her cottage kitchen. The woman who had killed herself was reincarnated in her grown-up daughter Annie.

'Annie!' I cried. And we fell into each other's arms. We kissed on the cheeks three times, and suddenly her lovely eyes filled up with tears. People waiting to buy their crisp, hot loaves looked surprised.

'What has happened to you?' I asked.

'We sold the farm,' she said, 'and my father lives at Dozulé. He works for a dairy combine.'

'You remember me?' asked M. Maignier, advancing with his young friend from under the naked branches of the pear tree.

'Yes,' I answered. 'How could I forget you?'

'I have brought my friend, Michel Robert from Gonneville. He has a farm of his own but he needs more grass. I wondered whether, now that the Déliquaires have gone . . .'

Buying grass was a technical term. It meant that you leased your land to somebody who in the strict sense of the word was not your farmer. M. Robert had his own farm at Gonneville. He merely wanted to have more grass for his cattle. An arrangement of this kind did not pass before a notary. It was a word of mouth transaction which had the effect in law of making you yourself the farmer. For tax purposes you were assessed according to what you would have earned had you had cattle of your own. The land was supposed to bring in so much per acre.

This system, perfectly legal, was being resorted to increasingly by owners whose farmers providentially left them. The obvious advantage was that the land became yours again to do with as you wished – to keep or to sell. In short you were mistress of your destiny. A slight danger remained, but a very slight one. Such arrangements in principle ran from April to November, and were verbally renewable every year. If the grass was sold to the same person for more than three years at a time, he could seek to prove legally that the understanding had

64

become permanent. In fact, because the person who bought your grass did not live on your land, he seldom sought to make trouble.

Mr Robert's offer had the effect of making me reach an immediate decision on Berlequet. I would sell it. I would thus never again have the problem of having to keep up buildings which I was not sure of getting back at the end of a lease. The difference to my peace of mind would be considerable.

The village was full of small local estate agents but curiously enough none of them produced a prospective buyer. Was the menace of the road sufficient to put them off? Or was there something else?

January was always the most difficult month of the year, when we were most likely to have snow and ice. But though at times I did suffer from a sense of loneliness, winter on the farm was not at all the ordeal that many people not accustomed to country life supposed it must be. To begin with both my husband and I had a passion for forestry. We cut down trees, the old way, with a long two-handled saw or with an axe; we divided up the trunk into three-foot logs which in turn we split with a sledge hammer and heavy iron wedges; we made faggots and stored our wood in six-foot walls and the kindling wood round the base of ciderpear trees. The telephone kept us in touch with two continents and we read voraciously. The big log-fire that burned night and day in the big, low room kept the house alive. We did not suffer from the cold but I continually dreamt of the London streets which I missed horribly. Our son and his family were either in New York, Singapore or Washington. He who at the age of eight in London had been momentarily but spectacularly a film star, flew from Kuwait to Tokyo, from Paris to Melbourne, on business of a modernity I never even tried to understand. He was everything I could most humbly have prayed for.

One Saturday evening of this cold January, French television, which at times was excellent, showed us a film about the lemurs of Madagascar, those small mammals like monkeys but with pointed muzzles.

Whenever Madagascar came into the news it evoked for me memories of my Protestant pastor at Clichy who had once been a missionary there and who at the end of the First World War taught us a hymn in Malagash which, though incomprehensible to a little girl, he made us sing at a peace celebration in honour of President Wilson. Alas, I never had an opportunity to visit this former French possession but often in later life, before taking the Channel steamer at Le Havre, I would stroll along the ocean quays and at one particular spot there used occasionally to be seen a white cargo ship of very elegant lines that bore the name of the island's capital – Tananarive. Watching the lemurs in the film jumping from branch to branch with their young tenderly clasped in their arms delighted me. What fun the film operators must have had! When Carol Reed was making *The Fallen Idol*, there was a scene in which my small son, as the foreign diplomat's little boy in Graham Greene's story, is taken by the butler and the housekeeper, Sir Ralph Richardson and Michele Morgan, to the London Zoo. Because of this important sequence we lived for a time in a caravan in Regent's Park. We shared our mid-morning buns with the llamas but whenever Périnal, the famous French camera-man, responsible for this picture, had a moment to spare he would rush over to the panda's cage in the hope of photographing the touching antics of this much-loved animal. My son and I saw in the panda merely an adorable, cuddly Teddy Bear come to life but Georges Périnal studied it with the same deep love for animal behaviour as he showed for idiosyncrasies and comportment of human beings which he captured so remarkably in his films.

I had found it difficult to make friends with Georges Périnal, a moody man and something of a genius, inclined to melancholy. But if one caught him in his moments of ecstasy in front of the panda he was apt to divulge something of the agony in his heart.

'Why are you so sad?' I asked him one day.

'I'm not sad at work,' he said. 'Only all the rest of the time.'

He put a hand on my son's blond head and exclaimed:

'You are fortunate to have this boy. I lost my son at the age of twenty-one. When I'm behind the camera I think about my work but as soon as I turn the key in my front door and have to face my wife then grief and despair choke me. I can sometimes forget. She, never. It takes a man some twenty years to form another himself. Then in a few moments, perhaps after an operation, in the course of a war – it's all over!'

At about this time also, I had a friend called Paloma – Marie Saquet was her real name, a strange character whom I first met in Green Park during the Second World War. In her youth, as one of the famous Gaiety girls, millionaires were at her feet. One of them, after all that time, was still in love with her – no longer because of her beauty (she looked like a tall, angular bird) but because of the diverting contradictions in her character and her wit which made conversation with her full of pleasurable surprise.

I never quite knew how to take her. She could be rude at one moment, generous the next. She would berate a taxi-driver then, when he was on the point of rebelling, give him a one-pound note with an enchanting smile. We had been walking down Bond Street where with some much-prized coupons I had bought a box of chocolates which I shared with her. I see her still dressed in what she called her cassock, a long, black, woollen sack with a zip running all the way up – even to the neck which, in her case, was elongated. She wore on this a cameo depicting the Virgin Mary, and the whole effect was so patently absurd that I almost blush with shame at the very thought that I could have been seen walking beside her along this fashionable, elegant street. But how piercing were her dark eyes – like those of an eagle searching for its prey.

She was oblivious to how people thought she ought to dress and to occasional amused looks in the street. She was convinced with some truth that she was a superior being, and if she suspected that anybody when addressing her lacked respect she had a devastating gift for turning the tables on them, so that those who started by laughing often ended by making a wry face. There was, on the other hand, a quality of fantasy about her which resulted in frequent changes in personality – one never was quite sure to whom one was speaking – country girl, Gibson Gaiety girl, lady of leisure or fairy-tale princess. She was at ease wearing an apron as she was in finery and feathers.

All this is merely to relate that on that particular day, after leaving Charbonnel and Walker, the chocolate shop, she said on a sudden impulse:-

'Let us cross the road, my little rat, and inspect the shoes in the windows of Hellstern!'

I was accustomed to this appellation. 'My little rat' was an endearment. As for Hellstern, it was at that time one of the smartest and most expensive shoe shops in London. As I suffer from a certain timidity, I objected:

'But his shoes are all hand-made. They are marvellous but far beyond my purse!' I added: 'On reflexion I have never worn shoes made to measure.'

'That only shows how stupid you are,' she said. 'Had you always bought shoes made to your measure you wouldn't now suffer from your feet. Consider how much better tempered you would be. When I was young, shoes, like dresses and skirts, were made to measure. They gave one individuality.'

By this time we had crossed the road and were inspecting the beautiful array of delicate shoes. But Paloma scarcely looked at them. She said:

'What are you waiting for? Let's go in!'

After sweeping into the shop ahead of me, she sat majestically on a comfortable chair and allowed her old string bag (which she invariably carried with her) to sink down on the thick carpet. A neat little woman came forward to meet us.

'What has become of you?' asked Paloma. 'I haven't seen you for ages.'

I felt tricked. So they knew each other! But wisely I remained silent. Later Paloma would assuredly explain matters. The two women talked for a while about nothing in particular after which Paloma rose, took her string bag up and as her dark, enquiring eyes looked slowly at the beautiful objects in the shop, she exclaimed:

'I like that leather bag. Is it hand-made?'

'Yes,' said the woman. 'It's a lovely handbag made by one of our cleverest craftsmen – but expensive.'

Paloma turned to me:

'What do you think of it, my little rat?'

A warm wine colour, the supple morocco smelt delicious. I had not seen anything so beautiful since the war.

'It's magnificent,' I said.

Paloma turned to the saleswoman who had remained all this time looking at us with a grave expression. Then she said:

'I'll take it. Find me a pen and I'll write you out a cheque.'

When the handbag had been wrapped up and handed to her, she opened her old string bag and pushed the parcel up against a pound of rice she had bought in Shepherd Market. She liked to feed the pigeons who congregated on the window ledge of her apartment overlooking the British Museum. A few minutes later we were back on the pavement of New Bond Street.

'You know,' she said, referring to her friend in the shop. 'That little woman is truly miserable. I doubt if she'll ever smile again. Her only boy, when not quite twenty-one, was killed during the Normandy landings. He had been spared until the last moment – and then suddenly it was over. Over for him and over for her. What do you suppose is left for her? You were surprised, weren't you, even a little shocked, to see me buy that very expensive handbag? You know quite well I shall never use it. It was because of her that I bought it – to help give her the impression that what she's doing in that silly shop is useful. Do you suppose that selling shoes and handbags is any compensation for losing your only son? That's what war does to us, my little rat. You are fortunate. Imagine if your son had been a little older.'

We had reached Piccadilly.

'I am going to leave you here,' said Paloma. 'I shall jump on that number 38. I've seen enough of you for one day.'

'Why don't you hail a cab?' I asked. 'That string bag of yours is both awkward and heavy.'

'Don't be a fool,' she said. 'Who would I meet in a taxi but my own reflexion in a broken mirror? Whereas in a bus I can have the pleasure of staring at a lot of idiots!'

I had been waiting for permission to go to France. The war was not quite over and one needed all sorts of permits – but now at last I was to leave. Paloma telephoned. 'I've a dreadful cold,' she said. 'Come and see me and bring me a bag of Carolina rice. Jump into a cab. I'll pay.'

She was in her large bed and on the table beside her reposed a bottle of Chianti and a saucer full of silver half-crowns.

'Why all the half-crowns?' I asked, intrigued.

'Because they are so pretty, I can't prevail upon myself to spend them,' she said. 'Real silver like real gold is so lovely to the touch. One day they'll take them away from us. You'll see. Now the war is virtually over, those politicians are capable of anything. When I was young a sovereign was made of gold. They didn't cheat you in those days. Did you bring the rice?'

'Yes,' I said.

'Is it the best Carolina?'

'I think so. What are you going to do with it?'

'Give it to the pigeons, of course. Can't you hear them knocking their beaks against the window pane? It makes me miserable when I have nothing to give them.'

'If you only knew the trouble I had in finding this rice,' I said. 'In wartime. Imagine! It had to come across the Atlantic.'

'What business is it of yours what I do with it?' said Paloma. 'If I pay for it?'

'In other words,' I said, 'you merely wanted the rice, not my company. I'll be off.'

'When are you going to France?'

'Tomorrow,' I said. 'I see that you have unpacked your lovely new handbag but you haven't used it yet, have you? It's a shame to leave it neglected. Personally I would never have the strength of character.'

'It's too much trouble for me,' she said, 'to empty all the things out of an old handbag and put them in a new one. I would be quite lost. But as you are determined to go to France before even the war is properly over, take my new handbag with you. Use it on the journey. It will do it a power of good to be taken back to the country where it was made. It will be twice as elegant after a trip to Paris!'

So I took the new handbag with me to Paris. There I was to meet again Elsa Schiaparelli, the great Italian dressmaker, just back from New York where she had spent the war years. She had not only taken over her couture house in the Place Vendôme again but was living once more in the historic private house she owned in the Rue de Berri, recently abandoned by the enemy.

'Who were the enemy?' I asked.

'Italian officers,' she said. 'My compatriots!'

To celebrate the joy at our reunion, for I loved her dearly, she gave me a small bottle of her 'Shocking' perfume, the perfume, one of my favourites, the bottle shaped like a mannequin, a tiny masterpiece of the glassblower's art. How wonderful it was to recover by degrees the superfluous – nylon stockings, French perfume, nail varnish . . .

On the ship returning to England, enemy mines still floating in the Channel, I clasped to my bosom Paloma's new handbag in which were my passport, my fortune and the bottle of Shocking perfume. But because I had doubtless failed to close the glass top sufficiently, nearly all the precious perfume flowed into the handbag.

Paloma, when I gave it back to her, sniffed appreciatively and said:

'Didn't I tell you, my little rat, that this handbag was in need of a trip to Paris?'

I started to panic about Berlequet. What if I could not sell it? Because now that I had decided to do so, I wanted it to happen immediately. I had never been able to learn the lesson of patience.

At heart, I think, I was ashamed to see it in such a sad state with windows broken, doors off their hinges, paint peeling, dead embers in the fireplace. I was appalled to reflect how unloved it had become after once, at the beginning, being so coveted. The ideal would have been to modernize it, to put in central heating, to instal a bathroom, to design a fine kitchen and to hang chintz curtains against the freshly painted windows. Here and there, inside the long, low dwelling house were vestiges of the shack, doubtless dating back to the sixteenth-century, which Groscol had inhabited – beautiful half timbering hidden behind boards or plaster. The dwelling house had no fewer than three front doors, another Norman custom because this style of architecture, built without foundations, without any form of cellar, never takes into account the obvious usefulness of a hall. Coming from outside you enter straight into the living room, the kitchen or the dining room. This was the great inconvenience in my own house. Strangers who knocked at the front door walked straight into the kitchen which infuriated me when I was cooking lunch or making a cake. The possibilities at Berlequet were immense. It is extremely tempting for a woman to dream of what a place like this could be turned into, given taste and a little money.

But as I was not going to live at Berlequet myself, the very idea of turning it into a jewel was, as everybody told me, madness. Property nowadays, to be economic, must provide homes for as many potential buyers as is permitted by the local planning authority. Why did I not sit on it for a while and then, perhaps in ten years time, sell it to a developer?

I suppose I was some sort of a poet. This was the very opposite of everything I believed. If the law made it impossible for me to rent a farmhouse to a farmer, then I would see that it fell into the hands of somebody who would love it, and turn it into the sort of place which I would take pleasure in looking at each time I passed by.

As it happened before the end of the winter somebody did fall in love with it – a coppersmith, a young man with a young wife, a schoolmistress, and two little girls. The young man's name was Buon and his dream, which matched mine, was to beautify the place by the work of his own hands. He was not only a coppersmith but also a carpenter, a stonemason and something of a draughtsman. The fact that he had no money to speak of, appeared to be no barrier at all. Any bank, he said, would advance it to him but could I not give him a tiny piece of orchard land so that he could grow fruit trees and perhaps keep an animal? And this for the two little girls would be ideal.

Somebody else gave me a final warning.

'The dwelling house should be sold to one person and the ciderpress and its dependencies to somebody else,' he said.

'Business is business. Money is what you want, isn't it? Two deals are better than one. And how do you know that a young man's dreams will come true? Once you've sold the property you won't have a say in what happens to it. Your prospective buyer can turn seller before two more winters are past. Then where will you be? Sentiment and money don't mix. That's why this lovely plateau is being turned into a wilderness of cement. Everybody wants to join in the merry-go-round. If you refuse to do like the others, you'll be left naked on the wayside.'

Before the first primroses came up, I was tired of the whole business. I told myself that these people doubtless had years ahead of them in which to scheme and to plan, whereas I must learn to count the days. I accordingly agreed to sell Berlequet to the Buons for the equivalent of £12,000 cash down from the bank, and no commission or expenses.

5

WHILE MY SON and his young wife, Lisette, (they had met while taking their respective degrees at Oxford – he at Lincoln, she at Somerville) were living in New York, they had their first child, a baby girl, whom they called Dominique.

Now, having earned a very short holiday, they were to fly to England (where Lisette's parents lived) and cross over from Southampton to Le Havre by the night ferry. Would we meet them?

As they were arriving early in the morning and I wanted to leave two hours for the journey by the new bridge that crosses the Seine at Tancarville, I trussed a fowl and before leaving in the car at 5 a.m. put it in a pot with an onion so that it would simmer quietly in the slow oven of the Aga stove. The problem of providing a hot meal for a hungry family with no help in the house, and myself absent all the morning, invariably called for advance planning. Until recently, to reach Le Havre, which from Deauville was only on the far side of the bay formed by the wide mouth of the Seine, one drove along the coast road as far as Honfleur, and then along the river bank, half mud, half brine, to where an old fashioned ferry took one across to the other bank. From here it took about half an hour to reach the docks by car.

The ferry had been replaced by the new bridge at Tancarville, supposed to be a great engineering achievement, and indeed the view from half way across was picturesque, on the one side towards the wide river mouth, on the other towards Rouen, the destination of much shipping. With no traffic on the road I reached Le Havre as dawn was breaking, and leaving the car in front of the customs shed ordered coffee and a hot roll in one of the new café-hotels that had sprung up along quays utterly destroyed by allied aerial bombardment during the war. Here, before the war, when the picturesque frontage was some two hundred years old, the Castels had their little place from which Yvonne's mother recuperated her precious store of linen. The bar in which I sat had neon lights and the colourful effervescence of pre-war days had disappeared, but the men who sat drinking their coffee and Calvados had not changed. Indeed the whole place smelt of this pungent spirit.

The quays in front of me stretched away to the distant ocean dock where the giant France was tied up waiting to make one of its final trips to New York, before being towed to a deserted creek along the river, where it was to remain like a common hulk, its paint peeling away, a miserable mockery of its former glory. Gone were the days of the ocean boat trains, the baskets of flowers and fruit, the gay streamers, the millionaires and the film stars. Nobody travelled by ship any more. The pride of the French merchant fleet would be offered to wealthy Arabs, like those fine office buildings along the Champs-Elysées, which discreetly passed into foreign hands. Gone too was the Red Ensign from most of the cargo vessels in the docks. The 200,000-ton tankers, that too often spilled their oil into the sea, sailed under a flag of convenience. The ultra-modern white vessel being towed in through the lock gate bore a Russian name and its place of registry as Leningrad. The Soviet flag was omnipresent.

I thought about these changes with a touch of sadness as the day began to dawn. I thought how excited I would have been to have found myself standing on the ocean quay in pre-war days waiting for my son, my daughter-in-law and my first grandchild to appear waving and gesticulating on the boat deck of some giant Atlantic liner which in five short days would have brought them in luxury across the ocean from New York. The Paris train with its hissing monster Pacific locomotive would be drawn up at the quayside to rush the passengers smoothly to Paris. The compartments would be warm and snug, the stewards in their white jackets would be waiting to serve hot coffee and *croissants* in the wagon-restaurant, the chef with his white toque would be standing on the quay, the employees from Cooks and

American Express would be all ready to greet their famous clients whose suites would be reserved at the Crillon, the Meurice or the Ritz.

I thought about Georges Périnal and the Pandas at the London zoo, and how the great camera man had put his hand on my son's head, so gently, so tenderly but with such infinite sadness, thinking of his own boy who had died at the age of twenty one. I thought of the little woman in the Bond Street shop from whom Paloma had bought an expensive handbag for no other reason than that in spite of her craziness, she was filled with compassion for a mother who had lost her son.

The ferry came in slowly from the open sea and was hidden by the cutoms shed. I stood on the roadside waiting. We were in Spring and the holiday crowds had not yet begun. The ship was not very full. The first passengers came down the gangway, clutching their passports and tickets in one hand, their luggage in the other. They looked enquiringly round the shed, advanced towards a customs official, then queued up in front of a little window to have their passports stamped.

They emerged on to the quay, sleep still in their eyes, looking rather bedraggled in the cold morning air. Women like men wore raincoats or duffle coats over pullovers and jeans; flat inelegant shoes, and nearly all were bareheaded, the women's hair flopping over their cheeks and eyes or tied back with a slide or a narrow bit of ribbon; the mens' hair long, unkempt and in appearance greasy. Some, after the long night on board ship, were unshaven, others wore beards. They looked round, undecided what to do or where to go. No Paris train was waiting for them to speed them on their journey. No helpful couriers from Cooks to give them news about hotel reservations. Not even a taxi or a bus. Many doubtless had their own cars on board ship but it would be a little while before they could be driven off.

Now suddenly I caught sight of my son and my daughter-in-law, and my heart gave a great thump of happiness to see them again after these months of separation, the wide Atlantic between us. My son looked tired, grave and a little wan but his light hair was smartly cut and I waved frantically and called him by name. He saw me and responded but where was my grand-daughter? Was she hidden by the straggling crowd or had they decided after all not to bring her? But she was still only a baby. How could she have been hidden by the crowd? Why was she not in her mother's arms? At seven months?

As they hurried forward to meet me, I saw that my baby grand-daughter was suspended in a sort of hammock fastened solidly to my son's back. I was utterly confounded. I could never have imagined that my first view of this important baby should be of her strapped to her father's back as if they had been Asiatics in Hong Kong! Pictures of Far Eastern ports floated before my troubled eyes. Could I be dreaming? Where were the costly frills and hand-made laces of my youth? The children's nurse in her veil and starched apron? The gangway leading down from the Atlantic liner with its red funnels and proud name – the *Mauretania*, the *France*, the *Bremen*? All the laughter, the gaiety, the cries of recognition, the smart luggage, the colour, the welcome to a different land?

Was this what age did to one? But how could I comprehend that brains, success and love should make their way towards me so humbly in this drab crowd?

We drove off through wide, empty streets, past warehouses, quays and huge refineries belching forth flame and smoke to the canal that borders the muddy banks of the Seine estuary. There was so much I wanted to ask but the questions became entangled in my throat and the answers, because we were not yet all three attuned to one another, were unsatisfactorily, guarded.

But here in my small car, asleep in her strange contraption barred with metal, was Effie's great-grand-daughter for whom, as the future woman, I dreamt such eager dreams. The mud of the Thames at Brentford had given place to the mud of the Seine, not very distant from the river's mouth. The shriek of tugs could be heard far off through the morning mist. I recalled how bitterly shocked my mother-in-law had been when in the fatal summer of 1940 I had come back from France like a pennyless refugee, tired, wan, bedraggled, holding tightly to

77

my bosom the baby boy with whom I had fled before the advancing might of the German army. Here he was beside me, this erstwhile baby, grown-up, rather tight-lipped, grave, important, the successful American business man, whose baby girl was almost exactly the same age as he had been when I brought him to my mother-in-law in her pretty, prosperous house in the English home counties. How bitterly she had resented my poor clothes and pathetic failure dragging behind me the loss of my country, the shame of my own destitution. How uncertain had been my future.

How could one hope to bridge the misunderstandings between one generation and the other? Those eternal comparisons that are endemic in a long life? Was the past better than the present? Would the present seem better than the future? Would I have time left to discover the latent character in the little girl asleep in her hammock? Would I feel compensated by the brilliance of her future for the fears that choked me when, alone in my orchard house, I felt the creeping intrusion of the town? The disappearance of all I loved.

It was not easy at first. The boiled fowl saw us all round the kitchen table and the cattle looked up lazily from the field. They were no longer Georgette's cattle. Her cows had been sold. She bought her milk, like I did, from the Levanniers or else from a shop in the village. She and I were not quite the friends we had been during my mother's lifetime. We smiled at each other in the street, even passed the time of day, but gone were those intimate conversations that we had at the kitchen door facing the brought milk can. When owner and tenant have parted they see each other in a different light. As strangers. There remains also a tiny shadow of resentment – on my side, that she had thought so little of the land that she had left it with an insult; on her side that the owner is by the very nature of things – an enemy. The excuse for class hatred, even in a modern world.

Mr Robert was now legally though unofficially buying my grass. He was to pay me quite a generous income in three instalments every year – on 1 July, 1 October and when the cider apples had been gathered on 1 November . His cattle were tall and powerful and when they raised their heavy necks to flick their tongues over the lower branches of the apple trees, the entire tree shook. I would turn my eyes away quickly, hating to see pear tree, apple tree or cherry tree maltreated but aware of my own dreadful impotence. I was angry at the damage, angry that I was such a coward as to accept it. So I would avert my gaze and try to think of something else. Yet nobody loved the cattle more than I did with their gentle ambling, their lovely eyes under long lashes, the noise they made tearing at the grass under my window at nights when I could not sleep.

My son listened politely to what I had done, spoke of what was happening in New York City, touching lightly on politics in case we might differ on them. Meanwhile he watched jealously over his young wife – as my husband had watched over me when both young we visited my parents-in-law at Brentford, springing to my defence if he felt that there was the slightest occasion for it. I had basked in the sunshine of his protection, feeling safe. Though Effie never did rebuff me. But when one is young one is dreadfully alert for the word that can sting, for the glance that can humiliate.

Now that my son was beginning a family, they took over the cottage that I had built before the war at right angles to the main house. It comprised a living room, two bedrooms, a modern bathroom and a small kitchen. Originally thatched, it now had a slate roof like my own but it had minor disadvantages. Whereas the big house, facing southeast, had the sun most of the day, the cottage only had it in the afternoon. The mornings were apt in spring and autumn to be cold, and there was no central heating, only electric fires. The main room had an open hearth into which we had put a wood stove.

The baby girl took most of Lisette's time and she was an excellent mother, but my grand-daughter was much too small for me to get to know her in so short a time. Indeed on this first visit we established no bond between us. This was natural. All her affection was for her parents.

We lunched all together in the big house at midday, and as this was the important meal it required considerable work on

79

my part, which often taxed my strength. I prayed desperately that I should live long enough to see this new mind awakening to the beauty of the world about her. My dream was to have her for a whole summer, perhaps, when at eight or nine she would be old enough to give me some impression of what the girl grown to womanhood would eventually become. Would her interests be so very different from what mine had been at that age? Was a little girl essentially feminine from the start, as I had been, or could it be true that children of both sexes were, unless otherwise influenced, alike in mind and spirit? This piece of modern philosophy profoundly shocked me but I needed to know. I have never in life willingly accepted a statement that I have been unable to prove. My little grand-daughter was a New York girl, at least by birth, and she would doubtless grow up in a boisterously new, harsh world.

I was impatient to see the result.

Deauville was no longer the small, fashionable resort of romantic evocation to which writers, dressmakers, actresses, painters and playwrights, in short the intellectual and wealthy élite of Paris, were convened every August by Mr André. They would arrive in Bugattis, Hispano Suizas and Rolls Royces or by special train. The prettiest mannequins in the capital deserted Longchamp and Auteuil to parade at the races. The King of Spain sipped his 'rose' cocktail at the Bar du Soleil.

By looking carefully one could still admire the virginia creeper on the walls of the unique Normandy Hotel. The elegant white casino, the Royal Hotel and the Printemps store are unchanged, at least from outside. But the modern equivalents of Coco Chanel, the Duke of Westminster, the cartoonists Sem and Forain, the playwright Henri Bernstein, the old Aga Khan, Venizelos and Mr Selfridge, if they exist, are lost in the crowd of people-of-all-sorts who have descended upon the camping sites all along the coast or have just bought themselves on twenty years' credit one of the many thousands of new apartments that speculators continue to put down on every grain of sand, every pebble, every available blade of grass.

Deauville, to all intents and purposes, has become a great summer dormitory town not for commuters but for the owners of secondary or tertiary residences which they have bought partly to enhance their social status, partly in the hope of selling them in a few years' time at a profit.

Virgil contemplating the building of Rome could not have imagined the speed with which these once-green orchards have given place to immense apartment houses with weirdly aristocratic appellations to inflate the egos of prospective purchasers. Even poor Marie-Antoinette has been dragged from her tumbril to flatter the brave republicans who will inhabit these palaces of cement and steel.

For all this Deauville was my shopping town. I bought the grain for my chickens there because the little man who owned the shop sold forage for the racehorses. But I also went to Deauville because of the yacht *Sarah Munro* which docked there every spring and which became for me a sort of home from home.

I came to know (and to love) its owners in the strangest way.

One summer when I had come over from London to stay with my mother on the farm, I received a letter, written by hand in violet ink, from an American woman called Theresa FitzPatrick who had read *The Little Madeleine*. She was, or had been, connected with a famous American monthly magazine and was on the point of making a pilgrimage to the shrine of Sainte Thérèse de Lisieux. As she supposed that my farm was not far from Lisieux, she was anxious to come and see me. She lived in Rhode Island and the name of her house was picturesquely 'The Little Schoolhouse'.

Her letter, I confess, put me in something of a quandary. I was touched that she had liked the book but I was not at all pleased at the thought of her descending upon me at the farm. Matilda, my mother, had never wished to read what I had written about my girlhood. As we received all the London newspapers and magazines at the farm she was perfectly aware of it, but even when the Americans sent somebody over to try to negotiate film rights which, owing to certain stipulations on my part, came to nothing, she pretended ignorance. After her death I found the copy of the book which I had sent her tied up with string and paper and tossed with some other rubbish on top of her wardrobe. She had never even opened it.

Matilda had an inflexible character. If at times she was not altogether displeased by the turn which our lives had taken, she never showed it. But the one thing she did not want, was to be reminded of the dark, difficult days of her early marriage. How could I allow a complete stranger to come into the house and discuss in my mother's presence a subject as intimate as this? Mother-daughter relationship is delicate enough at the best of times – and as I have inherited from Matilda an inferiority complex and a hot, sudden anger at the realisation of my inadequacies, I foresaw most unpleasant complications. Besides, I was afraid of her. What daughter is not secretly afraid of her mother?

I was in this state of acute embarrassment when the news reached me that Theresa FitzPatrick and a friend were to arrive at a certain hour by train. My son, if I remember rightly, still at Oxford, was of no great help. My literary indiscretions were not of a nature to advance his academic career and when he was on holiday on the farm, as he then was, he tended to be more patient with his grandmother than with me. Nevertheless I managed to explain matters to both of them, and having arranged for the two American women to be fetched at the station, I betook myself down the road to the sea for a long, lazy day on the sands.

That evening, on my return home, fearful of what awaited me, I found my mother jubilant. Never had she met such delightful people! She might, of course, have guessed as much. Had she not always had a predilection, dating from the days of Mary Pickford and Pearl White, for Americans who were so friendly and open-hearted? They all went together to fill a basket with new-laid eggs from right under the hens, for lunch they boiled them, drank cups of strong tea, and Theresa (whom my mother was already calling by her Christian name) had recounted so many tales of her American girlhood that, said my mother, she had the impression of re-reading *Little Women*.

Relieved by the way things had turned out, I dismissed the whole matter from my mind, but if Theresa had accomplished her pilgrimage to Lisieux and met Matilda who, after all, was the heroine of *The Little Madeleine*, she had yet to meet its authoress – and she was not a woman to do things by halves.

Back in my London apartment, the phone rang one day. It was Theresa inviting me to lunch at a women's club off Piccadilly.

I found an exquisitely groomed little woman who, though literary, had a distinct dress sense. She wore a well-cut skirt and a very pretty pullover which, she explained, she had bought from Anny Blatt in Paris. 'I told her that I had been to see your mother on the farm,' she said, 'and we talked about you. Anny Blatt is, indeed, as remarkable as you claimed in one of your books. I have come to the conclusion,' she added, 'that the world is full of clever women. It consoles me for not having married.'

Politely I allowed her to do the talking. She had been right to choose this pullover whose pink wool softened what was strong and uncompromising in her features. She revealed herself to be both erudite and forceful, accustomed to authority in that complicated world of politics and literature in which it is never easy for a woman to succeed without losing her femininity. Like many journalists her conversation showed her to be equally at home with people of every class and interest. I had seldom before heard a woman discourse with such knowledge on the difficulties and pitfalls of a profession with which for so long I had been intimately concerned. That the world of newspapers and magazines was so soon to experience deep modifications was already a disturbing certainty. Not least was the gradual debasement of popular taste which was to horrify those who, like Theresa, were creatures of culture and high principle. Just as the last orchards were slowly disappearing from our seaside plateau, so the last great daily newspapers in all the great capitals of the world were disintegrating before a veritable explosion of change, the serious paper, in an attempt to cling to life, transforming itself into a tabloid; the magazine, so long a symbol of American culture, tending to disappear.

Matilda was right in loving in Theresa her stories reminiscent of *Little Women*. But in both cases they were recounted with a purpose. Theresa's in order to illustrate how those principles that directed her life were first formed.

'My father,' she said, 'was my hero. The man in my life. He was superb, gay, deep, scholarly, always (at least in my eyes) youthful. One day he took me driving with him in his gig, the varnish and the paint sparkling in the morning sun, the mare spirited. We set off at a fine pace and I can clearly see my father with his Stetson at a rakish angle on his head, the heavy gold of his watch chain reflecting the light, a comforting, imposing figure which meant everything to the little girl that I was – house, schooling, future – an unshakeable, ever-enduring force. We had each had a sip of Madeira wine before setting out, as was the custom in mid-morning in those days, and now he was smoking an enormous cigar that in the open air smelt delicious. Suddenly, without warning, my father stood upright in the gig, and holding the reins in one hand, removed his cigar from his mouth with the other and hurled it away, saying: 'That, Theresa, is the last cigar I shall ever smoke, and the sip of Madeira wine we took before coming for our drive will be for me at least my last taste of alcohol. A man who respects himself must never become a slave to habit. I have come to enjoy these indulgences too much. Today I break with them!' Resuming his seat with a gay laugh, he whipped the mare and off we drove into the country.

'This scene, so clearly remembered, taught me that even the strongest men have their weakness. Fortunate are those who, like my father, have the will to overcome them. He has remained an example to me. When I found myself between what was expedient and what I knew to be wrong, I was fortified.'

But Theresa, as her name implied, was of Irish descent, and as her recent pilgrimage to Lisieux suggested, was a fervent Catholic. She was profoundly shocked when reading about my girlhood that though baptised into the Catholic church I had fallen so quickly under the influence of the Protestant school to which my mother sent to me when I was little more than five. I did in fact gain great comfort from the reformed church. I loved our school at Clichy, was confirmed there and learnt to admire

84

the pastor, M. Maroger, and his brilliant children who were later to be an inpiration to me.

'But why did they send you to a Protestant church school?' asked Theresa.

'Merely at first because it was in the same street.'

'Was that the only reason?'

'We were poor," I said. 'The Roman Catholics were always asking, and we had nothing to give. The Protestants gave without ever asking for something in return. That can make a big difference when pennies are important.'

'It strikes me as being a very down-to-earth argument,' said Theresa.

'Perhaps, but they gave me a most valuable grounding,' I explained. 'They even gave me my first holiday at the seaside. That counts for a lot.'

'I was tempted to scold your mother that day she gave me lunch at the farm,' said Theresa, 'but I saw her in such agony from arthritis that I had not the heart to do so. I would not, for all the world, have given her any more pain. She has enough like that. But with you it's different.'

'You mean that you want to scold me?'

'I am scolding you. You'll see. In the long run you'll go back to the church in which you were baptised.'

'I'm not sure about that,' I said. 'My heart is big enough to find a place for both. Indeed as things have turned out the two of them are inextricable. Added to which my husband's father was a Church of England clergyman.'

'And your son?'

'He went to Downside and married a Catholic girl.'

'There was a time when I had everything,' said Theresa. 'A large house, a vast number of friends, a great deal of influence. But they all disappear and then one is left alone. Not alone in my case. I have God, and if something prevents me from going to Communion, I am deprived of a pleasure.'

'I read in a book,' I said, 'that Mrs Gladstone, the Prime Minister's wife, very Church of England, said something like that of herself when, because of illness or her husband's official business, she was prevented from attending matins.'

'I am glad that you accepted my invitation to lunch,' said Theresa, 'and as I like to feel that my friends get to know one another I shall write to a New York couple who own a very pretty house near Dozulé where they spend a few weeks every summer. Do you know that part?'

'Dozulé? I buy my baby turkeys there, and sometimes also my grain. It takes me less than half an hour in the car.'

'They are Hélène and Bill Leonard,' said Theresa, 'and their village is Putot-en Auge. I think you'll like them.'

And so, sure enough, that very same August the Leonards rang up from Putot-en-Auge. 'About two miles beyond Dozulé on the road to Caen' they said, 'and then turn left by the cider factory.'

Dozulé was a small market town which until the Second World War had played an important role amongst the farming community. Every Tuesday morning, which was market day, farmers drove up in their buggies to sell their butter. Before leaving home the farmer's wife would wrap her mound of butter in a clean linen cloth and place it with her eggs in the gig. Most small towns and even villages had their regular market days but Dozulé was a butter market. When the farmer's wife arrived with her precious mound of butter, an expert would taste it for quality and put it on the scales. There was great rivalry amongst farmers' wives to surpass one another in the quality of their butter. Some women had the gift just as certain of their menfolk had green fingers in their orchards or a positive genius for making cider that tasted better than anybody else's. The art of butter making had practically disappeared and nobody sold it any longer in this manner. It was all too much trouble. The co-operatives bought the milk which they collected outside the farms and the farmers received a cheque at the end of the month. They thus dispensed with the time and labour that formerly went into cream and butter making. Cheese making on individual farms had become equally extinct. Camembert and Pont L'Evêque were made in factories.

The selling of the week's butter at Dozulé had required in the days of the horse and buggy (which continued until the war) quite an expedition. Farmers who arrived there early would transact their business during the morning over apéritifs at café terraces after a visit to the baker for large sticky buns for the children. There was also a cattle market and another for pigs and fowls. Many dealers and their customers would lunch at the fine old coaching inn where the food was renowned. Then in the afternoon everybody would drive home.

The cattle market, like the butter market, had disappeared. The town was almost entirely destroyed during the war. Rommel is said to have passed through several times. Modern shops line the main street and on market day which, as before the war, is on Tuesday, horticulturists display their potted flowers along the pavement and a little farther on there are stalls for clothing, fruit and vegetables. The chief innovation is that farmers' wives who no longer have time for broody hens (even if the hens were willing to co-operate) buy their chicks from the specialists who produce them in vast quantities in incubators and sell them when a few weeks old. The same thing applies to ducklings and young turkeys. All these soft, fluffy little things are brought in cages in a lorry, unloaded (still in their cages) on to trestles so that prospective buyers can inspect them at their ease. There was a woman in charge of these whom I loved to watch, a woman who had nothing in common with the peasant women of former times. She was still young, tall, beautiful in a dark, bewitching way, with eyes and lips made up like those of a film star and long, pointed, varnished nails of deep crimson, and the most elegant clothes, not to mention shoes with four-inch heels. This *volailleuse* as people called her would thrust her beautifully manicured hands into the case from which the customer desired to buy chicks or ducklings, bring out with incredible dexterity males or females according to choice and then thrust them into one or more cardboard boxes which she would then proceed to tie up with stout string. It was at this juncture that she showed her greatest skill. Taking up a short, sharp knife she would slash into the cardboard, at the top and at the sides to make apertures through which the fluffy birds inside could breathe during their journey to their new home. On a hot day the rays of the sun would be reflected on the blade of the knife as it cut swiftly this way and that – but never once did it touch the prisoners inside. She was a great artist who worked with precision and speed so that before the morning was over hundreds of fluffy things were carried off in their cardboard boxes to outlying farms. The picture she made of clever young womanhood reminded me of what Theresa FitzPatrick had said: 'The world is full of clever women!'

Both young chicks and baby turkeys need special feed and when the women had bought their new consignments one would see them make for the grain merchant's shop which looked like something out of a German picture book – a narrow triangular corner shop, the door of which was always open to reveal inside rows upon rows of grain in jute sacks whose open tops each had a shining aluminium shovel with which the grain merchant would dispense the required amount. The grain merchant's movements were as slow and studied as those of the *volailleuse* were swift and feminine. Whe he was measuring out the grain, oats, barley, corn, or even sunflower seeds into a brown paper bag he would add or subtract with his bright little shovel over the weighing machine in order to give the customer only the exact weight. One had the impression that like some modern Père Grandet he was loath to see his precious hoard diminish – every grain of corn was like a golden guinea. This was a scene that dated from pre-war days, something that was bound before long to disappear. Most modern farmers had their requirements supplied wholesale by the co-operatives that collected their milk. The era of the old fashioned grain merchant, like that of the village blacksmith, was over.

Two miles beyond Dozulé on the road to Caen, the Leonards had told me. This main road had, in fact, become a secondary road. The town had just been by-passed by one of those huge four-lane motorways along which you could travel nearly as fast as by an express train, and which no pedestrian was allowed to cross. The building of roads gave employment, and they were being thrust, unwanted, upon the countryside because once a small market town was by-passed it lost all touch with the outside world. The motorist no longer stopped to buy a loaf of bread or something that caught his attention in a shop window. He used the new motorway. But not the giant truck with its deathly load of chemicals, its oil, its twenty-ton load. These continued to go through the town because the companies refused to pay the motorway toll. Dozulé, for its unfortunate inhabitants, had become a death trap.

At the cider factory we turned left. The countryside we entered was utterly unspoilt; the road so narrow I hoped not to meet an oncoming car. This was one of the puzzling things about the problem of rural areas. Just here and there one had glimpses of heaven.

The house was called 'Courtehaie', a small, unpretentious house facing an orchard beyond which was an uninterrupted view over little squares of grazing land. One came upon it by accident, there being no village in the accepted sense – merely an occasional cottage with a garden and a low wall. It was, with its pleasant white veranda, the sort of house one could have found anywhere on this side of the Atlantic or the other. English books and French books lined the walls. There were comfortable English settees and china brought back from the Orient. It was the summer home of a family whose members were attuned to life in Paris, London, New York. These people have a different charm. They almost forget in what country they are, what language they should speak.

My recollection of this first visit is confused. I am not at my best with a drink in my hand, which I never touch, trying to make small talk. I am doubtless too tense, introspective, only at ease in the company of one other person. I must accordingly try to recall highlights – such as my first glimpse of Bill Leonard, handsome and agreeable in a welcoming, smiling American way, his wife, Hélène, modern offshoot of old French nobility, full of softness and dignity, making one feel that one's arrival was something that she had been anxiously looking forward to – a gift I have always envied but never been able to achieve. Switching from one language to another, with never the trace of an accent, she introduced, imparted news, asked questions. Her daughter by a first marriage, Jacquine (who disliked it when strangers called her Jacqueline) was, or recently had been, secretary to Barbara Hutton. As I looked at her bending over her young husband, Patrice de Rochambeau, most illustrious of names, I felt as if I were looking at an illustration of one of those fairy tales we read as children which end with the words '... and they married and were happy ever afterwards.' So beautiful was this girl even in this modern world when beauty is not rare. To meet a Rochambeau is to set one's imagination racing, as would a descendent of Sir Walter Raleigh or the Duke of Wellington. In America the name is as much revered as that of Lafayette. But, I regret to say, the Comte Patrice de Rochambeau was in the throes of toothache, and his chief desire at the moment was for his wife to discover him some dentist who was not on holiday on a Saturday afternoon at the height of the Deauville season. 'I have some English friends I would like you to meet...' Hélène Leonard was saying, piloting me gently out into the veranda. This English couple owned a small boat at Deauville and they had brought along with them a retired military man anxious to describe to Patrice Rochambeau his exploits during the Normandy landing. 'A choppy sea with devilish strong currents. Before 8 a.m. as we landed at June Beach... The third Canadian Division. From Courseulles to St Aubin . . . You see what I mean?' The boat owner's wife who persisted in mistaking me for an author whose books, she claimed, her daughter delighted in, had cornered me, and I had not the courage to tell her that the author she was mistaking me for was not a woman at all but a man. 'My daughter will be so thrilled when I tell her!' she said, continuing to savour the fruits of her imagination.

From the other side of the lane a cow was gazing at us with affectionate interest. How did we appear to her, we gesticulating humans holding glasses in our hands? She lowered her long lashes that even Barbara Hutton in her youth would have been jealous of, and ambled off behind a thin curtain of birch saplings. But a moment later, she was back, unable to resist another look. On the lawn the Rochambeau's young son, and Timothy, Hélène's son by her present marriage, were chasing each other round an apple tree. These are my only memories of that first visit. On this hot August night, I drove back through the small market town of Dozulé. The market place was empty and the grain merchant had folded up his shutters and closed his door.

A day or two later the English couple who had brought their boat to Deauville invited me to pass by if ever I was going that way. This, before long, I had occasion to do, and after spending some time on their boat, I was taken to visit friends of theirs on a much larger ship – the *Sarah Munro*, where I found myself being introduced to the owner as the writer of somebody else's books. Fortunately this information made no effect on anybody, and I was able rapidly to shake off this embarrassing confusion in the world of minor literati. Thus it was that thanks to Theresa FitzPatrick I was finally to have this glimpse into a different world.

6

THE LARGER YACHTS that visit Deauville have a pretty, tree-lined quay of their own where they can plug in for electricity, water and telephone, and along which they can park their cars. This is one of the few spots in this once so fashionable resort to retain its former, quiet dignity – a sort of 'millionaire's row'. Even thus, a bursting desire on the part of simply everybody in the nation to own, for prestige purposes, not only a secondary residence and one or two motor-cars but also a sailing boat, is gradually taking away the exclusivity. The turgid waters of the basin are alive with tiny craft whose owners are often taking to the sea for the first time. They democratize the scene though adding colour to it.

The view towards Deauville is marred by the hideousness of the marina built out into the ocean, but on the other side runs the muddy, narrow river Touques which divides Deauville from its twin city of Trouville and which is still lined at high tide, as in the days of the painter Boudin, with small fishing boats whose nets are often to be seen spread out on the quay. Here, several times a week, under the trees, market folk come to sell their produce so that it becomes a riot of colour – the fruit, the flowers, the vegetables, the butter and cream – and the fish of the previous night's catch. The town itself, built on a hill, towers over this scene, and overlooking the ocean is the beautiful old-fashioned cream-coloured casino which, according to rumour, has been bought by the Japanese.

The *Sarah Munro* was, at this time, unquestionably the most renowned of the large yachts that regularly sailed into Deauville. It was strong, solid, with comfortable deck space and a large cabin in which a picture of Sir Winston Churchill was the first thing that every visitor noticed. The story was that Sir Winston insisted during the Battle of Britain on going up to watch the nocturnal raids on London from the roof of 10 Downing street which so alarmed his security officers that they persuaded the Admiralty to bring the *Sarah Munro* to Westminster Pier. They thought that the Prime Minister would be far safer cruising up and down the Thames during an air raid than on the roof of 10 Downing street.

Sir Winston and the *Sarah Munro* were old friends. This 70-ton ketch built in Scotland just before the war had been owned by an M.P. whose daughter was Winston's godchild. In due course it was to carry out at least two evacuations from Dunkirk and was then purchased by the Admiralty or, at all events, taken over for the duration of the war.

Bud Mitchell, a keen yachtsman and an old Cambridge man, was on the point of leaving for South Africa one day when he saw an advertisement in the *Yachting World* saying that the famous ship was up for sale. He cabled an offer which was accepted and found himself the new owner. The ship was reconditioned and powered with a 120 hp diesel.

Bud Mitchell, whose father was head of a great engineering firm, and his Swiss born wife, Erni, who was once a skiing champion, made the *Sarah Munro* their summer home. Erni's large family, who all spoke German Swiss and had for generations been mountain folk, more or less ran the Swiss village Grindelwald. If you asked her what time of year she liked best in her native village, she smiled deliciously and said very gravely: 'All times!' Nevertheless like the Leonards, Bud Mitchell and his slim, beautiful wife were never long in one place. Bud's mother, whom we were to call 'Blackie' lived at Clopton Manor, near Kettering. She would come for a fortnight on her son's ship and then in September they would visit her. Afterwards it might be a business trip to South Africa – finally winter and glorious spring in Grindelwald.

Friends arranged to berth their ships close together. Next to the *Sarah Munro* would nose in on some June morning the twin screw ketch *San Lucar* which flew the Belgian flag. The Smeets with their two pretty young daughters would make the journey in leisurely fashion from their home town of Antwerp in two days. Seen side by side the *Sarah Munro* and the *San Lucar* looked much the same size. To go from one ship to the other one seldom needed to use the gangways. Most people climbed or were helped over the sides.

The long pleasant summer evenings on the deck of the *Sarah Munro* with Bud handing round drinks, his guests discussing racing or polo, the Smeets bringing news from Brussels, talking, reading the London papers, sometimes enjoying the lively reminiscences of Bud's mother Blackie, hearing how one or other of the Smeets girls had danced with the young Prince of Wales over for the Polo, sometimes gave one the disturbing feeling of living once more through the last days of an era which one had imagined already gone. Was it the present? Was it the past? Only the future would tell.

On a Saturday morning in November of that year, I read in the *Figaro* that the funeral service of Elsa Schiaparelli, the great Italian dress designer, was to take place that same afternoon in the tiny village church of Frucourt, near Hallencourt, in the Somme, and that she would be buried in a place reserved for her on a lonely hillside.

The weather was bitterly cold, and it was already late. I had no idea where Hallencourt was, or if it was possible to get there in time. The Somme for me represented the grim battlefields of 1914–18 and the immense cemeteries with their thousands of British dead over which still floated the Union Jack.

Was it reasonable to attempt such a long, cross-country journey on icy roads in a small car? Probably not, and there was so little time – and yet the desire to be present grew as I sought to finish the housework. I consulted a map. Hallencourt appeared to be just south of Abbeville through which I had thundered so often in boat trains between France and England – and just a little farther than where I would have to go was the forest of Crécy which everybody knows about, because of the Hundred Years War. Edward the Third of England, after invading France through Normandy, would have led his long-bowmen along much the same route as I would have to take, crossing the Seine at about the same spot as where it was now spanned by the bridge of Tancarville.

Now, cramming keys and money in my handbag and taking a warm fur coat, I set off on the long journey. Why had I been so moved on reading this short paragraph in the newspaper?

I saw myself again as a young married woman setting up my first home in a long, unheated apartment on the third floor of a new building at the corner of Beauchamp Place and Brompton Road in the London of the early 'thirties. We had leased what was then known as a 'maisonnette' flat for my mother over a chocolate shop a few doors away, so that I could run out of one apartment into the other in a matter of minutes. Matilda had by this time abandoned most of the clientèle for whom she had worked in Soho. On the other hand because I contributed to an important social and political column in a London evening paper, and because there was seldom a night when I was not obliged to attend a new opera, a theatrical first night, a political reception or some diplomatic function, my mother used all her genius with the needle to make me the most exquisite dresses. Occasionally she would fit me in my apartment; more often I would run over to hers. I would undress and the fitting would begin.

I felt a positive horror to see my mother kneeling at my feet with her mouth full of pins. I don't think I ever overcame this revulsion though she took the same pleasure in dressing me as I took pride in wearing her superb creations. There was a fitting one day that remains vivid. A copy of the magazine *Vogue* was open on her sewing table. I walked over to look at it. 'What have you been studying?' I asked her.

'There is quite the most fascinating photograph I have ever seen,' she said, enthused by my interest. 'Look carefully!'

It was a very modern photograph of tall french windows against which hung billowing waves of white organdie at the bottom of which sat, tiny by comparison with the height of the curtains, a small woman dressed in black.

'See!' exclaimed my mother. 'just like a fly in a bowl of cream!'

I laughed.

'What fun!' I exclaimed. 'Who is she?'

'An Italian woman called Schiaparelli whose work is

beginning to monopolize the news. It's time you took notice of her. Her dresses have a touch of genius and it's so refreshing to see the ideas of a woman designer, cleverer than all those men.'

In fact, her name was not unknown to me. A modiste had said to me some days earlier: 'She's the Picasso of fashion'.

Not long after this I was invited to a lunch at Claridges at which she was to be present. Like Molyneux and Worth she planned a London house and had already chosen a salon in Grosvenor Street. The fly in a bowl of cream accordingly took voice and shape – deeply expressive eyes in a face far too full of character to be even vaguely pretty. Her English was fluent but with a strong, though enchanting accent and a voice almost as vigorous as that of a man. One looked at her with growing interest as on a Florentine mask. I told her that I had liked the photograph in *Vogue*. 'Yes,' she said, in a matter-of-fact way: 'Christian Bérard took it and he's one of the most interesting men of our time. His designs for the theatre are remarkable. A genius in his way. I didn't want him to show my features. I'm far too ugly. So he made the curtain very tall and me very little.'

After this I began meeting her continually. She had a passion for the theatre, and would point out that creating a dress for an actress to wear on the stage was an opportunity for a designer to see it spring alive, whereas when a private customer bought a model in the Place Vendôme she might take it off to the other side of the world in which case the creator might never see it again.

She had sympathy and affection for Kurt Weill who just about the time of my marriage had done the music for Bertolt Brecht's *Dreigroschenoper*, known as the *Threepenny Opera*, a transposition to nineteenth-century London of John Gay's *Beggar's Opera*. Their mutual enthusiasm resulted in an operetta they called *A Kingdom for a Cow* for which Kurt Weill wrote the music and Schiaparelli designed the clothes and probably some of the scenery. They set great store by this production and took their roles seriously. The First Night was the usual impeccably dressed gathering of Society and the arts, and when Schiaparelli, attended by Kurt Weill and a little knot of friends, entered the foyer of the Savoy Theatre they created much interest; but by the end of the first act it was clear that the subject failed to please. Later at supper in the Savoy Grill it was fun to listen to the dress designer and the musician pouring out their hearts on the inevitable consequences of what was taking place in their respective countries, for they tempered their tears, which were hot and real, with thrusts of sardonic wit. When a page came in with early copies of the morning papers brought in a cab from Fleet Street, the lack of understanding on the part of the critics perplexed and angered them. It would need several more years before English public opinion was to feel concerned with what was happening in Germany and Italy.

Quite apart from this, Schiaparelli's character was hard for the young woman I then was to understand. There was nothing loveable about her, but the more I got to know her the more engrossed I was in her intelligence, her creative genius and what was detestable about her nature. I never had the impression that she liked me but we developed a singular satisfaction from each other's company. She was to become one of the great adventures in my life.

There was no mistaking her aristocratic origin. She carried it high and one was immediately aware of it. Born in the Corzzini Palace in Rome she browsed as a little girl amongst the volumes in the vast library which belonged to her father, the distinguished Orientalist. People who took her for little more than a successful and often sensational dress designer were surprised and perplexed by her deep knowledge of comparative religions and Eastern languages. Between her father and her uncle, one of Europe's most famous astrologers, she had a rare schooling. At her father's death the books in the library were given by her mother to the State – something that remained a source of angry resentment.

She was baptised in great pomp at St Peter's in Rome though everybody, including herself in due course, regretted she was not a boy. Not unnaturally in these circumstances, fascinated by ecclesiastical vestment, she was to make a strange discovery. By merging the cardinals' purple and the bishops' violet a new colour which nobody had ever suspected came to light but one that so shocked people at first that she called it *Shocking Pink*, and this very quickly became synonymous with herself throughout the world.

She had a most intelligent secretary in Paris who, like myself, had once worked at the Galeries Lafayette store in London's Regent Street and with whom she retained all her life a love-hate relationship, but without whom she was quite lost. Her name was Yvonne and she was invariably kind to me. One day while we were looking through some materials under the Place Vendôme we came upon a roll of exquisite satin that Schiaparelli had managed to have dyed in her beloved colour. Yvonne cut just enough from this to make me a scarf which I was later to wear when Eduardo Malta, the famous Portuguese painter, while on a short visit to London, did my portrait. But this scarf in Shocking Pink gave him more trouble than anything else in the picture. He claimed that the correct mixture in oils was impossible and that the necessary colours simply did not exist in his palette. I own today both the portrait and the scarf, the latter being one of my greatest treasures.

But the aristocratic side to her nature, the immense popularity she at one period attained, her wit and often her sarcasm were only facets in her make-up. Married young and unhappily before the First World War, she migrated for a time to America where she was to experience a mixture of dire penury and unbounded love for her little daughter, Gogo, whom she was to nurse through polio and make the motive-force in her extraordinary life. When a woman of intelligence has tasted all the different emotions that a chequered existence can offer she can never be a bore.

Her immense success in the 'thirties marked a period when the world was still full of famous women. It would be idle to recall by name even a few of them. Most have disappeared with the sands of time. But every single one in her moment was a star in the firmament – whether in the arts, in the theatre, in Hollywood or in Society which last, before crumbling to nothing, possessed a vast, fairylike importance which influenced music, painting and literature. This was a world shortly to be extinguished for ever. It explains why the Paris couturier, as we knew him or her then, has ceased to exist. The picturesque, individual customer has gone. Fashion today is for the masses.

The war fell as a curtain on the world that Schiaparelli had built. And she, like so many others in Paris, bowed herself out and fled to America. Her known views on Fascism would have spelt her death. Some blamed her for going, others sought to put out that she had been a spy, but there was nothing else that she could have done. My husband, flying over to Paris after the declaration of war, bumping over housetops and trees, flying only a few feet above the waves of the channel, allegedly at an altitude which would have made it difficult for the enemy to shoot an aeroplane down, saw her once when all the lights in the Champs-Elysées and the Place de la Concorde were dimmed into an impenetrable dark blue glow. A year later she had closed her firm and her private house and fled.

One morning during the Battle of Britain I saw an entire display window of Harrods, the great London store, full of Schiaparelli perfume, lipsticks and toilet soap shaped like a heart and wrapped up in Shocking Pink. This great consignment was a prize of war, seized when one of our warships intercepted a French ship on its way to South America. I went in to the perfumery department and bought a Schiaparelli lipstick whose bright little metal case remains with me until today. When in 1945 we both returned to Paris, she to her home and couture house, I on a visit, I showed it to her, and I fancy she was pleased to reflect that what had been stolen from her establishment had led to a naval engagement and a prize of war on the High Seas. This, incidentally, was the occasion when she gave me that small bottle of perfume which I was later to spill over Paloma's new handbag.

From this time onwards I was to know her better. She was pleased to be back in Paris but bitter against her 'enemies' who had either slandered her or taken advantage of her absence. We went down into the basement under the Place Vendôme where she kept her materials and where she had taken advantage of the popularity of the English duffel coat of coarse woollen cloth which Field Marshal Montgomery had worn to make one of her own imagination for the wealthiest and most elegant of her customers, Daisy Fellowes. Taking it up she held it for my inspection under the frosted pavement glass which let in a shaft of grey light from the street above. The wool was dyed Shocking Pink and the hood lined with lynx fur! The effect was breath-taking and the softness quite extraordinary. She made me try it on to savour quietly both the strangeness of her invention and the surprise on my features. She told me that her daughter, Gogo, was married and that she would soon be a grandmother. Schiap herself, as we all called her, had not physically changed. Her features were too strong to suffer the ravages that come too quickly to most women, especially to those who are prettiest. She wore a mauve turban under which her superb eyes shone fiercely. She often gave me the uncomfortable impression of a snake about to strike. I was once again under her spell but remaining as it were at a safe distance. Some time later I happened to be dining with friends when a very important fellow guest, speaking of her, exclaimed: 'She is one of those rare gifted women unable to say a kind word about anybody. We all get our share of her venom but the trouble is that what she says is nearly always correct.' She would laugh at me in an almost unkind way because I did not share her occasional liking for vodka. 'Are you still on your tomato juice and tonic water!' she would exclaim.

One afternoon I looked in on her in her office in the Place Vendôme. She wore her fiercest, most frightening look, not a hot rage but a cold one. The sort that moves mountains. She opened the huge window that gave on to the famous square with a strength and brutality that only anger can create. All the papers on her table began flying about in the sudden draught and her many telephones appeared ready to shake with fear. 'What on earth has come over you?' I asked. 'Let's get out of here!' she exclaimed. 'Let's get out of here and go to a film. I want to see that Japanese thing again, the one I've seen half a dozen times already, but every time it strikes one differently.' We went to a nearby picture house, and as soon as we had settled down, she lit a cigarette, doubtless to calm her nerves, and then another. Afterwards as we walked out into the street, I asked her:

'Why were you so angry just now in your office?'

'Because the place stunk of tobacco smoke,' she said, 'and I can't stand smelling those Gauloises my secretary smokes. I love her but I don't like the smell of her cigarettes. That's all. So to mark my displeasure I throw the window wide open so that she will shiver in an icy cold blast, but believe it or not she just doesn't understand.'

'But you smoke quite a lot yourself,' I objected. 'During the film just now you smoked at least two cigarettes, if not three.'

We had arrived outside her couture house. She turned on me angrily and said:

'How dare you stand there nagging! I have work to do.'

Some years later a London evening paper asked me to go to Gstaad in Switzerland where Schiap was staying, and write a series of articles about her. I found her in a villa she had taken for Gogo who was by now the mother of two little girls. A comfortable chalet in which all the armchairs and settees had been covered by Schiap in mohair Scottish plaids, already bore the mark of her good taste. I slept under the same roof as Field Marshal Montgomery, who could be seen on occasion walking through the snow in a duffel coat of the kind that had inspired Schiap to make the one in Shocking Pink for Daisy Fellowes. Schiap on the other hand arrived to pick me up every morning wearing a coat made from the skin of a bear, or perhaps of two bears, but the fur was shaggy and untrimmed, black and lustrous, and when she opened it, I generally saw her clad in Shocking Pink and everything about her smelt of that delicious perfume. Amorously cuddled in the hook of an arm would be her white Tibetan dog, Gouru-Gouru, who adored her. I appreciated the beauty and the good taste that sat so lightly on Schiap's person. 'For every year you grow older,' my mother said to me, 'become a little more careful of your person, more meticulous in the way you dress.'

We walked meditatively through the snow, enjoying the cold, mountain air but that morning Schiap was worried about one of her small grand-daughters who had a temperature, and none better than she knew how little signs can be the prelude to serious ills. However the English nurse had assured her that all would be well and after a while the invigorating air calmed her fears. We watched some ski-jumping that clearly bored her: 'Let's go into town!' she said.

The shops amused her. Already a favourable exchange allowed them to display the sort of goods that might have been considered luxuries elsewhere. Schiap bought a blouse of peasant design that could perhaps be entirely transformed and executed in a different material for her boutique in the Place Vendôme. Her mind was constantly on the alert for such occasions. 'Do you think it's really pretty?' I asked her. 'No,' she answered, 'but I shall make it so.' She bought some black cherry jam and a box of caviar for cocktail time at Gogo's chalet. 'People invariably turn up at the last moment,' she said. 'You can come too, if you like.' 'No,' I said, 'Like the Field Marshal, my neighbour, I feel like an early night. I shall sew.' 'Sew!' she exclaimed, almost derisively. 'There's something I have never known how to do. Besides, it would bore me. But what I always have been good at is draping a material round me and pinning it into the shape I want. Oh! How amusing! A shop full of walking sticks! I shall buy one for Gogo.' The shop was indeed filled with every kind of walking stick, umbrella and Alpenstock, and as soon as Schiap explained that she wanted something for her daughter who had once had polio, the owner went to infinite trouble to please. But first we installed Gouru-Gouru on a chair – he appeared only moderately to like walking through the snow, though in traffic we were careful to take turns in carrying him. My companion chose a stick with carvings of edelweiss for Gogo and I bought a rather simpler one for my mother. Armed with these we returned very gaily home.

True to my intention I retired early, partly because I was starting a cold, partly to economise dinner because living had proved much more expensive than I had expected, and I wanted to send as much as I could to my mother in France. But as I did not feel like going to bed I cleared the table and began to cut out a nightdress.

Suddenly in a cloud of *Shocking* perfume, Schiap and Gouru-Gouru broke into the room. 'Oh! That cocktail party!' she exclaimed. 'I couldn't have stood another moment. And I don't think they will ever begin dinner. So here I am!'

She did not even glance at what I was doing but perversely began taking enormous interest in the lampshade on the table. 'These Swiss women are full of ideas,' she exclaimed. 'Just look how clever this shade is! You probably never noticed. It is cut just like the cotton petticoat that a cancan dancer wears. I must have one copied in Broderie Anglaise, what the Americans call eyelet embroidery, and then if it were starched, it would keep neat and fresh! Well, I must run. Are you starting a cold?'

Alas, it was evident, and I thought longingly of all those warm woollen sweaters which I had admired in the shops in town that morning but which I knew very well I could not afford. I was beginning to feel hungry and would have given a lot for a glass of hot milk.

I got up late the next morning and decided because of my cold to keep away from Gogo and her daughters at the villa. Schiap, I knew, had an appointment. It was one of those ideal winter days when a hot sun shines down from a blue sky on to a white world. On the ice rink in front of the hotel a very pretty girl was executing pirouettes and figures of eight with consummate skill. She had the rink to herself and I sat down to watch her. It was nearing lunch time and it was as if the village, so busy and colourful, had suddenly become empty. I felt desperately lonely, and as I looked at this lovely girl performing so gracefully on the ice, the light shining on her blonde hair, I had the uncomfortable revelation that I was no longer young – no longer young like this girl who was so full of life and movement.

Later that day the owner of the hotel, discovering that I was unwell, sent her maid round with a note, inviting me to take tea with her. The annexe of the hotel in which the Field Marshal and I lodged was none other than the owner's private house. On being led into her presence I found a middle aged Swiss woman, physically not unlike her two famous compatriots,

Mme Ritz, the widow of the great hotelier and Mme Schwenter, the wife of the Director of the Meurice in Paris. These Swiss women had great distinction, and formed a very definite aristocracy of their own, governing adroitly and expertly larger establishments than ever a private hostess could have dreamt of. Their linen, their pillow cases and bedspreads were watched over with loving care, and their bone china and silver cutlery would have graced any of those historic English mansions that were beginning to be thrown open to the paying public. From the windows of her drawing room we looked down on her garden in which the Field Marshal, wrapped up in a plaid on a deck chair, was enjoying the sun shining on a snow covered world.

'Success finds me increasingly lonely,' said Schiap when I told her of my day. 'When a woman succeeds in a profession, she wins, to some extent, a victory over men – but at what price! She is apt to find "this peopled earth a solitude," to quote Shelley. Love is the price that women pay for brains and independence!'

'Would you rather have had it otherwise?'

'One has no choice. Many men fear me. Others admire or envy what I have achieved but none, I suspect, experiences in my presence that particular sentiment I dream of evoking. I am not alone in this. Many women are ill-loved or ill-married. They would be wrong to suppose that being talked about is compensation. There are moments when I long for a man's protection. I am mad enough sometimes to envy those scatter-brained girls who come knocking at my door for a job. They will doubtless experience satisfactions that may never come my way. Can you see me scream the place down and climb up on a chair at the sight of a mouse?'

These disjointed memories of Schiap came back to me as, having crossed the Seine by Tancarville Bridge, I drove rapidly east, leaving Fécamp and Dieppe on my left. The journey was taking longer than I had feared. I would never reach Frucourt in time.

It was in her house in the rue de Berri in Paris that I

remembered her best. The term 'house' would be a misnomer unless in the sense that such former residences of the nobility in London, like Crewe House, Grosvenor House, Spencer House, were merely houses. Schiap's house in the rue de Berri was one of those seventeenth-century mansions with its porter's lodge, its forecourt and its quiet, spacious garden, a mere stone's throw from the Champs-Elysées. Success had allowed her to return to something of the magnificence of the Corzzini Palace in Rome where she was born. Her early married penury in New York was far behind.

For me, her house was an enchanted castle. I had the impression of being ushered into the presence of Catherine the Great. I am still childishly impressed by grandeur and what is beautiful. I know that I shall never attain anything beyond my modest present. Daylight filters through wide windows.

On crimson upholstered armchairs repose the portraits of her two little grand-daughters dressed in white organdie with wide sashes – not of blue or of rose, as might normally be the case, but of Shocking Pink! The paintings she loves best in the house are all propped up on Louis XIV chairs so that when, like a queen, she rests on her sofa against cherished cushions and furs, the paintings all about her are on eye level. On the wall above her hangs the problem picture by Picasso in which both she herself, and many of her friends saw her strange character personified. Its interpretation is beyond me but she says: 'Surely it's clear enough!' I would try again. In the centre of the canvas is a cage. Underneath it a green carpet on which lie a number of playing cards. Outside the cage a fierce bird of black plumage defiantly beats his wings. Was it supposed to be Schiap beating her wings? Inside, a sad looking white dove stares at a green apple. This picture is mixed up in her mind with a prediction her mother once made that unless she was careful she would end up in a garret with nothing to eat but a crust of dry bread. Most of our mothers give us similar warnings!

Behind her would be the forecourt; in front of her tall wide windows open out into her garden which communicates, she says, with the famous *Couvent des Oiseaux* so that from time to time she hears them singing divine music to the Virgin as in her youth in Rome. Her part of the garden is full of hydrangeas which people at various times have given her in pots to decorate her house.

She used to have our lunch laid on the corner of a small table which was never in the same place. Sometimes the table would be in the middle of the room; at other times in some obscure corner. The idea was that it must be made to face whatever picture or objet d'art she wanted to fill her mind with on that particular day. Lunching with her tête-à-tête was always something of an ordeal. Inevitably I was aware that she was ready to criticize any faltering on my part. To sting! Her Italian servant would very respectfully bring in a dish of spaghetti into which she would pour a mixture of olive oil, tomatoes and ketchup, this served with an almost completely raw steak which she claimed was invigorating for the muscles! I found it difficult to stomach this food. But there is a price to pay for everything.

'Did you enjoy yourself last night?' I asked her one day. I had been at the Place Vendôme when she gave instructions for an evening dress to be ironed in readiness. It was a mauve model from the recent collection, very décolletée.

'No,' she said, 'I didn't enjoy myself but I would have enjoyed it a lot less if I hadn't been invited. At those diplomatic affairs one always meets the same people.'

'The dress you wore was from your latest collection,' I said. 'It must be fun to have the loveliest clothes in the world to choose from. Even if you did design them all yourself.'

She had taken her coffee into the bedroom and was winding a mauve turban round her hair preparatory to going back to the office. Without answering she looked me expertly up and down and said:

'How curious! You are made like me. Your shoulders are too narrow in comparison with your hips. On reflexion we are built like Greek amphora vases – the ones they find in wrecks at the bottom of the sea. The ones in which they discover traces of ancient wine. Our bodies are not a bit fashionable and I'm glad that Gogo is not made like me. It's always difficult to overcome a defect. You have to learn to cheat. That's what great dress designers have to do.'

Suddenly she exclaimed:

'I shall give a cocktail party for the people who invited me to that elegant reception last night. Would you like to come?'

'I have nothing pretty to wear,' I said. 'I practically live in a pullover and a skirt. It's so much easier when one is working, and when I need to go and see people I have no fear of making them jealous, if I'm less elegant than they are.'

Schiap looked hard at me. I never knew her to laugh but she said in an authoritative voice:

'Simone will find you one of my own dresses. I have something in mind and as we are more or less the same it will scarcely need to be altered.'

'Oh!' I said, interested. 'What sort of a dress?'

'A dress I have worn often and which I love.'

Often, in Schiap's language, when applied to a dress doubtless meant three or four times at most but at least she had loved it enough to keep it preciously in her wardrobe instead of allowing it to finish up in a boutique sale.

'The colour will suit you,' she said.

Her dress – my dress – was of dark foulard, and because of the graceful curve of the pockets, and the way it clung tightly to my body, it looked like a closed umbrella. As my dress was admirably fitted, the more I wore it the more I was in love with it. A dress signed by the great Elsa Schiaparelli, one she occasionally wore herself, was enough to invest me with enormous self-confidence. Wearing my blue foulard dress, I felt an important person. If I were to see somebody looking me up and down, I could whisper to myself: 'Maybe my dress does not please that person but nobody will alter the fact that it was designed by one of the greatest dressmakers in the world and because of that nobody can possibly speak ill of it.'

So I no longer feared criticism. I was above the crowd. My spirit was as light as air, and I actually felt beautiful, for I knew – yes, I knew – that my dress was a masterpiece made by the cleverest hands in Europe. I was like a man bearing in his arms a first folio of Shakespeare. You cannot laugh at that man, for he carries a treasure which invests his person with a halo.

107

Oh, how this lovely dress showed to advantage what was good about my body! The girls who fitted me, kneeling round me, pinching here, adding there, had reached the perfection of magicians in fairy tales. I felt about this dress what I felt about truth in literature, that when normally so unsure of myself as I write, I have drawn the character of a living person, described some trivial but entirely true action, I have hoisted myself, because of the veracity of my facts, above the criticisms of the cruellest critics. A critic may say: 'This character is hateful. That action is base,' but he can never write: 'She is a liar! She writes nonsense!' for though her prose may be imperfect, it is invested with the halo of truth.

'I shall be equal!' I told myself. 'Equal to the best of them.'

I had a big diamond clip and I pinned it against my shoulder. The party proved wonderful and the traffic was held up from one end of the Rue de Berri to the other, the *sergents-de-ville* whistling and waving their white batons, their dark blue capes floating behind them.

I woke up from this rêverie to see the words on an illuminated road sign:

Abbeville – Six Miles.

According to the map it was about here that I should leave the high road and find my way across country to Frucourt. The time was ten minutes to three and I was getting desperate. A woman in a café, when I mentioned Schiaparelli, reacted immediately. She knew about the funeral and took great pains to explain the way. I thanked her and drove as fast as I dared along a lonely, narrow country lane.

I must now try to recall the strangeness of my last farewell to this exasperating genius.

The village was tiny but a few cars were parked in front of a small twelfth-century church over which towered the battlements of a medieval castle. The service could only just have begun. I was met at the tower by the berobed, behatted figure of a beadle, all in blue and gold, holding his tall wand in his right hand, with which from time to time he would give a tap on the ground. The church was so small that though there could only have been a very few people, it looked full. There were spluttering candles everywhere which bathed it in a mysterious mixture of light and shadow, and the smell of roses and incense was pungent. A couple of dozen villagers sat in old fashioned boxed-in pews with small carved doors; their sombre clothes helped to put this part of the church into a grey, misty obscurity. Beyond the altar rail everything was a blaze of colour and vaporous heat, the more important mourners tightly wedged in the choir stalls facing the coffin surrounded by wreaths and mountains of fresh flowers, that spilled over the stone floor. Led by the beadle to a choir stall I accordingly found myself on the fringe of this enceinte. Somebody was playing a harmonium which had been installed beside a make-shift stove rigged up because of the icy weather. I now noticed something the like of which I had never seen. As the hot air climbed up from the stove into the ancient beams and rafters it set a-quivering a great, unbroken sheet of cobwebs that hung above our heads in one solid but ethereal mass, dark, alive, breathing, ghostlike. This fairy canopy pulsated with the even, metrical beat of a human heart. No human hands could have weaved it. Not even the most adroit collection of Paris *cousettes* could have sewn it together; not even my mother with her gift for joining together bits of valuable lace. It was so fine, so delicate, so theatrical that I found myself half wondering if I was in a church or watching a Wagnerian opera. How Schiap would have loved it!

I tried to discover known faces amongst the very few people facing the coffin. Could the pale little woman wearing a stole made of two immense black fox furs, her features in shadow, be Gogo? Which of her two daughters whose portraits I had seen in the Rue de Berri in their white organdie dresses and wide sashes of Shocking Pink, was the tall girl beside her? I had not seen them for so long. But here, almost exactly beside me, could only be Yvonne, Schiap's faithful secretary who had been so kind to me, who had cut off from that precious roll of Shocking Pink satin sufficient for the scarf in which I was painted by Eduardo Malta. We looked at each other hesitatingly. Could it be that we were so few to bid her farewell?

The short service ended. We filed past the coffin sprinkling holy water; were invited to kiss some relic which, because of my tears, I hardly perceived. Slowly we filed out into the cold November afternoon, waiting for the coffin to be brought out on a hand trolley so that it could be wheeled in front of us to the nearby hillside where the open tomb was waiting.

I smiled at Gogo wrapped up in her huge fox furs.

'Do you remember me?' I asked.

'No,' she said.

'When I came to Gstaad to be with your mother?' I whispered, yearningly.

'No,' she repeated.

There was not a glimmer of recognition on her pale face. I had wept for Schiap. I was weeping for myself now, to discover how little I had counted in all that had gone before. How desperately unimportant I was. How utterly lonely and unknown!

I looked up at her daughter.

'You are Marisa, aren't you?' I asked. 'Do you remember your sixth birthday party in the Rue de Berri?'

She looked at me suddenly interested. But how could I tell her? This was how I saw it at the time:

'Two small sisters come and settle beside me. We are friends. The party is being held in honour of one of them whose birthday it is. It is also the birthday of their little white dog. During tea the two sisters smiled at me. They were the only ones to break through the wall of voices and laughter which divided me from the rest of the room. They wear hydrangea-blue, embroidered cotton dresses with wide satin sashes of ruby red. As soon as they sit on the cushioned floor their dresses spread out round them like huge powder-puffs, the tips of the shoes peeping out like rabbits' ears. The elder sister is six and her maternal instincts cause her to take up her little sister and arrange her on her lap, encircling her tightly with tiny white arms, as she would lovingly hold a doll, and though the conjuror has started to pull things out of a hat, she continues to clasp the living doll, keeping quite still for fear of disturbing her. She will

110

be elegant but also, I reflect, an excellent mother, and I derive great joy in watching the way she peeps from time to time into her small sister's face to see how she is enjoying the show.

'The conjuror goes on with his tricks but the smaller of my two friends remains as quiet as the older one who, of course, is as proud as a queen. I am sure that the little sister finds the big sister's arms infinitely comforting. Now we have the puppet show. Young voices are raised. All these children are bilingual and they jump from English into French with complete ease. They are enjoying themselves in a quietly sophisticated way. Their laughter is already elegant, perfectly modulated and controlled, and there is never an unnecessary or ugly gesture. Clearly they are accustomed to being in rich drawing rooms, surrounded by lovely things, and it will be some years yet before they learn that there are poor children whose ways are very different from theirs.'

By now the coffin had been brought out on its chariot, and was being wheeled along the village street which almost immediately became green, hilly country specked with snow.

Here on the flank of the hill was the open, waiting tomb and beside it the slab of jet black Italian marble which would eventually close it. This polished marble was in itself a thing of rare beauty but as if to render this strange woman's story theatrical to the last, her long, powerful scrawled signature was embossed in gold upon it.

ELSA SCHIAPARELLI

just as it appeared on her perfume, on all those lovely ephemeral, feminine things that were seized by the British Navy as a prize of war and displayed so proudly in the window of a Knightsbridge store.

The Comte de Forceville, whose title dates from the days of Charlemagne, and whose castle was catching the last rays of the November sun, touched me lightly on the shoulder.

'My wife and I were her friends,' he said. 'She asked to be buried here. In the castle, where she stayed so often as our guest, we have prepared a few refreshments and a glass of wine.

Will you not join us?'

'I wondered . . .' I said. 'I wondered why she had chosen to rest here.'

Thus it came about that this handful of mourners met in one of the great rooms of this *fief comtal* round a table laden with good things. Our distinguished host, sometimes speaking English, sometimes French, was clearly anxious for our last memory of Schiaparelli to be gay – as indeed her life had been. They had first known each other in New York before the war. Then the Comte de Forceville was imprisoned in Germany but escaped to follow General Patton into the Ardennes.

Turning to Marisa I asked:

'Where is your sister? She married Anthony Perkins, didn't she?'

'She's expecting a baby,' said Marisa. 'That's why she isn't here.'

'Tell me something else. What happened to Gouru-Gouru?'

'He died,' said Marisa, 'but the Tibetan I have with me here might almost be a reincarnation. My grandmother was so certain that what she loved would go on for ever.'

The Comtesse de Forceville, in navy blue pants, said:

'Yes, it was really I who got to know her first. We were living in New York where my husband was connected with a firm of Wall Street brokers.'

She looked at my plate anxiously:

'Won't you try some of the chocolate cake?'

'I have done,' I said. 'It reminded me of Vienna.'

The Comtesse de Forceville smiled happily:

'Oh! I'm so glad,' she said. 'I made it myself.'

7

A T FIRST I FELT convinced that I had been right to sell Berlequet. The Buons were delightful and it was a joy to hear children's voices and to see with what skill young M. Buon began turning the place into everybody's dream of a self-contained fief. He made windows and doors, put in little panes of glass, ripped off the ugly wallpaper to reveal magnificent beams which he cleaned and polished, turned the long attic, in which Jacques had once kept his hay, into a playroom for the two little girls, and re-cut the Caen stone of the main fireplace so that it looked quite new, the sort of meticulous transformation that one would have supposed that only a professional stonemason could have done.

M. Buon was, indeed, supremely professional in everything he undertook. Though when he first arrived he introduced himself as a coppersmith, he had clearly worked in the company of carpenters, stonemasons, bricklayers and welders. He filled one with admiration for the modern equivalent of the medieval craftsmen, and I much enjoyed looking in on him of a morning while he was sawing or planing in front of the long dwelling house which soon began to shine with fresh white paint. A former bedroom was turned into a modern kitchen with a new door and two large windows, one facing the courtyard, the other an orchard at the back. As in so many modern houses the family used the kitchen as a dining room so that the food could come straight from the oven on to the table. In summer the door was always open so that going to call on the Buons was both amusing and instructive. The entire electrical system was rewired and as they continued to burn logs in the living room which was half-timbered and panelled I gave him permission to cut down, within reason, what he needed in one or other of the small woods on the estate, both for his carpentry and for his fuel.

Mme Buon was a young schoolteacher who was successful in exchanging her post near Paris for one, at least of a temporary nature, in our village school. Her two little girls thus had the advantage of being taught by their mother. At this juncture M. Buon was more often at home than his wife. Perhaps wisely he thought it more important to transform their new acquisition into a thing of permanent beauty rather than to be away all day on a building site or in a coppersmith's yard.

But from the first I suspected that his wife was not altogether happy to be away from Paris. The more M. Buon became enamoured of this small paradise in which there was almost everything necessary to capture a man's heart when he is adventurous and clever with his hands, the more there crept into Mme Buon's mind little twinges of regret for the undoubted advantages that a great capital offers to a young and pretty woman. Mme Buon's parents lived in Dieppe where her father, a renowned chef, owned a small hotel which faced the shingly beach of that famous seaside resort. Often in summer she would go there with the two little girls while her husband remained at Berlequet making new improvements. There was so much to do – the house itself, the stables, the outhouses, the cider press, the laundry, the garage, the rabbit hutches all at eye level, the poultry yard – and, of course, the kitchen garden. No sooner was one building renovated than M. Buon began turning his attention to another. Then also what a temptation for a man who sees himself the master of all this, not to go shooting rooks with a gun and to push as far as the woods with a saw and an axe to cut down a dead tree with which to make floor boards or a window frame? One sensed that he enjoyed every moment spent indoors and out, looking with pride at the result of his handiwork or enjoying the new-found wonder of a dewy morning or a crimson sunset.

Back from Dieppe, Mme Buon would bring the two children round to my place for tea and bread and jam. She lacked friends in this still relatively unspoilt corner of damp grass and apple trees, and in her natural femininity regretted that her young husband could not exchange at times his manual gifts for more

114

intellectual qualities. In point of fact she was the owner of the farm. Indeed the sale had been retarded for some days because she had insisted with reason that the contract be drawn up in her name – not in his. She was thus not only mistress of the domain but at this precise moment the only wage earner, her husband having discontinued his trade to embellish her property. The situation was modern, in the extreme.

Though as a woman my instincts were towards Mme Buon, I watched fascinated the emergence of a new and prettier Berlequet. It was the manual genius of a M. Buon that I, alas, was unable to contribute either to my own house or to my two gardens. In return for my supplying him with wood and lumber, M. Buon occasionally came round to trim a fence or dig up potatoes but this ended when he announced that, like his wife, he was going out to work. He had been offered a post in a school for backward children in a neighbouring town.

This, alas, did not work out as either of them had hoped. The improvements at Berlequet hung fire. Mme Buon remained the owner of the property and very much mistress of what she surveyed. As Mme Schiaparelli had once pointed out there are perils attached to a woman usurping all the privileges of a man. She may find herself forced to pay the price. In this particular case her husband announced that he wanted to leave her and marry somebody else.

Mme Buon came more often to see me. We were brought temporarily together by a common bond of femininity. I love the countryside but though I might have liked to have been brought up as a child in the country, I certainly would not have wished to spend the crucial first years of married life away from the intellectual and social opportunities of a great city. A young woman's mind needs to be loved and admired, and allowed to unfold in a milieu that is not entirely composed of gurgling brooks and apple trees.

After the divorce had taken place I surveyed my own fallen pride. Why had I not left the sale of Berlequet to a hard-headed business man who would have waited patiently to obtain the best possible price? Mme Buon was free once again. She was in possession of a greatly enhanced property, a salary more than sufficient to allow her to complete her mortgage and two adorable little girls. She was still young and very pretty. Her intelligence was far above the average. One might suppose that she had all the aces in her delicate, firm hands.

But if she had the qualities, she also had the disadvantages of being a woman. What on earth could she do with this suddenly quite vast domain which would need a man to keep it in running order? In a little while something would go wrong in the house, the stables would need urgent repairs and all the vegetables in the garden would run to seed. As it was, M. Buon had neglected things since the certainty of a divorce had become clear. The paint was not quite so fresh, the lounge not quite finished and she had been compelled to get rid of the poultry and the rabbits because she was not always there. He had come by night to take away what belonged to him. The tools and the lathes were no longer there.

I was angry with her when she told me one evening that she had decided to sell it. I had allowed her to have it at less than its value because of the fun of possessing so near to my house young and friendly neighbours. I had even thrown in that small orchard full of cherry trees because it did not seem fair to allow two clever little girls not to have an orchard of their own in which to run wild, safe from the cattle, lovely in spring when the fruit trees were in blossom. She looked at me curiously and said:

'But I bought it. It's mine.'

'Anybody might buy it,' I objected. 'The place could become an eyesore.'

'I'm sorry,' she said. 'But what would you do in my place?'

'But surely you'll miss it terribly. The swings you fixed up for the children on the front lawn? The apple logs in the stone fireplace? The kitchen with the two wide windows and the modern electric stoves? The chickens . . .?'

'I hated the poultry,' she said. 'Their feathers make me feel ill.'

'What will you do?'

'I don't know,' she said.

The first thing she did was to have oil-fired central heating put in. This was something that in my own house I had never been able to afford and once more, in my small feminine heart, I felt bitter. The operation proved, of course, much easier at Berlequet than it would have done on my farm. The buildings were for the most part modern and there was plenty of room for the oil tank. In addition to this, tanker-lorries could drive straight in whereas I was connected to the lane by a grass track. I was more or less cut off from the outside world in icy weather.

I saw much less of her after this. The house was let for a while and then one day I saw a bulldozer making an aperture in the holly hedge leading to the forecourt. This hedge was very old and of great beauty. Hitherto there had only been a small gate opposite the house. Because I wanted the place to look nice, I had, before selling it to the Buons, commissioned M. Longuet the carpenter to make a new one and to paint it white. This had cost me a great deal of money.

I asked the workmen what they were doing.

'This place is being divided into two separate properties,' the foreman said. 'One family will have the house and the garden. What remains – the cider press, the outhouses, the cartshed and that small orchard with the young trees – is to be sold apart. The beginning of suburbia, what? The place was much too big before. Whoever sold it as a single property must have been crazy. This way it will be worth double – maybe three times what it was worth before.'

How could I have been so abominably outwitted?

Bud Mitchell sat in a canvas chair in the front part of his ship peering through binoculars at a cormorant perched on the very top of Trouville's ornate town hall. The great bird remained so perfectly still that it hardly looked real.

'Comes here every year,' he said, laying the binoculars on the green leather-bound copy of *Lloyds Register of Yachts*.

'He,' (I meant the cormorant) 'appears to have frightened off the gulls,' I said.

It was high tide and small sailing craft were fussily going out to sea.

'No,' said Bud Mitchell, 'at this time of the evening they congregate at the Polo Ground. They'll be back in an hour. You'll see.'

The *Sarah Munro*, with her main anchor far into the harbour, rode very gently on the tide. Erni, Bud's lovely Swiss wife, wearing a yachting cap and a Hermes silk square, a collection of Krugerrands playing golden music from her wrist, was arranging glasses on a tray for guests who invariably sauntered over for pre-dinner drinks. Max Aitken, Lord Beaverbrook's surviving son, still chairman of Beaverbrook newspapers, had just come in on a slim sailing ketch anchored at the foot of the customs office.

'He'll be along,' said Bud, as his wife removed a basket of cherries I had picked for them at the farm earlier in the afternoon. They were late in the season but it had been a good cherry year. I had put the basket and some roses from the garden on the highly varnished lid of a narrow bunker.

'That bunker,' said Bud in reminiscent mood, 'used to store the coal that Sir Winston Churchill burnt on winter evenings in the saloon.'

'You mean that he had a coal fire – like in a house?'

'Exactly like in his drawing room. He was that sort of man. During a raid he would sit in the middle of the Thames by a nice coal fire, smoking a cigar.'

'It's a pretty tale,' I said.' By the way, did you ever know the real Sarah Munro – the little girl after whom this ship was christened?'

'Only once – she came into my life like a ghost,' said Bud. 'I was sitting in front here just as I am now – but outside Cowes – and a pretty blonde rowed up in a dinghy and called out: "May I come on board?" "Why, yes, of course," I said. How could a man say no to a blonde? So she came aboard and said "You are Bud Mitchell?" "Yes," "Well, I'm Sarah Munro!"'

'What else?' I asked.

'Nothing,' said Bud. 'I never saw her again.'

Albert (his name was Albert Sheaf), Bud's captain, came up from below, rubicond and smiling.

'Mix yourself a drink,' said Bud, 'and bring me one too. The bell's gone.'

Erni had arranged the roses in a tall vase in the saloon. It was a very gay room with comfortable furniture, lots of cushions, a small library of books, nautical and otherwise, a well-stocked bar and Sir Winston's picture scowling down on everything. Over the entrance, Bud had put a notice that read: 'Beware! Men drinking.'

'What happened to Winston's fireplace?' I asked.

'Oh, I chucked it away,' said Bud. 'Replaced it with central heating – the same kind they use on London's double decker buses.'

'How strange! I thought they heated buses from the exhaust.' Bud looked shocked.

'Dear me!' he said. 'How ignorant you are. All the passengers would be asphyxiated.'

'There goes the cormorant!' I said, as the great bird flew away and out over the Channel.

'Yes,' said Bud, pointing towards Deauville. 'And here come the gulls. Polo must be over for today.'

My bedroom formed the corner of the house. It had two large windows, one facing east, the other south. Each had a single pane of glass so that the view was framed as in a picture frame.

The window facing east revealed a great stretch of country-side that had virtually not changed in three long centuries, not since Mme de Carpentier's beautiful château was built in the reign of Louis XIII of France. The château is what, as a little girl, I dreamt a château should look like. It was the castle of every little girl's fairy tale, tall, narrow and elegant. The castle out of which the young Prince clad in white should ride in the morning.

Standing in front of this window I saw my own home-orchard, with its apple trees, sloping gently down to the stream. From there, the ground rose steeply until above wood and grazing land shone the castle in all its dazzling beauty. Not another building defaced the pristine beauty of the scene.

Every morning the sun rose in Homerian splendour, its rosy fingers exactly behind the castle as if about to clutch it in hot

119

embrace. Often the light was so blinding that the castle disappeared altogether from view and only the red piercing light remained. Then the woods that were all about the castle took on different colours. The woods were still theirs as in feudal days. 'Fifty hectares of woodland, fifty hectares of pasturage,' one of the family once said to me with a smile.

After this the sun would move round until in mid-morning it faced the other window that overlooked the quince tree in my flower garden – the one that every autumn gave forth great baskets of golden fruit.

Down on what had once been marshland facing the sea, great white apartment buildings, in shape vaguely reminiscent of the new Paris hospitals of my youth, were rising almost overnight. Then, like the spread of some dire disease, they would be followed by others, creeping nearer and nearer to the outskirts of the old village.

We all talked money – not so much that the bread we bought at the baker's in the morning cost the equivalent of over £1 or that a fillet of cod cost even more than that – but we talked about other people's money. Ours, the money the char earned, she and her husband – 'Think of it, my dear. He and I together only make a million a month!' But the char and her husband were (comparatively) such small fry! 'You know who bought all that land for a song thirty years ago – and now they say he's worth . . . !' In our village the equivalent of one million sterling was hardly worth talking about. Forty million or fifty million! These were the sort of sums that had made Rockefeller or Morgan household names. Was it possible that a single village of such complete unimportance in the intellectual formation of a new world could comprise such a staggering collection of multi-millionaires!

The ridiculously small sum for which I had sold Berlequet mocked me from its modest resting place. My women friends no longer discussed hats, dresses, lipsticks or hair styles. They wore pants or jeans, drove their own cars and bought gold. Goaded by their shrill advice, I had some years earlier scraped enough from the housekeeping money to buy myself (not to be completely left out in the cold) a kilo of gold at $35 an ounce. It seemed a stupid thing to own, lying there in a dusty corner, not even earning its keep. But now suddenly as all about me, like the roar of the mighty Zambesi, I heard the cries of an entire nation rejoicing in the fact that they alone – alone amongst all the countries in the world – had been proved right, I began to feel an uneasy, unbelieving concern in this effervescence, this jubilation as the media noted triumphantly gold's daily ascent towards $200 an ounce. Soon it would roar past that!

'Supposing,' I told myself, 'supposing that instead of only having this one bar, I had put all the money from Berlequet into gold!'

I still went down on occasion to the sands but curiously enough every year I seemed to have less time for those former lazy afternoons discussing feminine trivialities in front of the bathing tents. The garden, especially the kitchen garden, was becoming too much for me. If I neglected it for a few days it became a veritable jungle. On this particular afternoon I had stolen an hour in which to sunbathe and was walking back through the village along the one-way street which leads to the church.

Just this side of the Crédit Agricole bank was a small empty shop whose drawn blind hid its dusty nakedness. Hither when first I came to the village would come all the local ladies for their ceremonial hats – gay hats for weddings, black hats for funerals. Just as soon as any known villager died, all the ladies would hurry to Mademoiselle Yvonne's little shop.

Yes, she was another Yvonne but I suppose it must in those days have been a popular name.

Nobody ever referred to Mademoiselle Yvonne otherwise than as Mademoiselle. It was her title. She had two armchairs in her tiny shop, one for herself, one for her customer, for no lady would have come in just to buy something. When the doorbell tinkled it was first and foremost a social call. Though Mademoiselle was primarily a *modiste*, hats were not her only business. She sold sweaters, skirts, stockings, not only nylon but wool and cotton, and occasionally boned corsets or stays with good, solid suspenders. She knew to a nicety the requirements in ladies' apparel.

When I was first in the village she had a friend who helped her in the shop but the friend died – and Mademoiselle carried on the business alone. Her living room was through a narrow curtain between the stacked boxes in which she kept her wares. In this minute parlour she took her lonely meals. I used principally to visit her for what was then known as Marygold knitting wool, but in spite of its name I doubt if it was English.

She had her own tales of the German Occupation. They were delightfully Old Maidish, the sort one might have read in *The Girls' Own Paper* if that had existed. She and a neighbour, while shaking their carpets in the narrow street, had exchanged some piece of gossip so droll that they had laughed like schoolgirls. At that very moment there passed a number of German soldiers who, supposing that the two women were laughing at them, nearly marched them off to jail. 'Think of it!' she said. 'We were so frightened that I went to lodge with friends in the village of St Pierre Azif which, being away from the coast, was less dangerous.'

It occasionally happens that the place to which one flees for safety turns out to be more dangerous than the spot which one has left. So it was in the case of Mademoiselle. She and another friend had gone for a walk in the country one evening when they tripped over something hard. 'What was it?' one asked breathlessly.

'It was something very secret,' Mademoiselle would explain in a hushed voice. 'A secret weapon – something like the equipment needed for those human torpedoes!' There would be a quiver in her voice, and we were meant to understand that this might have been the end of her and her companion.

Happily the two women escaped unseen and a few days later the equipment disappeared.

I remembered these things as I walked slowly towards the church.

Our church was not particularly beautiful from the outside. Inside it was very comforting and it had a lofty roof and some nice stained glass windows through which filtered the afternoon sun.

I experienced at this moment of my life a great need for solitary reflexion and it was my habit when I was passing near the church to go in for a few moments to pray. The changes that were taking place in the village, the feverish preoccupation with vast sums of money – sums bandied about until they ceased to have any meaning, the destruction of so much that was beautiful, one's own feeling of smallness and helplessness when faced by problems that baffled Presidents and kings, the certain knowledge of my own descending star, my inevitable end, weighed heavily upon me. I needed something or somebody to lift me up out of this morass. So I would kneel in a dark, cool corner of the church and bury my face in my hands.

There was nothing new in this. It was not a sudden revelation. I have seldom walked past a church without going in – caught a distant glimpse of a churchyard without feeling myself drawn to its moss-covered graves or illegible head-stones. These were not sad but marvellous moments. When, in Milan, I went into the cathedral to pray I had the good fortune to find myself listening to a cardinal whose deep-set piercing dark eyes and beautiful voice proved later, to my great surprise, to be those of Pope Paul VI. I must have been afforded on that occasion the gift of tongues. His Italian was of such simplicity that I was able to understand him with the same ease as if he had spoken in English or in French.

Well, here I was, quite absorbed by my thoughts in a dim corner of our village church when somebody tapped me lightly on the shoulder. I looked up to see our village priest of whom I really knew nothing except that he had come quite recently to us from the adjoining town of Blonville and was called the Abbé Duvieu.

'Do we know each other?' he asked.

It was a question he had the right to ask. I was, after all, in his church. As a new priest, he was doubtless anxious to become friendly with his parishioners. Nevertheless I wanted no misunderstanding.

I probably know more of you than you of me,' I said. 'I live up on the plateau, just above the village. My husband and I are English. He was the son of a Church of England clergyman. So you see, I am, and am not, a true member of your flock.'

'You mean that you only come here occasionally to attend a wedding or perhaps a funeral, and from time to time, to pray?' he asked, interested.

'Perhaps more than that,' I said. 'Sometimes also to Mass. There is so little difference any longer in the two rituals. But, of course, though we can attend the Feast, we would not presume to partake of it.'

'It would be sad indeed,' he said, appearing to turn the matter over in his mind, 'if you were figuratively to knock at the door and find it slammed in your face.'

'Not quite that,' I said, 'but sometimes it hurts.'

We walked out together into the sunshine and he talked about Rome and his regret at never having been there. I told him how I had once attended a Pontifical Audience of Pope John XXIII. 'There was a Spanish woman,' I said, 'who wanted to touch the hem of the Pope's garment. She was very angry because she had been badly placed. Turning to me, she exclaimed: "Don't think for a moment, Madam, that I am going to worry my head about putting you to a little inconvenience. Consider that I have come all the way from Barcelona on foot with a letter from my parish priest, and that one of those men dressed in red took the letter away from me, and instead of placing me at the foot of the throne, from where I could easily have thrown myself in front of the Pope and implored his special grace, they have put me here. My parish priest will be furious when he learns what has happened. Look at my feet!" She showed them to me. They were swollen, obviously to several times their normal size, and were swathed in bandages. When the Pope, having blessed us all, returned to his chair to be carried back on the shoulders of his bearers to the Vatican, the Spanish woman gave a leap forward to throw herself at his feet, but the Palatine Guards, who had anticipated her move, barred her way with their bayonets. Her dark eyes flashed in anger, and when she felt a soldier's restraining hand on her shoulder, tears of frustration rolled down her cheeks. But as the Pope, seated high on his chair, passed us, the woman tore herself free, and jumping up, seized the hem of his robe and tugged at it with all her might. The countrywoman next to me cried out in Italian: "She has touched him! She has touched him!" and all of us thought of the woman in the New Testament who came behind Jesus and touched his garment, saying within herself: "I shall be whole!"'

'How very fortunate you are,' said the Abbé 'to have seen the Pope. I seldom have time to leave my parishioners. To be a village priest is a very exacting task. My only indulgence is a love for old furniture. I had a beautiful old house at Blonville and was broken-hearted to leave it. But it was the will of God.'

'If ever you come my way,' I said, 'I will give you an English cup of tea.'

Some ten days later the Abbé was to be seen walking briskly down the muddy rut to my house.

'I put your case before our Bishop!' he exclaimed. 'He bids me hasten with the good news. From this day forth you will both be fully admitted to the joys of Holy Communion. When may I expect you?'

'At 8 a.m. on Sunday,' I said.

We seldom, if ever, missed early Mass on Sundays after that. Except in the height of the season, we met there the same little group of native-born villagers who exchanged discreet little nods and smiles. In summer the sun which rose from behind the château to envelop that lovely façade with its rosy fingers, shone at the very same hour through the stained glass windows of the church with such fierce beauty that it often blinded us to the view of the Abbé Duvieu at the Elevation. Sometimes the local watchmaker read the lesson, at other times his wife, at other times the bearded young upholsterer who stitched new velvet on valuable antique chairs. Also just a minute or two before the church clock struck eight, the people from the château marched in one after the other to occupy the front pews. One of the daughters and her husband, a former cavalry officer, ran a riding school and arrived, as in old days, in riding breeches and habit – and when during the week they came with their horses riding round the Point, they would wave to me as I stopped the car to let them pass.

One fine October morning while in the orchards all about us, little groups were picking up cider apples shaken down from the trees by men with long poles, Mme Robert arrived leading a cow by a rope. On going to meet her, I saw that the animal had blood on its head, a broken horn, a cut above an eye.

'What has happened to your cow?' I asked.

'We don't know,' said Mme Robert. 'It's just possible that a bull from a neighbouring field may have attacked her, but there was no sign of a break in the hedge. She's quite old and we ought by rights already to have sold her but she's a nice animal and we never had the heart to part with her. When I used to milk her by hand she was the quietest of the herd.'

We led her to the front of the house.

'She's had a bad shock,' said Mme Robert, 'and was doubtless blinded by her own blood. I fear she may miscarry. That's why I'm bringing her here where she'll be all alone in your home orchard. I was going to ask if you would mind keeping a friendly eye on her?'

'Of course not,' I said.

'We are all so busy picking up the apples,' said Mme Robert. 'It's back-breaking work.'

'The Levanniers have a machine.'

'Yes, it belonged to Jacques Déliquaire. I'm not sure how much it helps. It's a noisy, smelly thing. Could you give me a pail of warm water and something with which to wipe the wounds of this unfortunate animal?'

'Anything in the warm water?'

'A drop of disinfectant. Her name is Rita.'

We drew the warm water, found a sponge and began dabbing the wounds, but though it seemed to relieve her the blood kept running and it was some time before we could safely let her go.

'She might become bored,' said Mme Robert. 'I'll look in later in the day to see how she gets on.'

I thought it rather wonderful to be put in charge of a wounded cow, like a hospital nurse, and I kept on running out of the house to see if Rita needed me. The blood on her wounds began to congeal but she was covered by flies and I felt rather sick. Nevertheless she made a speedy recovery and except for the broken horn appeared to be none the worse for her adventure. She was certainly not bored. When she was not busy making friends with M. Levannier's milking cows on the other side of the hedge, she would come to me, as if glad of human sympathy.

That evening at milking time Jacques Déliquaire rounded up the Levannier herds. We greeted each other politely. He informed me that the Levanniers were helping their parents in the Eure and that he had promised to replace them. Clearly Jacques was intending to keep up his rural interests. I stood watching him from the cherry trees in my kitchen garden admiring the scene, surprised because he seemed to be following one particular animal, occasionally touching her flanks with a hazel stick.

'What's the matter with her?' I asked. 'Is she ill?'

'No, blind,' said Jacques. 'But she gives a good milk yield and seems quite happy with the others.'

During the next few weeks, as the trees began to lose their leaves, I noticed that Rita came to me regularly every evening at dusk to ask for her crust of bread and her half dozen apples. When sometimes after dark I would go out into the orchard, as was my custom, to pick up dead wood for the fire, I would suddenly hear her heavy breathing and find her beside me, putting her damp muzzle against my arm.

The cold weather set in, the boughs were bare and the bread we put out for the birds in front of the house had to be changed several times a day. They would often eat their way through a four-pound loaf and for the first time since the previous winter I would hear the distinctive call of the robins which flew in from the woods and never were to be seen in spring or summer.

Then came the snow and when, before breakfast, I went to let the hens out, the forecourt was white, not yet thick but enough to change the whole aspect of the farm, and to make me wonder with some trepidation whether I would be able to drive up to the lane in the car. Snow could imprison us.

I used to collect the eggs after tea every afternoon, and it was always fun to count them, rejoicing if there were many, disappointed, as on these cold winter afternoons, when there were few. Then, before closing up for the night, I would follow one or other of the hedges down to the stream, looking for the last eating chestnuts, the last walnuts, any Canadian russets still hanging on the trees. On this cold winter evening the whole countryside was white with only the occasional marks of a rabbit or an adventurous hen to disturb the even smoothness of the by now quite deep snow. This was the moment of the day I liked best with everything so still outside, the knowledge that a log fire was waiting for me in the big room with a book, or perhaps a film on television.

Down by the banks of the stream, there had once been a stretch of marshland where, before the war, I had tried to grow mustard and cress. Brambles had grown here during the Occupation; water-thyme, flowering rush and what is known as *Policeman's Helmet*, or *Himalayan Balsam*. On my return I had cleared the brambles all by myself, a tremendous task for a little woman but which had amused me because of the feeling it gave me of successfully accomplishing a task – and I then had a nurseryman plant two rows of Italian poplars in the hope that they would dry the soil.

Now these very tall trees stood bare and very upright in the fading light, giving me a sense of satisfaction and pride. But what on earth was that dark, greenish mass lying sack-like on the snow but from which seemed to emanate curls of steam mounting into the cold air? Tiggy, the New York cat, leapt ahead, then stopped, cautious, sniffing from a distance. The snow-covered ground fell gently towards the tree-lined stream – and now I became aware that Rita was laying beside her new born baby, licking it clean.

Calling Tiggy, I hurried back to the house, my rubber boots crunching into the powdery snow. Taking up the telephone, I dialled Mme Robert's number. After a while it was her little boy Eric, just back from school, who answered:

'Eric, is your mother there?'

'No, Mme Henrey, I'm alone,' he said. 'They are milking.'

'Eric! I have tremendous news. Rita has just given birth to a baby. What I fear is that she will be cold on the snow. What am I to do?'

'Leave them as they are,' said Eric, expertly. 'I'll tell mother just as soon as she's home.'

Half an hour later, having left their car at the top of the orchard, Mme Robert and Eric came down the rut carrying a bundle of hay. I got into a warm coat and went with them down to the stream. Here, they cleaned up the bull calf and stood him up on his slim, unsteady legs:

'It's a fine boy!' Mme Robert exclaimed triumphantly. 'How fortunate we are! I was so afraid that Rita would miscarry. Do you know, Mme Henrey, I think it may be in part thanks to you – the way you looked after the poor, wounded animal.'

'What are you going to do with them now?' I asked anxiously.

'Leave them both here just as they are.'

'In the snow? With night coming on? With this cold wind from the north?'

'They will be better here than anywhere else,' she said. 'Far better than in a stable. At least, they will breathe good, healthy air. No fear from infection.'

I thought it cruel as, with my window wide open, I listened to the familiar sounds of the night – cruel to leave a new-born babe in a bed of snow, and once or twice I was for dressing hurriedly, taking up a hurricane lamp and covering Rita's baby with a rug. As grey daylight revealed familiar objects in the room, I got up and looked out of the window. More snow had fallen during the night. All my footsteps would be covered. A pale sun was rising slowly from the direction of the château. Now against the barrier of the flower garden I recognised the patient form of Rita. Rita all alone. Oh! The worst had happened. Her baby bull calf had died in the night!

Raising her large, watery eyes, Rita was begging for her early morning crust of bread. I gave the usual ration, then another piece out of pity and watched her ambling off to a dip in the terrain near the trunk of an old apple tree. There to my joy lay her baby, nearly as white as the snow, fast asleep.

I kissed him gingerly.

I'll call him Jimmy, I thought.

Later that morning, walking over to the Levannier farm

129

where Mme Levannier left my milk can hanging to the netting in front of her house – the square brick house – I heard her washing the churns. She came out, and seeing me, exclaimed:

'All this snow! Would you believe it, Mme Henrey!'

'The cow with the broken horn has a bull calf, and Mme Robert insisted on leaving it out all night,' I said, 'Should she have done that? Is it not cruel?'

Mme Levannier laughed.

'On the contrary,' she said. 'That is the best way to give a young animal a good start in life. If you want him to be stong and healthy in all weathers, bring him up in the open air! Don't worry about your bull calf. He's doing fine. I caught sight of him this morning when I was rounding the cows up.'

At midday Mme Robert and her husband arrived with some fifty bundles of hay, all tightly secured with thick hemp. They were perfect squares and could be built up into a solid wall.

'As Rita is feeding her baby, she will have the right to have two a day,' said Mme Robert. 'One in the morning and one in the afternoon – but not the two together. She would mess them up.'

Now that I had officially become Rita's guardian, I kept strictly to this arrangement. The cats were delighted by their mountain of hay in which they both played and slept. Rita was never late for breakfast and when she saw us having tea in the kitchen in the afternoon she would come to the garden gate and call vociferously for hers.

Thanks to Rita and her baby I spent a very pleasant winter for no other reason than that I felt myself indispensible.

8

THE FOLLOWING SUMMER a rumour swept across the plateau that the Levanniers had decided to leave their farm. We did not immediately question them. This may appear strange but the news, if it was true, had such grave undertones for us that we may have feared to receive confirmation from their lips. Curiously enough we had become almost accustomed to the idea that one day, perhaps after our death, the road might appear like a snake from the east and devour strips of woodland and orchard on its speedy journey to the west. We increasingly told ourselves that even a great road is not the end of the world. Indeed by isolating the greater part of our pasturage on the far side of it, and transforming it into a green belt, we might find ourselves (if still alive) with something like the beauty of an African game reserve where nature and beast together are allowed to pursue a relatively calm existence. Nature fenced off and tolerated. A concession to what God had made.

But the break-up of the Levannier farm, or should I say that of Mme Bompain who owned it, was something much more immediate and fraught with dire consequences. It sounded terribly like a death sentence to the whole plateau. Because once they had marched off with their cows (if that was what they intended to do) what could take their place but the bulldozer?

Rumour starts in curious ways. It is tortuous, seldom direct. I had heard a suggestion – never made directly to myself – that a wealthy speculator had enquired about the possibility of buying not only Mme Bompain's forty-odd acres but also my own so that he could have a really worthwhile area on which to build a garden city high above the village. My reaction had been to exclaim that my land was not on the market. 'What matter?' people said. 'Mme Bompain's is.' If rumour is often insistent and devious it is seldom entirely correct. It was conceivable that if the Levanniers really intended to leave, Mme Bompain might decide to let the farm to somebody else. There were supposed to be laws guaranteeing farm preservation.

However, the distant menace of the road one day, the more direct threat of a major disruption the next, began to weigh heavily on my mind. Early summer lost some of its charm.

Then suddenly my son and my daughter-in-law decided to entrust me with the care of their seven-year-old little girl, Dominique, for an indefinite period. They had just come back from Singapore and while busy house-hunting in Washington D.C. where they intended at least temporarily to live, they felt that the country air, the calm of our orchards and the opportunity it would give her to speak and write French perfectly (as was the case with all our family) would be good for her.

But what would Dominique, intelligent, much travelled, think of me?

The room we called her father's because he had always occupied it when young was small, half-timbered, with a great stone fireplace and a narrow sixteenth-century window. The fireplace where once bats used to hang was filled up and now had bookshelves. I made up her bed, supplied her with a sophisticated German radio and put flowers by her bedside.

This room was next to mine (or ours, when my husband was there) and indeed one could pass from one to the other – as the cats had been quick to discover – through a tall, narrow cupboard.

We said prayers and kissed her good-night. Would she dissolve into tears for her parents, for her baby brother from whom she had not yet been separated? I was full of anxiety, and tiptoeing back to our own room slipped into bed with a book.

The house was very quiet. 'Leave a light burning,' she had asked me. I had done so, shading it with something on the side. She was coughing a good deal and ever since her New York days suffered from asthma. Indeed this was one of the reasons that prompted her parents to make this experiment. Would the sea air prove good for her or bad?

I read a great deal at night. When alone I would read for hours. When my husband was there he complained, and I was obliged to limit my reading and occupy my mind with much less intellectual problems, like what on earth would I give them for lunch the next day. Thus in the darkness or when the moon came looking in at the window by my bedside I would go through all the well-tried possibilities – sirloin, saddle of lamb, roast pork, fish, and then I would enumerate these all over again. Food had become a trying repetition. 'If she had been brought up by an English nanny,' I told myself, 'she would eat anything'. But as it was, I had already been warned that she was difficult. Perhaps in Singapore she had been accustomed to Chinese food. What sort of food did the Chinese eat?

After a while I heard soft footsteps in the corridor and switching on my bedside light, I saw our door very slowly open to reveal our little grand-daughter in her long nightdress.

'I was afraid – all alone!' she said.

Her bright, inquisitive eyes were taking in the scene in front of her – the big double bed with my husband and myself, the bedside lamps that I always covered with silk or chintz, the mauve cupboard, the little pink bathroom, the water-colours on the green papered wall, the one of the squirrel eating an apple on a white table cloth and those of Effie, my mother-in-law, when she was a little girl, one of them showing her just like Dominique at seven or eight in a long white nightdress. Our black cat, Poupée, so small that to save her life she was delivered by a Caesarean, lifted her head and blinked. The room was bathed in a soft glow.

'Would you rather come into this bed?' I asked.

Her sad, puzzled expression was replaced by an immense smile. In three leaps she was in the bed, her little arms round my shoulders.

'Can I stay?' she asked.

'I'll sleep in my own room,' said my husband. He had a room of his own with books, table, typewriter, and a big window overlooking the garden. The little girl stretched herself out comfortably beside me, stroked the cat who began to purr, and in a few moments was fast asleep.

With my window wide open to let in the cool breezes of the hot July night, I took up my book again and with my little grand-daughter snuggled into my crooked right arm, I re-plunged myself into Lady Cynthia Asquith's 1915–18 diaries.

The three of us quickly learnt to live together. The joy the child brought into my life is indescribable. I caught myself breaking into peals of laughter, something I had not done for years. I am followed with enthusiasm when I go to feed the chickens. The corn, almost worth its weight in gold, disappears at an incredible speed. I go into the kitchen garden. On my return I find Dominique sitting on the edge of the feed bin surrounded by the entire farmyard as she distributes largesse! The chicks climb on her shoulders, over her face, perch on her head, follow her in clouds wherever she goes. The turkeys try to knock her over while others dance a mad ballet all about her feet. She laughs, begins to recognise them, to give them names. She goes out into the orchard to talk to Rita, to embrace Jimmy. She is entirely without fear. Even the operation of taking the linen out of the German washing machine and hanging it out on the long lines in the forecourt where it will dry and bleach in the sun becomes new, exciting, punctured with laughter and cries of *Grand'mère*! The revolt I had felt upon reaching the age of seventy is metamorphosed into warm happiness at the re-discovery of a new, small, starry-eyed myself, an almost startling example of a woman in embryo.

French television brought her familiarity with a language in which, proficient though she was, she had not hitherto lived in daily contact. She was now discovering its common usage – in the news bulletins, the cartoons, the parlour games, the films, and in the presentation of ballets and operas, not only French but German and Russian. Like most little girls of her age her dream, momentarily, was to be a ballet dancer, and like Isadora Duncan, she improvised graceful poses and barefoot dances with flowing draperies. In the village shops she showed no nervousness, going in alone to buy the bread and the *croissants* at the baker's, the milk in Mme Legoff's little general store where her poise, her rather strange accent and her politeness surprised. Questioned, she told them that she was born in New York City had lived for some time in Singapore. Her unconventionality gave her a charming little personality of her own.

I was not so naïve as to believe that she was any prettier or any cleverer than any other young person of her age. The miracle she accomplished was not on others, or on herself, but on me. It was I who felt myself opening out under her influence. I was being given a new and exciting phase at a moment when my heart might well have turned to summer dust.

My son's teddy bears were ranged in rows in his bedroom and were to discover once again the pleasure of being hugged by little hands, kissed by warm lips. This one had lived right through the Battle of Britain, had been squeezed by nervous baby fingers when heavy explosives and incendiaries rained down upon our apartment in Shepherd Market, blasting the smooth road surface of Piccadilly, starting fires all along Curzon Street, sending the glass from our window panes piercing the opposite walls like cruel daggers. That one had been taken in the push pram along Jermyn Street when on a cold November morning the houses on either side had been rent open, revealing half-suspended baths, beds hanging from ceilings, smashed offices and shops emptied of their goods which were strewn upon the ground, broken, half drowned by the water of the firemen's hoses. What other baby had been taken after every raid in this part of the West End to be shown the damage? Where else could we have taken him, we who lived all through those days and nights in the centre of the battlefield? How normal it had seemed to him! What stories these animals stuffed with sawdust would have to tell! How needful to a child's start in life this juxtaposition of the tragic with the comic; sadness with beauty.

The novelty of being allowed to do the shopping herself in the village, not merely to ask for what we needed but to go in all by herself unaccompanied by a grown-up, resulted in her fixing up a little shop of her own in the garden. I found myself obliged to pay for my own produce. Two rather elegant young Parisian career women walked down the rut one day to ask if we would sell them the little house that my son owned beside his orchard and in which the dairy maid had lived. They would have liked to rebuild it and turn it into a weekend home. They found Dominique in her shop wearing the numerous necklaces, bracelets and rings that she acquired for a few francs in surprise packets outside the village newsagent's. The little girl looked at the two young women who displayed a similar fondness for contemporary costume jewellery. The two women looked at the little girl. All three were not so very different under the skin. On discovering the reason for their visit, I explained that the house in question was not mine but belonged to my son. He had already refused a number of offers. Then one of the young women said to Dominique: 'I see you have a shop. Perhaps you would sell us some new-laid eggs?'

One of them was a men's hairdresser in Paris, the other sold package trips to Madagascar and Tahiti. 'No part of the world is far enough away to satisfy the present clientèle,' she said. 'They think no holiday worthy of them unless to the other side of the world. This season our demand is for the Himalayas.' Dominique having sold them two dozen eggs and watched them depart, suddenly exclaimed: 'Grand'mère, I have charged them three francs too much! What shall I do?' 'Run after them with the money,' I said. Minutes later she returned with a contrite expression: 'They wouldn't accept the money,' she explained. 'The prettier of the two said that I was to buy myself another piece of jewellery!'

In the cool of the evening, we would either go down to the sands or drive to Deauville to look in at the Printemps store or discover what guests Bud and Erni were entertaining on the *Sarah Munro*. The little girl learnt to love the ship and would ply the long-suffering captain with questions that he never failed to answer with happy patience.

The ancient mariner in the person of Albert Sheaf, captain of Bud's ship, the *Sarah Munro*, was telling stories to the little girl about his youth at sea. He enchanted her and she liked his voice and his round, smiling face.

'Are these true stories?' she asked.

'They are true,' he said, 'but nobody would believe them today so you can think of them as fairy tales, but don't repeat them to the grown ups. They would be shocked.'

'Why shocked?' she asked.

'Because all my stories are about rich people.'

'Is it wrong to be rich?'

'No, everybody is more or less rich today but the rich people I am going to tell you about are of the wrong kind.'

'Pirates?' she asked hopefully.

'No, but they were mostly rich dukes and wealthy lords, a race that is altogether taboo.' He smiled. 'Only the Queen is tolerated.'

'Go on!' she said. 'Tell me about the first one.'

'The first one was known to his friends as Bendor – Duke of Westminster. I went to him in my early twenties. He had two ships and kept two crews going, so even for a Duke he was very rich. The name of one ship was *The Flying Cloud*, a four-masted schooner with two diesel engines and a crew of some thirty-two. This was a new ship built in Livorno, Italy – of some six hundred tons.'

'And the other one?'

'The other one was called the *Cutty Sark*, which had been built as a naval ship in Canada. He used it to go to and fro on fast short trips. It had no sail, just a diesel, and a crew of twenty.'

'What did he use the *Flying Cloud* for?'

'To relax on.'

'Were you the captain?'

'Alas, no, at twenty-one a man is seldom captain. My job was very modest. I was launch man but it gave me the opportunity to meet interesting people as we cruised down the Dalmatian coast and round the Greek Islands – people like Mademoiselle Chanel and the then young Winston Churchill.'

'When shall we come to the story?'

'Sometimes we would drift along slowly close to the land so that the guests could sunbathe. The Duke was very unhappy because he had just lost his only son. It is sad for any man to lose his only son – but sadder still for a Duke. That is something I won't try to explain. but the Duke's sadness did not alter the

137

fact that when he wanted something done, nothing was allowed to stand in his way. One day in Venice the ship was going so fast along the canal that all the gondolas with their romantic poets and youthful lovers, and all the busy vaporettos began bobbing up and down like corks in a tub. 'Your Grace,' I said timidly, 'soon all these unfortunate ships will capsize in our wake and people will be drowned. Shall I tell the Captain to slow down?' 'Slow down?' cried the Duke, 'why, certainly not. I have a train to catch. Buy the canal and turn everybody off it!'

'Could he have done?'

'Yes, I think he could. He could buy almost anything in the world. Mind you, today this would be thought very immoral.'

'What else did he do besides wanting to buy a canal with all the ships on it?'

'When we were cruising in the Mediterranean he used to go for a bathe every morning before breakfast. Sometimes Winston Churchill would go with him. When they were in the water you could always tell one from the other because the Duke always swam with his brown trilby hat on.'

'Why?'

'I don't know. It was a fad. He would leave his cigar behind – but never his hat.'

'After breakfast what happened?'

'We would go on shore, and I would go with him. He never carried money on him so every time we left the ship, I drew £100 which was replaced as soon as we got back. We were generally back in time for dinner but once His Grace went into dinner with his friends, nobody knew when they would come out. Sometimes the meal would go on till the following night. Occasionally he would send out a message: "Go and get a band on board. We want music." Often Mademoiselle Chanel was there. I don't suppose anything like this could happen today.'

'Go on!' said the little girl.

'After the Duke, I went to an even stranger man, a wonderful man like the ones you read about in story books, strong silent men who move mountains. This one was a baron – the first Lord Moyne. He owned a ship called the *Arpha* in which he made several trips up the Baltic, but one day it hit a submerged wreck just this side of Riga. So he came back home and bought a much larger, faster ship, a former Newhaven-Dieppe cross-channel steamer, to which he gave the name of *Rosaura,* and in which he travelled to distant parts of the world.'

'What did he look like?' asked Dominique. 'Everybody knows what a baron looked like in the old days.'

'This one was tall, thin and what is known as an ascetic. He never smoked and I never saw him touch alcohol. I don't even think he cared a lot what he ate. Food was not a passion with him. He was a dreamer with a stubborn mind. Not the sort of man you dared argue with or contradict. He liked to be alone. If a stranger came near him, he would move away. If another ship berthed near his, he would lift anchor and sail away. It was wonderful to be his companion. I never knew from one moment to the next what he would say or what he would propose. Suddenly he might get up and exclaim: "Let's go to Tahiti or to Greenland!" And off we would go.'

'Did he swim like the duke with his hat on?'

'No, he fished. We fished with a net or with a line in every river, every ocean. Yes, he owned a trilby hat but it was not for swimming. He kept it in his Rolls, and his chauffeur was not allowed to put petrol in the tank without first filtering it through the crown of the trilby hat. This was something apt to surprise the people at filling stations but the Baron didn't mind – even if there was a queue of motorists behind.'

'Did you catch big fish?'

'Big fish and small fish. We went right up the north-west coast of Alaska amongst the glaciers and pea-ice. Pea-ice are tiny pieces no larger than peas on a pod. He was talking to me one day when I brushed a whole lot of pea-ice off the rail. "Albert!" he said reprovingly. "You'll scratch my varnish! Have you the remotest idea what a long, tedious business it is to apply varnish on a boat?" "Yes, sir," I answered. "It's part of my job!"'

'What else did he do, except fish?' asked Dominique.

'He collected birds and strange animals and brought them back to zoos. One day he got it into his head that he wanted to look for the famous Northwest passage.

"Albert," he said: "We ought to go and look for it."'

'What's that?' asked the little girl.

'A dream that mariners have always had – oh, way back since the fifteenth century. They wanted to find out if by going right over the top of Canada amongst the ice floes and the bitter cold, they could succeed in passing from the Atlantic into the Pacific.'

'Did they?'

'They did and they didn't. There was an Englishman called Sir John Franklin in the early years of Queen Victoria's reign who set off in a ship called the *Erebus*. With him went another man called Captain Crozier in the *Terror*. A little band of brave men. Not a single one survived but they had pointed the way. Later navigators found traces of their passage. Of course now we have aeroplanes.'

'Did you do what he said?'

'Oh, come! Imagine his Lordship trying to crash his way through the ice in our cross-channel steamer, trying to follow in the wake of the *Erebus*!'

'So you prevented him?' asked Dominique, wanting to give grandeur to the Captain.

'The ice prevented him, not I. But he was a determined man. Once when we were off the west coast of Scotland, he exclaimed:

"Albert! I want to go ashore!"

"You can't, sir. Not here. Because of the rocks. You'd damage the launch."

"Albert! Didn't you hear what I said? I said: I want to go ashore."

"Very well, sir," I said.

Well, it cost him half a new bottom for his launch but that didn't worry him. He had gone ashore at the moment he wanted to.'

'He must have been very rich,' said the little girl, dreamily.

'Very,' agreed Albert, 'and yet he was careful in funny ways, sometimes in quite absurd ways. In the 'thirties when I was first with him, Britain went off the gold standard. In other words it was the first of those currency devaluations that happen every other day now. His Lordship heard about it on the radio when we were cruising on the other side of the world.

"Albert," he said, "this is a very serious matter!"

"Yes, sir," I said.

"We must economise. I may find myself one day with no more money."

"Yes, sir."

"Go down and see the chef, and find out if he has any kippers. We must all live on kippers for the next few days. See that I am served a kipper for my supper."

"Yes, sir.'"

'Personally,' said the little girl. 'I don't like them because of the bones.'

'I don't like them very much either,' said Albert. 'Fortunately it did not last long. But he was like that. In strange ways, careful with money. One Sunday morning we were ashore in Scotland, and as I had no money he lent me two coppers with which to buy a Sunday paper. I forgot all about it until eighteen months later when we were back from a long cruise in the South Seas. He made me a present of £50 which was quite a fortune in those days.

"Oh, thank you, my lord," I said.

"Yes," he said, "but don't forget that you owe me tuppence for that Sunday paper I bought you in Scotland. You must learn to be careful with money."

I gave him the two coppers, laughing.

"No," he said, "don't laugh. My father always taught me this. Be careful with money, Albert."'

'What happened to him?' asked Dominique. 'Did he lose all his money because of the devaluation?'

'Oh, no,' said Albert. 'There was no fear of that but something worse happened to him. He was assassinated in Cairo towards the end of the war.'

'Haven't you any other stories?' asked Dominique.

'Yes, plenty. You remember the *Flying Cloud*, the Duke of Westminster's ship? I went back to it for a time but though the Duke still owned it he had chartered it to an American, a very sick man who needed plenty of fresh milk, butter and cheese

141

every day.'

'On a ship?' asked Dominique.

'Exactly, on the ship. So we bought two Jersey cows, built cowsheds with padded sides and engaged the champion milkman of England to look after them. The American had his wife on board – a charming woman, and we set off for the Mediterranean. But by the time we reached Syracuse in Sicily, the weather was so hot that because of the cows we were infested with flies. I went on shore to get the mail, and on my return I found the American offering a halfpenny a fly to the assembled crew. In addition to this, he said, he would give a prize of £2 to the one who caught the most flies! By the end of the day the crew were smashing, and hitting and clambering all over the place, even chasing flies to the top of the masts. Of course, when it came to counting them, all the flies were stuck together and nobody could be sure who the winner should be. I don't remember what happened to the £2 but we got rid of the flies and the crew were delighted to have had such a financially successful day.'

'Where did you go after that?'

'Eventually the American and his wife left us and the ship was laid up for a time in Venice, off St Mark's Square. Then I went home to England where I met a shipping agent who asked me what I was doing.

"I'm on holiday," I said.

"Would you like to go to South America?"

"I shouldn't think so. Why?"

"It is that Thornycroft have built a new cattle boat for a firm on the River Plate and they want a crew to take it down. You should go. It might be fun."'

Albert smiled and said:

'So I went.'

'Go on!' said the little girl, implacable.

'No,' said Albert. 'Not now. I have other things to do than tell fairy tales to little girls.'

'Just this one more.'

'Very well,' said Albert. 'We put in at Las Palmas where the crew had a chance to go ashore. Two days out from there, it was a lovely hot day and I was washing my shirt in a tub on the deck when the soap slipped through my fingers and fell through a grid on to the deck below which would eventually be for the cattle. With my hands still full of soap suds I quickly jumped down into the hold. In the darkness, I became suddenly aware of eyes fixed on me. I thought of strange, dangerous animals – lions, tigers. I was terrified. Instinctively I sought to lay my hand on a weapon, something that might have been left by workmen in the empty hold, but even as I turned round, I saw other eyes staring at me from dark recesses. Two pairs! Three pairs! Four pairs of eyes! It was like some horror film. How many wild beasts could there be? At what moment would they decide to spring? Summoning up all my courage I clambered back to the deck above and ran to fetch help. What do you think we found?'

'Quickly!' urged Dominique. 'What?'

'Stowaways from Las Palmas, wanting to go to South America. They had slipped on board while the crew had gone ashore.'

'What happened to them?'

'We decided to put in at Freetown and dump them there. As for me, once I had safely handed the ship over to its new owners in South America, I returned in luxury at the company's expense on the liner *Alcantara*.'

I had been meaning all that summer to ring Hélène and Bill Leonard at Courtehaie to discover if they had arrived for their usual summer vacation from New York. We did not often correspond, generally a card or a letter at Christmas but I had learnt that Hélène's beautiful daughter Jacquine had divorced Patrice de Rochambeau and was now married to an American millionaire, a head of a great international cosmetic firm.

Perhaps because my grand-daughter occupied so much of my time, I had kept on putting off my summer phone call. Then one August day, on opening the *Figaro,* I had a shock. Young Patrice de Rochambeau had been killed in a Paris suburb while driving home from an evening appointment. It was night and his car must have skidded and hit another vehicle.

I could imagine with what emotion the Leonards and

Jacquine herself must have heard this news, because quite apart from their own affectionate relationship, was there not a son, Jacquine and Patrice's little boy, heir to the title and who by now would doubtless be a young man?

I immediately put a call through to Coutehaie. Hélène answered the phone. Yes, she said, they were all in a state of shock. The funeral was to be early the following week and Jacquine, of course, had come over from America. I reminded her of that evening when we had all been on the terrace of her house at Courtehaie when poor Patrice had that terrible toothache, and how we had all searched for an available dentist. She said:

'Come early one evening to tea in the middle of next week. We shall all be back from the funeral.'

'Will your daughter be there?'

'Yes, I'm sure she will. I know that she will be glad to see you.'

Before ringing off, her husband, Bill, came on the line to thank me for ringing.

On the appointed day I drove to Deauville to buy Hélène a small box of the home-made chocolates that I knew she particularly liked and towards evening we set off for Dozulé. We were met by Hélène, her tall, good looking son, Timothy, and Patrice Rochambeau's son who looked almost the same age as Timothy. Whereas my house is reached by a rut, there is not even that, over the well kept lawns at Courtehaie. One drives over the grass and the car in damp weather leaves tyre marks.

We were warmly welcomed, and Hélène and the boys showed us over the new cottage they had lately built not very far from their own house but in the same orchard. Built to their own design, it had the loveliest rooms and American taste and comfort, and a patio that looked across a very large pasture field to thick woods on the far side. It was the sort of place that made one long to do likewise.

After this we walked slowly over to their own house, and for the next half hour we talked in a desultory way, first in the living room, then on the verandah. I was puzzled by the fact that her husband Bill was not with us. Nor even Jacquine. I thought at first that Bill, at any rate, might have gone out to visit friends or perhaps to buy a packet of cigarettes; that we should see him arrive at any moment across the lawn. Finally I said to Hélène:

'Where is Bill?'

'Bill had to leave in a hurry last night,' she said. 'He couldn't allow Jacquine to go to the funeral alone. They barely had time to catch the French *Concorde*. They ought to be in New York any moment now.'

'I just don't understand,' I said. 'I thought the funeral was over. Was it not to be last Tuesday?'

Hélène looked at me in a puzzled way.

'Don't you know?' she asked.

'Know what?' I repeated.

'Jacquine had no sooner arrived to bury her first husband in France than we received an urgent message from America that her second husband had died suddenly. It meant going immediately from one funeral to the other – over three thousand miles apart. She was – I suppose you could say – twice widowed in a single week.'

'How terrible!' I gasped.

'So Bill had to take her back to America in the *Concorde*. She was in no fit state to travel alone.'

While Hélène was saying these words the phone rang in the living room.

'Excuse me,' she said.

On her return she explained:

'It was Bill ringing from New York. They have both arrived safely.'

'Oh!' I murmered.

Hélène said:

'It will all take a long time to unravel. He had interests in a dozen different States in America.'

'Yes, I suppose he had,' I said, thinking of the immense fortune that the name of his firm evoked amongst people all over the world.

The two young men, about the same height, perfectly brought up, grave, exquisitely mannered, stood side by side looking out across the recently mowed lawn to the distant countryside.

I asked softly:

'What will happen to them?'

Hélène poured herself out a cup of tea and said:

'We hope to go for a cruise to the Greek Islands.'

Later in the month, I received a picture postcard showing the
St Sophia Museum at Istanbul. But it had not been posted in
Turkey but in Greece. The stamp bore the word *Hellas* and the
postmark *Mykonos*. On it I read:

'In spite of our hearts being heavy, we are making a marvellous journey.
A thousand loving thoughts from
Hélène and Bill.'

9

MY GRAND-DAUGHTER had small ears and a graceful neck, and when she put her hair up she could appear very grown-up. She took a delightful interest in all my small possessions, and I knitted her the prettiest pullovers, and made her smart little skirts of the same material as my own. At last I had somebody for whom I could knit and sew.

She would sit on a tiny painted Russian chair beside me after supper at television but as from girlhood I had been taught never to be idle with my hands, I could both work and watch. My sewing baskets were legion, of every shape and size, and full of ribbons and threads, of strips of material and other delights. She would rifle through them for her own use but I came against the problem of teaching her to sew correctly. She was left-handed and though very adroit, of necessity worked differently, so that it was as hard for me to show her what to do as it was for her to copy my movements. I despaired of translating to my left hand what my right was so accustomed to doing.

I found in her an astounding reflexion of my own girlhood, though she was less self-conscious. If not always careful to use a thimble, which is so important, she was quick to invent. She found one day a piece of *sparterie* in a work basket, the stiff white material from which one shapes a hat, and this she expertly bent to the shape she wanted, covering it with satin and a whole lot of tiny coloured ribbons and bows so that when she put it on her head, it suited her admirably. Wearing this she would go down the village street and into the shops, quite unconcerned by the interest she aroused, or perhaps certain in her own little mind that she looked nice wearing it.

I have said that we quickly learnt to live three together. Not the least of our surprises was her enthusiasm. My husband, in accordance with his own childhood, accustomed her to read aloud a chapter of the Gospels every morning from his mother's greatly annotated Bible, and these moments gave her immense pleasure. Her memory, like that of most little girls, was great. She would learn the loveliest of the old psalms in a matter of moments and could recite the twenty-third: '*The Lord is my Shepherd* . . .' and the hundred and twenty-first: '*I will lift up mine eyes unto the hills* . . .' with an ease that filled me with jealousy. When she used to drive with my husband down to the village in the morning to fetch the mail, the milk and the bread, they would manage to go through all the multiplication tables, and whatever new piece they were learning by heart, before arriving in sight of the ocean. Then she would do the shopping and together they would go to the foot of the black cliffs for a long walk on the lonely sands, and she would tell him stories about New York and Singapore.

At this time of the year, I sometimes had a telephone call from a Russian woman to whom I had given hospitality a couple of times in the cottage. Short, a trifle on the stout side but with fresh, youthful features she was apt to bark at one but without malice, and in everything she was scrupulously correct. Our relationship was strange. We were not in the true sense of the word friends, and indeed we seldom conversed together. We eyed each other approvingly from a distance but without any feeling that our secret ways could meet. She was from the Ukraine and a good Soviet citizen, and for this I admired her, for after all it was her country and her regime.

She had first come to our village when called from Paris to nurse a friend of mine who was ill. Nursing was her profession. She had a passion for sea bathing and would plunge into the ocean on even the coldest days when the beach was deserted and the waves turbulent. There she would remain happily swimming for several hours on end. Anybody else would have emerged thoroughly exhausted. To her it gave exuberant life.

One day, while she was still nursing my friend in the village, she told me of a wish to see something of the country inland. I

148

offered to show her the farm. She expressed much admiration for the orchards, the trees, the hedges but most of all for the silence. 'What would I give,' she exclaimed, 'to pass an entire night in the stillness of the countryside, go out into the fields under a canopy of stars, breathe in the fullness of this country air.'

'When, after you are back in Paris, you feel, between one patient and another, that you need a few nights in the country, phone me,' I said, 'and if nobody else is staying in the cottage, I will be happy to lend it to you.'

'Thank you, Madame,' she said.

She was always precise in her speech.

As I said, she took advantage of this once or twice, and now I again received a phone call from Paris. Was the cottage free?

The visit she now proposed to make me differed from the others in this respect, that she had just returned from visiting her family in the village in the Ukraine where she was born.

'I could tell you all about it?' she said hopefully.

I seemed to recall the lines of Thomas Hood.

> *I remember, I remember,*
> *The house where I was born,*
> *The little window where the sun*
> *Came peeping in at morn.*

'Yes,' I said, 'the cottage is free. When do you want to come?'

'Tomorrow,' she said. 'I shall arrive by the 11 a.m. train.'

I went to fetch her at the station. She wore her red coat and carried two enormously heavy bags full of make-up, skin cream and special food. As we drove through the outskirts of Deauville, she noticed all the new houses that had gone up since her last visit.

'These are capitalists' houses,' she said.

'Hardly,' I suggested.

'I don't mean in a derogatory sense,' she hastened to explain. 'What I mean is that you would need a lot of money to buy one.'

'I fear that is mostly the case,' I said. 'But suppose you tell me about your village – the one in Russia. How did you get there?'

'I flew to Moscow, just like anybody else,' she said. 'From there I took the night train to Kiev, a fourteen-hour journey in a very comfortable sleeper.'

'Oh, I'm sure of that,' I said. 'I travelled from Moscow to Leningrad some years ago in a beautiful sleeper. Their trains are very good.'

'I stayed two days in Kiev,' she said. 'The city, of course, is completely rebuilt. It's very noble in appearance. From there I took the evening sleeper train to Kremenchug, all along the banks of the Dniepr. We arrived at about breakfast time. I watched it a few moments later pull out of the station on its long journey down to the Crimea. Russia is very big.'

I agreed.

'At Kremenchug, I took a little local train to the group of villages in which I was born,' she said. 'This was not the most comfortable part of the journey but the roads are even worse, and covered by white dust that sticks to everything. Still, it allows you to imagine what roads all over Europe must have been in Napoleonic times.'

'Are your parents still alive?'

'No, alas, they are both dead. My mother died young. She was very beautiful and my father adored her but he was constantly unfaithful to her. After her death he married a woman that both my brother and I disliked. My mother used to come back in the spirit and haunt him. He was very angry at being pursued by her ghost. She even appeared before my stepmother and exclaimed: 'Don't rejoice at the thought of replacing me. You also will die early. Just like me!'

'Did she?'

'Yes, indeed. But these are village tales. I expect the same sort of thing happens in other countries.'

'So with whom did you stay?'

'With my cousin who is a school-teacher. Her husband works in an office. They have a little girl of eight. And, of course, the prettiest little house – with a garden in front full of sunflowers and roses – and light blue shutters!'

'It sounds horribly capitalistic.'

'So it is in a way but every family in the village owns their house. But with this difference from Europe. If all the members of the family put money away and don't get drunk they can easily finish paying for it within a year.'

'Do these houses look very different in other ways?'

'Personally I find them prettier – but that's a matter of taste. One always likes the sort of houses in which one played as a little girl. Let me describe my cousin's house – not by any means one of the most splendid. A large room in the centre and bedrooms on either side of it. Every member of the household has a room of his own. They are all on the ground floor – including the bathroom.'

'Have you forgotten to mention the kitchen?'

'A kitchen in the house? But there is never a kitchen in the house. That is what is so wrong about French houses. It is impossible to keep a house clean, – the paint, the curtains, your clothes, everything – with the steam and the smells from a kitchen, seeping in from the oven into the living rooms. In my village in the Ukraine, the kitchen is in a little building all of its own in the courtyard.'

'Where do you eat?'

'Out of doors in summer. In the garden in front of the sunflowers. It's very jolly.'

'Was there plenty to eat?'

She looked at me reprovingly.

'But just consider! Our village is in the middle of the wheat belt. They have never known such a good harvest, or so my cousin says. Oh, the bread! Great, round, golden, crusty loaves weighing some five or six pounds apiece. I had quite forgotten what real white bread tastes like! As for the markets, they were infinitely richer than here in France. But, of course, there is a dark side. . .'

'It sounded too good to be true,' I said.

'No! No! Not at all that way. But Madame, how they drink! The vodka, Madame! By the full glass. The women are beautiful, the little girls much better dressed than in France, their hair in plaits, embroidered blouses and the smartest little skirts – no jeans or pants for little girls, Madame! – no, not on your life, Madame. Starched aprons with beautifully coloured designs. So very feminine. But the women grow so stout. Is it the food or the vodka?' She sighed. 'That is what I meant by saying that there was a dark side.'

'Well, if that is the only disadvantage?'

'Oh, no, there are others. The intellectuals earn so much less than the skilled workers. There are too many of them. The men in my own family, for instance, were nearly all engineers. Well, to give you an example, an engineer earns some 200 roubles a month. Whereas a skilled worker would earn at least 500 roubles, if not more.'

'That's becoming the case everywhere,' I mused.

'The datchas in my village are worth about 5,000 roubles,' she said. 'And as it costs a worker very little to live, you have only to work it out for yourself. With an annual wage of 6,000 roubles, he can buy his house within a year. That's what I meant by saying that in France you need to be a capitalist. Fancy taking ten or fifteen years to buy a house in a village like this one, Madame? It's a millstone round your neck.'

'People spend money on motor cars here,' I suggested.

'Yes, I grant you that,' she said. 'In the Ukraine a motor car (they are very fine) costs much more than a house. Nearly half as much again. But the authorities do it on purpose. They don't want people to own motor cars.'

'They may be right,' I said laughing. 'There's something to be said for going back to the dusty roads and a horse and buggy!'

'Oh, it's not that way!' she said. 'Everything is very modern.'

'Except that there are no rich and no poor – no extremes?' She laughed again.

'In the small group of villages where I was,' she said. 'They call these groups *arrondissements* – I was told that there were no fewer than eight millionaires!'

'What?' I exclaimed. 'Millionaires in what?'

'In roubles of course.'

'And I who imagined that the people in my village were so unusually wealthy!' I said. 'Eight millionaires!'

'In addition to which,' she said. 'Lots of people have a fortune of one hundred thousand!'

'I am afraid you are going to find your stay in my cottage very dull!' I said.

But though the fish from the English Channel might not compare with the river fish from the Dniepr, my guest was supremely happy.

'The country of my birth is far away,' she said when she had arranged her things in the cottage. 'But I love these Norman orchards because what I appreciate most is solitude.'

The cattle frighten her. Once or twice I had to go and rescue her as surrounded by gentle but inquisitive cows and heifers she did not dare move. 'Take a light stick,' I said, 'and hold it very quietly in front of you. They will quickly amble away.'

She had been in the cottage for several days, – eating, sleeping, wandering out in the middle of the night. I had scarcely exchanged a dozen words with her. She was autocratic, not particularly friendly but I felt sorry for lonely women, and though I would not have tolerated a paying guest, I found it normal to offer hospitality to a comparative stranger.

While I was digging up potatoes in the kitchen garden, she came up behind me.

She exclaimed in her harsh, Slavonic voice:

'That's the work of a peasant, Madame!'

'True,' I answered, digging the fork into the thick, damp earth. 'What of it?'

She did not answer this, but went on:

'Did you read the copy of Gogol's *The Dead Souls* which I sent you last winter?'

'Yes, of course.'

'He was a native of the Ukraine.'

'I know.'

'You remember what I told you about people in my village not spending much of the wage – putting it away so that before long they had enough with which to buy a house of their own?'

'Yes, I remember. In fact, I found something of my own character in that of Tchitchikof who had that habit of stuffing everything he found in a big chest. My grand-daughter laughs at me because of my many baskets full of knitting wool and pieces of material. Mark you, she's beginning to do the same thing herself. My grandmother was something of a witch. Maybe I inherit this trait from her. How are you getting on?'

"I have been down to the sands once or twice. Everything is very peaceful in a turbulent world. It's time that we should re-establish moral standards.'

'You have no religion, I suppose?'

'No,' she said.

'What happens in your Ukrainian villages. Did any of the churches escape the war?'

'Not many but a few.'

'Are any in use?'

'Any that remain are used. In villages where the church was destroyed, the pope holds his services in a private house.'

'A house in which people live?'

'No, a house kept for that purpose.'

'Who attends such services?'

She looked at me, smiling, and said:

'Old people. People like you!'

I accepted her bland verdict without flinching. After all, I was old. One must learn to face the truth. I asked:

'Any others?'

'No,' she said. 'Not young people.'

'You did not go inside any of them?'

'No,' she said. 'Definitely not. But it isn't for that, Madame, that I am not shocked by what I see around me. Besides, I am quite terrified of death. The thought that I might cease one day to see the beauty of those clouds in the immensity of the sky, the trees in their foliage, the stars at night – no, Madame, I cannot accept the idea of death. Madame, will you be driving down to the village later on?'

'Perhaps? Why?'

'I will come with you. I might even bathe. You could bring me up again towards 6 o'clock.'

How did she dare dispose of me as if my car was a taxi? I put the potatoes I had dug up in a basket and laid my sickle on top of them. I felt as if I were the communist, she the capitalist. Did she even know how to handle a sickle?

But it behoved me to give honour where honour was due. I

154

had never seen anybody cleaning out a cottage as she could. With a scarf tied round her head, and a broom in her hand, she was a formidable figure. All the doors would be wide open, every pane of glass rubbed. The carpets were taken out into the yard and beaten till not a speck of dust remained. It was a veritable revolution. Yes, that was the word – a communist revolution. I said to her: 'What on earth is the matter with you? Was the cottage all that dirty?'

'No,' she said laughing. 'But I happen to have the curse, and when that happens I must let fly!'

As a private nurse she was apt to be engaged by wealthy patients. She did not find it at all strange to work for millionaires. This past spring, for instance, she accompanied a very rich woman to Madeira, a picturesque spot, she said, but what had impressed her most was that the sheets in the hotel were of pure Irish linen – 'and think of it, Madame, they were changed every day! Even in the richest houses in Paris linen sheets were a thing of the past too easily damaged in washing machines and with nobody any longer to starch and iron, as in the old days. 'When I slipped between those pure linen sheets in bed at night, shall I tell you what I dreamt of, Madame? Of cutting them up into dresses which I would embroider with coloured silks!'

'If you have the choice,' I asked her. 'Do you prefer nursing men or women?'

'I have no rule,' she said. 'Women are apt to spy on you. Men are easier to please, and more often manifest their gratitude.'

My grand-daughter knew where to look for mushrooms. At the right moment, especially after rain, they would be found in certain parts of the orchard, under or between the apple trees – never exactly in the same place, but in known areas. She would run swiftly from find to find, learning how to pick them carefully not to damage their delicate bloom. The orchard sloped down quite precipitously towards the stream so that going down was fun but coming back slow and exhausting. Down at the bottom, near the hedge, which was mine, that separated us fom the Levannier home orchard, that splendid fourteen-acre field with the square brick house and the stables at the top by the lane, I had planted a line of sweet chestnut trees whose prickly fruit fell into the long grass so that it was wise to handle it with care if the outsides were not yet split. These were treasures one found in that delightful period between the departure of the cattle and the picking of the apples. When the cattle were round the house they ate everything. There was no treasure trove.

Just now Dominique was learning to recognize every tree, almost every blade of grass. She knew where the blackberries were most luscious, the hazel nuts most abundant, and where the mushrooms were most likely to be found.

The stream was bordered on either side by tall trees, ash, oak, wild cherry and amongst them a great deal of hazel which, apart from giving one of those lovely, soft nuts, were valuable for staves, props, and tall forked poles for keeping up the linen on the two long lines in the forecourt. But hazel, once abundant in the hedges, was so plundered by city folk in search of the fruit, and farmers to make kindling wood, that it was becoming rare like all those other gifts which God made to the land and which men have wasted and allowed to become extinct.

Often followed by the cats, or even with a favourite chick in her blouse, Dominique would wander slowly down to the stream. By crawling under the barbed wire fence, she could scramble down on the mossy banks where the cool water gurgled over broken branches and ferns. Here grew the spotted orchids.

The stream, after passing on its course at the bottom of our home orchard, continued it meandering way through Mme Bompain's land until it lost itself somewhere under the road to St Vaast. Levannier's cattle would congregate at the bottom of his home orchard under the oak trees gazing at the clear water as it bumped its way over small boulders. All this was Dominique's terrain. She called it 'The Forest'.

One day we heard the sound of mechanical saws in the direction of the road to St Vaast. Everybody used mechanical saws everywhere. It had become the favourite pastime of idle farmers. But this noise, though distant, was harsher, more insistent than a single man could make with a single saw. We bore with it for a time, glanced over the hedge by the kitchen garden to see if any of the Levanniers were in sight, and finally decided that it must be somebody cutting down a big tree over against Rémy's farm. But when, after lunch, the strident orchestra grew to intolerable proportions, Dominique exclaimed:

'I'm going down to "The Forest!"

Half an hour later she came back in tears:

'There are men everywhere in Mme Bompain's bank of the stream sawing down all the biggest trees with giant machines!' she said. 'It's terrible! It looks like a battlefield – oak, ash, chestnut, everything!'

This, for my grand-daughter was her first great sorrow, as if in a fairy story somebody had cut down the enchanted wood, laying low the prince, the princess, the ogre, the singing birds and the witch's sugar plum house. This slaughter continued for some days, from morning till dusk, perhaps ten days in all – until no single tree escaped between the Levannier home orchard and the narrow, winding, powdery road to St Vaast. Oaks and ashes looked immense when they lay prostrate on the ground, their noble branches severed and the huge stumps, the base of these giants, running with fresh sap. The gurgling water of the steam fought to rediscover its true course over a desolation of broken boughs, chipped wood, uprooted plants, old petrol tins and all the other ugly paraphernalia of the workmen whose immense eight-wheeled trucks, ready to take the timber to the saw mill, were parked along the road.

'On whose instructions are you doing this?' I rather timidly asked.

'I have no idea,' said the foreman. 'The trees have been sold. My job is to carry out orders.'

I still took my milk from the Levanniers. Every morning in the lane their tall churns stood by the white metal gate and then from the direction of Andrée Pradeau's Bois Lurette farm, the heavy truck would arrive to collect them. Stupidly I was angry with the Levanniers for what had been happening at the bottom of their orchard, holding them in some way responsible. But no tenant would have been allowed to inspire such a massacre. I knew that it must have been done on the instructions of Mme Bompain, the owner of the land.

This event must needs have a deep significance. The entire aspect of this corner of the plateau had changed. The wood of tall trees through which the stream ran had hidden us from the road to St Vaast. It had given us all a deep country privacy, an illusion of being much farther into the depths of the country than, alas, we really were. Now, from the road to St Vaast one could look straight across the orchards to the red brick house, to my house also. Motorists passing along the road could peep at us. From a distance, of course, but it gave one this naked feeling. Worse still, the noise of the traffic, once deadened by the trees, now came clearer, more menacing. The birds and the beasts would suffer.

'What are you doing down by the stream?' I asked Levannier aggressively.

'Ask Mme Bompain,' he said. 'It's her land!'

'Oh, yes, of course, but as you are her tenant farmer, I presume you must know.'

'The woodland between the bottom of the home orchard and the road to St Vaast is not included in the farming lease. Besides you know as well as I do that a tenant farmer has no right to cut down forest trees.'

'Please tell me the truth!' I pleaded.

Mme Levannier came out from her buttery, wiping her hands on her apron.

'We are leaving at Christmas,' she said. 'Didn't you know?'

'There were rumours. I hardly liked to ask. What do you intend to do?'

'My parents are no longer young,' said Levannier. 'We shall link up with them. Actually I have been buying a few acres myself in that part of the world.'

I looked at the house, the stables, the milking sheds, the long undulating fourteen acres of pasture land running down to the water.

'What will happen to all this?' I asked, with a slight tremor in my voice.

'We are going!' said M. Levannier.

'Yes, you have just told me. Will there be another tenant farmer?'

'No,' said Mme Levannier. 'Mme Bompain is selling it for building land. Already one or two people have come to look it over.'

'Is that why they have been cutting down the trees?'

'Presumably. Some of those oaks should fetch good money. There was no point in studying the landscape if the whole place is to be turned over to the builders – now, is there?'

'So fast?' I exclaimed. 'So fast?'

'We shall be taking the cows away,' said Mme Levannier. 'I shall have no more milk for you after the middle of the week.'

'Wednesday,' said her husband. 'I shall take them away on Wednesday.'

'Where to?' I asked.

'To our place – our new place,' he said. 'We are building a new home for ourselves and the children. The land round here is no longer any good for farming. The owners have no other thought in their mind but how much they can sell it for – to some speculator. All the farms are going the same way round here, all because of our proximity to the sea.'

'What about the orchard on the other side of my home field,' I asked. 'Do you suppose Mme Bompain will sell that too?'

'That's different,' said M. Levannier, 'on account of the road which is scheduled to pass over it – right through it, one might say. Mme Bompain might try to sell the two little cowhouses at the top by the lane but the rest is Green Belt. It can't be built on. I might keep it myself for fattening cattle.'

'But if you are going away to a new farm?'

'I could fatten cattle on some of the orchards here. What's forty miles by car? One can be here and there, so to speak.'

'How much of the land would you keep for youself?'

'The fifteen-acre field on the far side of the road to St Vaast, the field known locally as *The Big Piece* – and the one on which we grow corn on the cob. These I don't want to give up.'

I turned away not to show my resentment. In fact, when a farmer tenant came to the end of his lease, he could pick and choose. Abandon this, keep that. Just as Déliquaire, having abandoned my farm, had kept my son's orchard.

But fancy Mme Bompain being free to sell the brick house and whole of the home orchard, all fourteen acres of it, for building land! What a fortune she would make!

I would forget it. I would wash it all out of my hair. I would take my grand-daughter to Deauville to buy her a new housecoat. This desire had been whispered into my ear.

'You must understand that in Singapore, it was very hot, Grand'mère, and I never wore anything but the lightest, flimsiest things. Whereas here we shall soon be running into cold weather. Do you think we shall have snow, Grand'mère?'

'Is that what you would like?'

'In New York there was snow. I loved it.'

She looked at me enquiringly:

'Where shall we go in Deauville to buy my housecoat?'

'We shall go to the Printemps,' I said. 'I regard it with something of the same affection as in London I regard dear Harrods. There are shops that follow one all through life.'

'You mean,' corrected Dominique, 'that you follow them?'

'As you please,' I said.

On our way into town, my grand-daughter asked:

'Does it happen to you sometimes, Grand'mère, to feel that you have nothing to wear?'

'I think it happens to all of us,' I said. 'A grown-up can wear a simple black dress, the one we all have in our wardrobe, and make it look smart with a diamond brooch, but that is something not yet possible for little girls. So I fully sympathize!'

The Printemps between the ivy-covered wall of the Normandy Hotel and the Casino is what gives Deauville the sophisticated city look. It lifts it from being just a summer watering place. We went in through the perfumery department which is particularly large and well stocked with a bevy of pretty young salesgirls in attendance. I am not sure why it is, but the perfumery departments in French shops have quite a different smell from those in other countries. Dressing gowns and housecoats were on the first floor. We went up by the stairs, and at the top found ourselves facing a life-size cardboard London police-man. A notice tells us that it is British Week, and indeed a whole department is devoted to English biscuits, toffee, tea and marmalade.

At this point Dominique leaves me in order to run off on her own to the right department. I watch her from afar, pretending the while to examine a display of French books both in hard and soft covers. A youthful salesgirl leads her to a place where housecoats of all kinds for little girls hang side by side, and she removes one or two to display them to her small customer. But my grand-daughter is not the kind of person to allow herself to be influenced by others. Courteously, she informs the salesgirl that she will make her own choice, and a moment later she has removed from the colourful collection one with a Chinese collar which presumably may remind her of Singapore, her small brother and her parents now in Washington.

When I next look up I see all the salesgirls grouped around her. Those from other departments have joined the one who is supposed to be helping her. What clearly amuses them is this very young lady with a mind of her own who addresses them most politely in a faintly American accent. Now she opens her purse and is counting her money. She is led to the cash desk while the house coat is packed between tissue paper and put into a carrier bag.

'Did you think it pretty?' she asked while skipping lightly down the stairs.

The lavender had never been finer. There must have been something about the soil that it enjoyed. When the bushes grew old and untidy, I needed merely to cut off a sprig and plant it at the edge of a rose bed for it to become a real joy the following summer. Every year I made sachets in white muslin, filled them with lavender and tied them with pink satin bows. These I would send to friends all over the world.

One summer Bud Mitchell brought his mother to lunch on the farm. Erni came also and so did Albert, the Captain of the *Sarah Munro*. It was one of those summer days when in spite of a blue sky, a cold wind was blowing in from the north-east.

Because I was sensitive of the honour Bud's mother was making me and extremely anxious to please her, I laid the table in the low raftered room and lit a fire of apple logs in the big stone fireplace.

The châtelaine of Clopton Manor, who in her youth must have been an exquisite brunette, was now an old lady whose husky, authoritative voice commanded respect. Short and slightly corpulent, she wore a yachting cap, a blazer and pants, and walked carefully with the aid of a stick. I liked the slight bark in her voice and her commanding ways. Character in a woman, just as in a man, makes up for age.

I wanted the lunch to be simple – roast chicken, a home-made trifle, and all sorts of produce from the farm, and I asked her to take the head of the table. She said: 'You may call me "Blackie"', and when I asked the reason she told me that it was the nickname given her because of her dark hair by the other girls when she was sent to school in Germany.

This lunch in the sixteenth-century room beside a log fire in the height of summer remains a delightful memory. All the doors of the little house were wide open and when, after lunch, I led her into the front garden she stood entranced by the immense bush of lavender, heavy with bees, which met her gaze. I remember Bud Mitchell, jovial, corpulent, like a merry Falstaff, beaming down at his mother, and her saying: 'He was such a pretty little thing when he was born that I likened him to a rosebud'.

'Oh!' I cried. 'Is that why you called him Bud!'

There were other summers when they came to us, or we went to them on the ship. That August evening when Sir Max, Lord Beaverbrook's son, came over for a drink from his ocean racer *Perseverance* which had berthed beside the customs shed on the far side of the pool. He struck me on that occasion, as we all sat on the foredeck, as everything that a great fortune and good looks can do to a man. Like Bud, he was a Cambridge man, and had been a keen yachtsman from his youth. But for me, having known London so intimately between the wars, he was more than this; he was the living continuity of the great newspaper empire his father had built up, a reflexion of England's grandeur in one of the most picturesque periods in her long and glorious history. This was the London that had just come triumphantly out of one war, was shortly to become an example to the world in another. As we all sat holding our glasses in the quiet of the evening under a sinking summer sun, some passing ray caught the big gold commemorative coin that Erni wore by a slim chain round her neck with the words written upon it: 'Never in the field of human conflict . . .' It was more than fitting in this forgetful world that Beaverbrook's only surviving son, still carrying proudly his father's empire, should find himself on the *Sarah Munro*, so evocative of his father's closest and most illustrious friend.

Just about this time there had been a very disagreeable incident in the narrowing world of Paris daily newspapers. There was a growing movement in the wind that a newspaper's policy should be dictated not by the owner but by the editorial staff – unthinkable in the days of Northcliffe or Beaverbrook, something that neither man would have tolerated, and quite rightly, for it was a step away from freedom. My husband was with us that afternoon, and he said to Sir Max very quietly:

'I don't suppose such a thing could happen in England but if it did – what would you do?'

'I would not tolerate it,' said Sir Max.

'The mere supposition is absurd,' I thought.

On that summer evening on the *Sarah Munro* how calm, how still, how endless everything seemed, this yacht that had been Bud's for twenty years, this little piece of England in a French port, the memories that we all must secretly have been turning over in our minds – while talking politely about unimportant things.

Other summers came and went. Then Bud told me that his mother had died and that Clopton Manor was sold. He gave me two slim volumes from her library – the elegies of De Bertin published in Paris in 1823 with the bookplate and crest of Duff Cooper.

'Oh!' he added, 'you might be glad to know that as I was going through some of her old diaries, I came upon an entry in which she noted the pleasure that one of your books had given her.

This was, of course, long before you met her. So when I first introduced you, I was not introducing a stranger.'

This was indeed sweet vengeance in my ears. I had not forgotten how, when I was first taken on board the *Sarah Munro*, the woman I had met at Dozulé persisted in taking me for somebody else.

The two little leather-bound volumes would be a precious reminder of Blackie. I looked out across the bay sadly. Bud's blue and white houseflag flew on top of the mast of the *Sarah Munro*, the Blue Ensign drooped limply from the stern. It was good to see it. It gave me the illusion of maritime power.

Dominique continued to be enthralled by the hens and the turkeys. She had not only invented a name for each of them but knew their characters, their idiosyncrasies, whether they had been born on the farm or bought at Dozulé market when only a few weeks old. One evening we heard the French Prime Minister, Raymond Barre, telling the nation that it was the government's aim to sweep away all the country's old fashioned ideas and turn it into a competitive industrial nation. That meant, of course, our small, picturesque, uneconomical farms, our cider apple trees, the last remaining poultry yards where the hens ran between the hooves of the cows and became broody. All the trouble we gave ourselves over our poultry was as old fashioned as milking cows by hand seated on a three-legged stool. It might still look pretty as a picture on the outside of a box of camembert cheese but modern children would not even believe it in a story book. Hens were industrialized, cider favoured alcoholism and no farm under 200 acres was economical.

The work I gave myself, the things we did, were ludicrous. We would buy half a dozen chicks at Dozulé to amuse Dominique who would bring them joyfully home in a box, but what could we do then? There might be one or more mother hens with their young clucking round her but she would certainly not adopt strangers, even if the new chicks were, in our eyes, undistinguishable from her own. She would fight them. The turkeys might kill them. So we would let them sleep in the kitchen at nights and feed them separately until they were strong enough to join the flock. I would give them milk in a teaspoon, as I did to any young bird who looked unwell or not strong enough to defend itself. How great were the dangers of a new day. Chicks I had cherished and loved would disappear completely. Had some large, black bird from the heavens swooped down upon them, carrying off its prey? I would feel miserable, tell myself that it was my fault. I should have foreseen the danger. A young turkey would wander off towards dusk to hide in a distant hedge, or even to spend the night in the boughs of a tree. The next day I would find a trail of feathers to show where the fox had swooped on her and dragged her away. Was I over-sensitive to take all this to heart? Was I so different from other women? Must it really come to pass that the world could only survive as a competitive industrial nation?

What my grand-daughter liked best was to collect the eggs in the evening and bring them home like Little Red Riding Hood in her big basket.

We sold a few but as they cost me a fortune to produce, several times more than their value commercially, we gave them away to mothers with young children who were otherwise unable to find eggs sufficiently fresh to boil. Dominique took over this meticulous business. No stranger in our village would have guessed, on turning in with his car to M. Hanrard's garage, that he had fallen upon a veritable nest of femininity. Lionel Hanrard was a good-looking man with a perpetual smile, who was father of no fewer than six girls in succession before at last being given the long desired son. His young secretary who worked in a glass cage between the petrol pumps and the garage had a little girl of her own who was her delight and her joy. Yes, with all the knocking and the shouting, the welding and the varnishing, and the hauling in of bashed cars at weekends from road accidents, this was the centre of children-land.

On the opposite side of the road Roginsky and his wife had, before the war, owned a shop where I bought much of the furniture for my newly-acquired farmhouse.

This included nearly all the beds, the tables and chairs and that tall grandfather clock in which my then farmer, Goguet, hid his illicit calvados.

After Roginsky's death, their youngest daughter Maud married a young man called François. Her parents' shop was divided into two smaller ones. Maud and her husband set up business in one of them; the other was sold to the Barbets who were watchmakers.

Let nobody say that the life of a young wife who stays at home with her husband cannot sometimes be bliss!

Maud adored her bearded young husband who in her eyes could do nothing wrong. His business was to repair valuable period furniture – Louis XV chairs, armchairs and settees, the sort that terrify me in wealthy homes when I am expected to sit upon them. They are so fragile. Their owners watch one so nervously. François would be seen with a light hammer in one hand, a dozen tintacks in his mouth, knocking against an upturned chair while Maud, on the other side, would be cutting out or sewing the rich brocade with which the chair or the settee was to be covered. Her huge scissors, her sewing machine (of the very latest kind), her rolls of magnificent material were a measure of her skill.

The Barbets next door in their watchmaker's shop, and Maud and François were the best of friends. Maud and François had six children; M. and Mme Barbet had five. There were times when the children spilled out from these two homes, poured across the dangerous high road and invaded the garage with its six little girls.

Maud had another occupation that delighted my granddaughter. She was responsible for arranging the flowers on the altar at church. Very few people still had gardens. On the other hand a great many marriages took place on Saturday afternoons and when this happened there were masses of flowers for the marriage ceremony that were still beautiful the next day – Sunday. But when there were no weddings we occasionally came to the rescue with roses or – in spring – with apple blossom.

It had become the fashion for many people to go to Mass on Saturday evenings in order to stay in bed on Sunday morning.

Though it might have been called lazy Christianity, it was doubtless better than skipping church altogether. But the original inhabitants of the village, that tiny core, would be found at Mass every Sunday morning as the clock struck eight. Maud would look appreciatively at the flowers on an in front of the Communion table and Mme Barbet would occasionally read the first lesson. She had a very nice, clear voice and it was pleasant to see her graceful, feminine figure walking up to the lectern.

Quite apart from anything else, it was comforting at a time when the countryside was being overrun with hordes of invaders, to have this opportunity of finding oneself for a few brief moments with people one had known since before the war. My grand-daughter, like myself, used to watch with wonderment the sun rising behind the coloured stained-glass windows depicting Christ walking on the sea and talking to the woman of Samaria. This early morning service was never very full. When the clock struck eight and the priest, who had been waiting for it, appeared from the sacristy, there were not more than some twenty people waiting for him: our friends from the château, in their usual places, a woman in the third or fourth row with three children, one a baby in arms, Maud and François, the Barbets, and Mme Javot, Matilda's friend who had been such a comfort to her during the last years of her life. But gradually from the back of the church would come the sound of new arrivals so that one would be almost surprised before the end of the service to see so many.

One August the Abbé Duvieu told us that he was going into a Paris teaching hospital for an operation. Maud's husband drove him there and brought him back some ten days later. We saw him walking down the village street looking much better, wearing a smart new suit. I stopped the car and he told us how much he was looking forward to seeing us the following Sunday. Towards the end of the week he went to Trouville to visit a friend of his, another priest, but when he reached the top of the stairs, he collapsed and died. I remember the date because it was the same day that Maria Callas died. So do those one loves and admires leave one without warning.

On this Wednesday morning, Dominique and I set off for Trouville. It was market day.

We were both determined to enjoy these picturesque open air markets before they disappeared from the countryside – and the one at Trouville all along the banks of the River Touques – between the muddy river with its fishing fleet and the tree-lined road, the little town with its old houses built in tiers – remained one of the loveliest. Dominique was radiant. She carried her new handbag in the crook of her left arm.

The claret-coloured box-calf handbag was in fact mine. I had bought it at Delman in New Bond Street but frequent use had made a small split at the side. In the course of a periodic bout of tidying up, I decided that I was tired of it and that I would courageously throw it into the fire. If I do not burn things immediately, I invariably go and retrieve them half an hour later. My grand-daughter saw me on the point of consigning the handbag to the flames, and called out:

'Oh, please, Grand'mère, don't do that. I would love that handbag!'

'Would you?' I asked. 'Why specially this one?'

'Because it's a handbag like the Queen carried in the photograph you showed me in the paper last week. The Queen carries her handbags in the crook of her arm and that gives her a very regal air. When grown-ups give handbags to little girls they invariably choose little-girl purses that do nothing for one's self assurance. They don't help to make one feel grown up. So to own a handbag made of real leather with a leather handle is something I have always dreamt of possessing. But how can one explain that to grown-ups?'

The nicest things about being a grandmother is that one is treated as an equal. One becomes the recipient of whispered confidences that even mothers do not always receive from their daughters.

So together we took some beeswax from that Norman convent where it is prepared by the monks, and rubbed it into the leather until it became supple and full of new life, the colour warmer, the smell delicious. I threaded a thick needle with nylon thread and mended the part which had split, and I relined the interior. Here indeed was a new handbag of real calf, shining as brightly as on the day when it caught my attention in the elegant Bond Street shop. I almost regretted having been so generous but the smile that my little girl gave me quickly made me change my mind. My little grand-daughter was becoming a young woman, with a young woman's desires. She stood in front of me in the smart pullover I had knitted her, wearing the short broken check skirt in the same wool as the one I was wearing myself, her hair pinned back to display her beautifully formed ears. Her new shoes completed this picture of sophistication. Did little girls really prefer the blue jeans that most modern parents felt sure was so much better for them? How could I resolve this difficult problem when my own grand-daughter, at the age of seven, was already anxious to have the sort of grown-up handbag that the Queen wore when she drove out of what Dominique called *Buckington Palace?*

Once a year, in September, a vast fun fair with swings and roundabouts occupies the space usually devoted to market day produce. Its lilting music dances over the Casino and the little fishing boats along the river Touques, and all the children ride on elephants or giraffes, or swing in gilded cages right over the river. As for the market, it is given a long narrow strip on the other side of the trees, reducing the space devoted to traffic. When all this is going on at the same time on a busy Wednesday morning, Trouville is indeed a gay place.

Behind the scenic railway and the Big Dip, and all the shooting ranges with their clay pipes and beautiful dolls, are the caravans of the families who travel all round France with the paraphernalia of a mighty fun fair. They plug in to electric cables for their light and cooking, and you may peep into these travelling homes where the stew smells good and all the little beds are made up and tidy for the children. Dogs strain on leashes, monkeys are tied to poles, canaries sing in kitchen windows. What wonderful dreams are conjured up by the sight of all this in Dominique's mind! How wonderful to change your school every time you travel between one town and another! Always to be on the road.

My grand-daughter wants to ride round and round on the

back of a giraffe. If while the music plays and she goes round and round, she is successful in catching hold of a suspended rope, she will win a prize. She says:

'Don't worry about the money, Grand'mère. I have what is necessary in my new handbag!'

On the farther side of the trees was the market – and here a large van unfolds itself when parked in the open air, to reveal a shop of surprising dimensions packed with every known form of cheese. Men and women in white stand at the back of this display, cutting and weighing the cheeses of your fancy. Because they are standing on a raised platform, they need only stretch out an arm to pick up this cheese or that. To those whose knowledge of cheese is limited to what is brought, often quite dried up, on a plate in an English country hotel, this sight is quite breath-taking. In spite of industrialization, every French province still makes its local cheeses, some from cows' milk, some from ewes or goats, some with herbs, some with garlic, some with dried seeds or vine leaves.

Dominique, having spun round for a while on her giraffe, is back at my side and we both look very small and slight in the face of such grandeur. Roquefort . . . Brie . . . Cantal . . . what shall we choose? Cantal is almost the same as English cheddar and for that reason I am partial to it. This morning as I watch the tall, good-looking assistant cutting me a large piece of Cantal, I think back to a cold November morning so very many years ago when as a little girl I first arrived in London after crossing the Channel by night in the Dieppe-Newhaven boat. Cheddar was what we had for lunch, and it remains, I suppose, a symbol of my love for the country of my adoption and marriage.

Dominique, meanwhile, had three francs burning a hole in her purse. This was the money the pretty young hairdresser from Paris had told her to keep for herself against a new piece of jewellery. Here, right next to the cheese stand, was one entirely devoted to those sparkling treasures that so excite the imagination of little girls.

'I would like to buy the whole shop!' she whispered as I joined her.

I would not have presumed to tell her that she was already

170

sufficiently bedecked – "rings on her fingers . . . bells on her toes." The little hairdresser from Paris had called her *La femme aux bijoux*, at which I had laughed because in my extreme youth in Paris there had been a song which went:

> *C'est la femme aux bijoux,*
> *Celle qui rend fou,*
> *C'est une enjoleuse,*
> *Elle ne pense qu'à l'argent,*
> *Elle se rit des serments . . .*

The little hairdresser, hearing me sing it, began to intone it herself.

'How curious,' she said, 'my father used to sing that song when I was little. He had a beautiful voice and put so much feeling into it that I began to wonder if the *femme aux bijoux* concerned was not my mother. I was delighted to think of her as being covered with bracelets and rings but what intrigued me was the idea that this could be responsible for seducing my father to the point of rendering him quite mad!'

Her father had sung that song.

The idea made me feel suddenly old. I recall a very elegant American woman saying to me one day: 'If you don't want anybody to know your age, never hum an old tune.'

After my grand-daughter had chosen a new ring, we continued to thread our way through the crowds. Many market folk attend regularly with their wares – at Trouville on Wednesday, at Villers on Friday, at Dives on Saturday. Thus as Dominique and I pass by we hear ourselves being greeted from every side. The woman who sells materials, for instance, whose husband was interned at the Auschwitz extermination camp during the war. Having miraculously escaped the gas chamber he returned to his native country to be charged with not having paid his income tax! I exchange a little local gossip with his wife and then go to buy some carrots for a stew.

These small things accomplished, I look round for my grand-daughter and discover that she has disappeared. I hurry this way and that, I fight my way frightened to death through the slow-moving crowd. I run to the roundabout and look despairingly at the giraffe bobbing up and down with another child on its back, I rush to the muddy bank of the Touques to search for her between the caravans where, in their respective kitchens, the women are making lunch. Dominique is nowhere.

I have left the highroad to the last. The traffic flies past and I see it as a deathtap. Did she panic and try to cross the road? What sort of a grandmother was I?

It was then that I saw only a few yards away from me a little girl whose poor little face was bathed in tears. She raced into my outstretched arms, and says:

'See what I have bought you, Grand'mère! A wooden platter on which you can cut the food for the cats.'

She looked up anxiously. Her eyes were swollen. So this was the reason for her disappearance. She had run off to buy me a present.

'Do you like it, Grand'mère?'

Her voice was tremulous.

'Of course I like it,' I exclaimed. 'I would not exchange it for all the gold of the Incas!'

10

AS IF NATURE were determined to complete what man had so savagely begun, there fell upon us that winter an unexpected tragedy. A tempest swept over our orchards with hurricane force, followed some weeks later by days and nights of deathly stillness as the entire countryside was imprisoned without light or telephone in snow and ice, the latter of such strange ferocity that the like of it had not happened within living memory.

Every winter brought its high winds, and more often than not, drifts of snow, but what took place that January, what began it all, was something so eerie that one had the uncomfortable feeling that Heaven was punishing us for what we had done to this once beautiful countryside.

On 11 January, the eve of Dominique's eighth birthday, a wind rose in the night that was soon howling round the house. We took no great notice of it. The evening had as usual been spent reading, writing, watching television by a beautiful, warm log fire in the low rafrered room. The house was so snug. It had stood up proudly for no fewer than four hundred years! We went to bed at midnight, even slept with the window wide open. On these occasions under warm blankets one feels as if one were at sea with an open porthole. There were no cattle in the field. Not even Jimmy or his mother.

But when we came down in the morning, the sight was almost unreal.

The wind, like a fearsome reaper with a giant scythe, had laid low several lines of trees from the top of the orchard right down to the stream at the bottom of it – a length of nearly a quarter of a mile. It was as if with every swing of a mighty arm, this ghostly figure had cut down thirty trees at a time. They lay, line to line parallel – uprooted, their heads and arms smashed but all pointing in the same direction.

It looked at first as if we, because of our position, had perhaps taken the brunt of the storm. The orchard looked a mess but it was not tragic. Most of the trees that lay uprooted were either old apple or pear trees – or, in quite another part of the orchard, fifteen or twenty plum trees that I had planted some twenty years earlier and which in fact had never given forth worthwhile fruit. Half a dozen elders on the hedge that separated my kitchen garden from the Levannier home field had fallen across the posts and netting that kept the cattle away. This was a nuisance because I would have to find manpower to put up new posts and netting over a length of about a hundred yards.

M. Robert arrived with a mechanical saw and cut into one-metre lengths as many of the apple and pear tree trunks as he could. I promised to go to the co-operative in Dozulé and buy stout chestnut stakes and netting for the kitchen garden hedge. The insurance said it would pay. The tempest was an act of God but if the elders had been dead that was quite another matter. Curiously enough, they were dead. Elder trees in hedges are a curse anyway. They stifle the hazel and the cherry, and one cannot even burn their wood. The insurance people came to look at the trees, confirmed their lack of life and offered me the equivalent of some £50 to redo the hedge – which money I promised to M. Robert in return for doing the work.

My husband and I set about sawing the branches of the pear trees and apple trees, and even splitting the pieces of trunk. It was hard work but we both had a passion for forestry – and so far the loss of the trees was merely financial. They could be replaced. We mounted two long walls of split logs against the back of the stables and congratulated ourselves that we had been able to do so much.

But less than a week later, snow began to fall, and there were rumbles of industrial strife. This began with a postal strike which was invariably a partial closure with the outside world.

For three weeks light snow and sporadic postal strikes made things difficult but I succeeded, towards the beginning of February, in persuading Laquerre to check the slates not only on the roof of the house, but also on those of the cottage, the stables, the cartshed and the old bakery in the kitchen garden. I was worried about their condition after the hurricane.

By this time the Levanniers had finally left their farm. They made no picturesque departure. They did not go off, as farmers did in the old days, leading their cattle and a cart with their belongings. Since early autumn, they had been gently fading out, selling very little, taking most of their livestock by truck to their new home in the Eure, emptying the house and the stables by degrees. The children had left our village school at the end of the summer term and by September they were already with the grandparents, going to a new school near the house their parents were preparing to live in. Christmas found all of them together. When the front door of the red brick house was open, you could see right through empty rooms to the farther fields.

Early in the New Year a young man accompanied by an Alsatian dog arrived at my garden gate. Polite and well-dressed, he enquired if the orchard with the two small Norman cowsheds was mine. I told him that it belonged to Mme Bompain who lived in Caen.

'Her tenant farmer has just left.'

'I thought of buying the two cowhouses,' he said.

'What for?'

'For a place in the country.'

'Could you live in a cowhouse?'

'They could, perhaps be adapted.'

'Are you aware that a major road is scheduled to pass over them in a few years time?'

'Not through them but between them. There would be just enough width to leave them standing, one on either side of the road.'

'Wouldn't it be rather unpleasant?'

'It depends. Proximity to a road is sometimes an advantage. I live in Paris. I'm a busy man. I would be glad to drive straight up to the door.'

'Would you get a permit to turn cowhouses into houses for human habitation?'

'Within limits. Oh, not very luxurious ones, of course.'

'Would you like Mme Bompain's address?' I asked.

'No, it's not necessary. They are in the hands of an agent. I shall have to think about it. But I was tempted by the price. They are relatively so cheap.'

'How much?'

'Twelve thousand pounds,'

'What?' I cried. 'Am I dreaming? Two cowsheds for £12,000! You call that cheap?'

'She has measured off exactly two acres of pasture land from the top of the field. The rest, by the stream, will continue to be leased to a farmer. What I have to consider, therefore, is whether two Norman cowsheds and two acres of orchard constitute a cheap package for £12,000.'

He smiled.

'I bid you good-day, Madame' he said.

In spite of what the young man had said, I felt pretty sure that nobody in his right mind would pay £12,000 for two cowsheds with mud floors, no windows and cracks in the sides. They were fit for cows but not for people. And I was pretty sure also that anybody foolish enough (in my opinion) to buy them, would only get a very limited permit to alter and add.

So I dismissed the whole thing from my mind, and indeed I never heard any more from the young man with the Alsatian dog.

But on 9 February, this is what I wrote in my diary:-

Postal strike – No telephone – deep snow and ice.

Yet, I was naïve, enough to believe that everything would have righted itself in a day or two, and indeed on the Sunday we went down as usual to 8 a.m. Mass officiated over by a new Abbé-Abbé Dominique Thiron whose father was killed in an air raid on Caen during the war and who had a number of Protestants in his family. He was an altogether fitting successor to our much lamented Abbé Duvieu.

But the snow continued all the next week until I began to wonder if I would be able to get up to the top of the orchard in the car. When the snow deepened, I left the car up by the gate all night, covering it over with a tarpaulin. Because the lane had little gradient, we were generally able to get away in the morning to do the shopping, buy the milk, the bread, the urgent provisions.

By Sunday morning even this was impossible. The doors of the car would not open. They were iced up. The entire countryside was white, the snow deep and soft underfoot.

Even this might not have been so strange. It happens everywhere. What was different from any other cold spell we had ever known, was the way the ice formed on the branches of tall trees and forced them down until they snapped and fell. All the tops of the ash, for instance, after looking like diamond bracelets, crashed one after the other into the hedges or on to the snow. The Italian poplars swayed, groaned and then broke in two. The trees that had not been uprooted in the hurricane of the previous month now suffered a different fate. Their boughs became brittle and snapped. Scotch firs came tumbling down. The drought of a previous summer had rendered many trees less resistant. Pollution from such distant sources as the oil refineries at Le Havre had for some time been affecting our forest trees.

This was the great avenging blow.

Much of Andrée Pradeau's estate, Bois Lurette, skirted the road to St Vaast, and here many of their finest trees crashed down on telephone lines and high tension cables, plunging all that part of the plateau into darkness. Power was then cut off at the main. We slithered down to the village on the Monday, past cars abandoned by their owners, past uprooted trees, past limply hanging wires – a scene nevertheless of matchless beauty, and wonderful silence.

Only slowly did the fact emerge that a large percentage of all the cider apple trees in Normandy were felled by the gale and ice. This was something that with foresight we might possibly have avoided. Hardly anybody during the preceding forty years had replanted. When an apple tree died it was cut into logs and burnt. The cider apple tree had ceased to interest the farmer who no longer drank cider at home. His farmhands might have done so but he no longer had any. Not only did he allow old trees to die but he greedily accepted money from the Government to cut down younger ones. After these turbulent weeks it was clear that only cider apple trees in the full vigour of their youth had stood up to the elements. The others paid the price of age and neglect. They were swept off the face of the earth. Orchards were becoming fields with just one of two odd trees. The character of the province was changed out of recognition. This was no longer the Normandy of the guidebooks, the Normandy of Lucie Delarue Mardrus and of Guy de Maupassant. What would take its place?

While the wind was blowing and the snow was falling, I had been intrigued to hear incessant knocking from the top of the lane, as if some spirit were busy hammering nails into wood. I could hardly imagine the presence of any human being in this snowbound, desolate part, and one day I put on snow boots and walked slowly and with difficulty up the track to the gate.

Here there was a gap in the hedge, and looking through it I found myself opposite a little man with slit eyes and an oriental face.

'Good day,' he said, 'My name is Tran Ngoc.'

With a serious expression, anxious to enlighten me, he spelled it out and said:

'You don't pronounce the "g" in Ngoc.'

I smiled.

'Chinese?'

'Vietnamese,' he corrected. 'Scene of the long, terrible war.'

I asked him what he was doing in Normandy on this icy day. He said:

'I am the new owner of the two little cowhouses against the top of the lane. I have just signed the contract and now I am putting down posts and nailing barbed wire to circumscribe the limit of my two acres of land. As I am all alone it is hard work but I shall manage.'

As, full of wonder, I gazed at him I saw all the unfortunate Vietnamese fleeing with their babies and their miserable possessions from the modern armour of the American army – fleeing from tanks, flame-throwers, jet planes. I saw again those harrowing scenes that we had been shown every night on television for months and months on end, and I was terribly moved. What on earth was this Vietnamese doing all alone in Normandy so very far away from home?

'If I can be of any help?' I said.

With his pile of stakes and the heavy roll of barbed wire, he looked pathetically small and inadequate for the immensity of the work he had undertaken. To stake out two acres of land all alone on a snowy, cold morning is no small task. I would so terribly have liked to help him. I said:

'You can see my house from here.' Then suddenly anxious for his health: 'You're not going to spend the night in one of those draughty cowhouses? You would be frozen!'

'No,' he said. 'For tonight I have found a room in an hotel. But if later I could come down to fetch a pail of water?'

Later that afternoon he arrived at the garden gate with his pail. He was shivering with cold but all smiles, having successfully achieved what he set out to do. 'Temporarily,' he said, 'I saved putting down stakes here and there by using well-placed apple trees. Do you think it will harm them, nailing the barbed wire against their trunks?'

'It won't do them any good,' I said, 'but others have done as much before you. What was important was to stake out your land. I saw two surveyors from Caen with their motor car at the top of the field a couple of weeks ago, but I was not aware that Mme Bompain had sold the land.'

'They drove boundary posts into the ground,' said Tran Ngoc. 'I merely had to follow them.'

He refused a meal but gladly accepted a cup of tea. He had come to Europe as a student before the war to attend a course of engineering in Paris.

'At the Sorbonne?'

He waved his hand negatively:

'Not the Sorbonne,' he said. 'Better places than that.'

His young wife, though born in France, was of his own race and they had two young children, a girl of about six and a boy of three or four. His wife was a school teacher. He was an engineer. He repeated this several times, anxious for me to understand

179

the extent of his qualifications. When the family was together they all spoke Vietnamese. In addition, of course, he and his wife knew French and some English, but they could retire behind the walls of their own language, and when the children played together that was what they spoke.

I saw in Tran Ngoc a symbol of all that lone determination that characterized his race, and I was quite overcome by the work that lay ahead for this slim, curiously elegant young man who expressed himself with a forthrightness and an assurance that I had been far from expecting.

'There's a lot to do,' he repeated. 'The wind blows through the half-timbering, the mud floor is strewn with damp hay and the place smells of cow dung but the roof is virtually sound though I intend to have a slater run over it and make it snug.'

'There's no water,' I objected.

'That won't be a problem,' he said. 'the same pipes that run through your land run through mine. I have already arranged for the electricity board to lay on current but in order to save money I shall dig the trench myself. I have a great deal of work ahead of me. I want at least one of the houses to be ready for my wife and the two children this summer. My only fear is that she may find the place too lonely.'

'Will you need to get a building permit?'

'I know the law,' he said. 'I am meticulously informed. I have limited rights, and anyway I intend to do everything myself. I have already applied for the building licence. I shall receive it shortly.'

There was a question I longed to ask him. How much had he paid for it? Twelve thousand pounds, he said.

'Was that not rather a big sum?' I asked.

He laughed rather sardonically and said:

'What will that represent in a few years' time?'

'And the road that is supposed to go between your two houses?'

'The road!' he said. 'The road! Who knows what will happen in five years' time? Who knows what will happen tomorrow? The road? Well, let it come. I shall still be the winner.'

He smiled, took his pail of water and I watched his small, slim figure disappearing round the bend of the snowbound track.

Were we now going to be colonised by these tough little men from the distant East?

By the end of March, the front garden was full of crocusses and daffodils, and the hedge separating the kitchen garden from the red brick farmhouse, as well as all the lawns, were full of primroses. In another week the cowslips would be out.

This, with early fall, was perhaps the loveliest time of the year. In London, during the worst of the aerial bombardments of 1940, I used to wheel my pram with my baby through the smitten streets as far as Cambridge Circus where Ernest Zaehnsdorf, the great bookbinder, would be found at the back of his showroom, all the windows of which had been blown out by repeated high explosives. He had a tiny office heated by an oil stove in which he tried to keep warm. His grandfather, Joseph, was born in Budapest a few months after Napoleon was sent to Elba. He grew up to the sound of the anvil in his father's blacksmith shop, but as a young man was apprenticed to a bookbinder in Stuttgart. After a few years he came to London, started a business of his own, and soon became famous. His son carried on after him, having widened his knowledge in Paris where he was trapped during the Siege while staying with his uncle, court jeweller to Napoleon III. This Ernest was a craftsman with the inherited cunning of three generations.

I would wheel the light perambulator into his office and he would brew me a cup of strong tea, and take down from the bookcases that stretched up to the ceiling some fine example of his work. There seemed so little chance of there ever being a tomorrow that he would often say: 'Take this one home and enjoy the feel of the binding. What is the good of keeping anything these days?'

One day in this manner he happened on a miniature copy of Mary Russell Mitford's *Our Village* published at the beginning of the century in the Temple edition by J.M. Dent which he or his father had bound in calf with some fine gold tooling. The date on the spine was 1906 which happened to be the year of my birth. I fancy that it was for this reason that he was anxious for me to have it.

181

Whenever I want to make comparisons between the country-side of today and that which our forebears knew, I reread such chapters as 'The First Primrose', 'Violeting' and 'The Cowslip Ball'. It is now rather more than a century and a half since Miss Mary Mitford, contributing to the *Ladies' Magazine*, described the meadows and lanes of Three Mile Cross between Reading and Basingstoke. I have already said that when I first bought the farm in Normandy, the lanes, even at my door, were filled with cowslips, primroses, violets and, in their season, wood straw-berries, and that they were occasionally, but not always, garlanded with honeysuckle and the wild rose. I doubt if there was very much difference between the Pays d'Auge and Three Mile Cross. They shared an incomparable beauty.

What is driving the last of the primroses away from our lanes is not merely the destruction of the trees and shrubs in them, but the close shearing of the hedges with devastating mechanical blades that uproot almost everything but weeds. The cool springs and babbling rivulets have been dried up. Left to itself the primrose multiplies but with its roots blasted out from the soil by motorized units of a rural council it is faced, even well away from the seacoast, with annihilation.

Curiously enough, in this part of the world, the modest violet is the bravest of these former country delights. When one comes upon a few on a mossy bank one kneels down to embrace them. But what has happened to their perfume which not so long ago lingered in this moist, heavy air? Is it really possible that in Mary Russell Mitford's day they burst upon her, these lovely violets, in tenfold loveliness?

'The ground is covered with them, white and purple, enamelling the short, dewy grass, looking but the more vividly coloured under the dull, leaden sky. There they lie by hundreds, by thousands. How beautifully they are placed, too, on this sloping bank, with the palm branches waving over them, full of early bees, and mixing their honeyed scent with the more delicate violet odour! How transparent and smooth and lusty are the branches, full of sap and life! And there, just by the old mossy root, is a superb tuft of primrose, with a yellow butterfly hovering over them, like a flower floating on the air. What happiness to sit on this tufty knoll, and fill my basket with the blossoms! What a renewal of heart and mind! To inhabit such a scene of peace and sweetness is again to be fearless, gay and gentle as a child. Then it is that thought becomes poetry, and feeling religion.'

Though she talks to me from so long ago, I have something else (but my love of wild flowers) in common with Miss Mitford. Strange as it may seem, to me also needlework is the most effectual sedative, that grand soother and composer of woman's distress. But if Mary Mitford has sudden desires for exercise and exertion, so have I. But alas, my meadows, so fresh and cool, and delicious to the eye and to the tread are not full of cowslips and all vernal flowers. There are dandelions, thistles, occasional wood sage and wild mignonette, buttercups and white mustard but there are not fields of cowslips any more. Golden marsh-marigolds do not grow on the margin of the little brook which runs between the ash and the hazel at the bottom of my orchard – what my grand-daughter, Dominique, calls her 'Forest', and I have no hope of seeing trout dart up the stream. Izaak Walton might have loved the brook and the quiet meadow but he would not have found any fish. As for me, when I laid down my needlework (or my knitting) it was to seek exertion in the kitchen garden pulling up weeds or planting potatoes and lettuces because I have nobody to help either in the garden or in the house – no more than a farmer can any longer find a farmhand. When my strength goes, my garden will become a jungle of bindweed like the garden in front of the red brick house since its tenant farmers have departed. Nobody will come to my aid.

Just before midday while I was in the kitchen preparing lunch, the cow bell from the Austrian Tyrol tied to my garden gate gave notice of a stranger at my door. Here was Tran Ngoc come to introduce his exquisite little Vietnamese wife and their two young children, a boy and a girl bearing between them a gift, and bowing and smiling profusely.

When the introductions had been satisfactorily concluded, the little girl handed up the gift.

'Vietnam toffee,' said Tran Ngoc, 'very wholesome. I hope you will enjoy it.'

I asked them if they had only just this moment arrived from Paris. Were they staying the night? In that case they must give me the pleasure of sleeping in the cottage. We stored the apples there in winter but here was spring and if they were cold there were electric fires.

'No,' said Tran Ngoc, very decided and forthright. 'We have much to do and little time in which to do it. We need water and a dozen eggs if you can spare them. I have brought a good deal of gear in the car, a carboy of gas and even a barbecue. If the cowhouse is damp, the children can sleep in the car but there is no need for you to pity us. We are accustomed to overcoming small difficulties. Besides we shall all enjoy the sweet country air.'

'While you are filling your pail with water, let me take your two children into the poultry yard. We have a mother hen with a family of three-day-old chicks. Would that amuse them?'

The two children each take a baby chick in their hot little hands and run around crying out excitedly in their native tongue. Mme Tran Ngoc informs me that she has a sister who is to be married in the summer and that they want to hold the wedding festivities in their piece of orchard in front of the house which her husband intends by then to render habitable. They will organise a summer fête. All the children will run about wild. There will be guests – other Vietnamese. It will be charming and picturesque.

I am beginning to be reconciled to the idea of exchanging the antiquity of these Norman fields for a new and no less colourful form of existence. Everything will be different but once one is prepared to exchange the 'lovely violets in ten-fold loveliness, the cowslips and all vernal flowers' for the strangeness of having Saigon on your doorstep, and the raucous sound of Asiatic children floating up into the morning air, life may still be very good. I am even beginning to look with a less jaundiced eye upon the new drive flanked by its newly planted trees between Andrée's Bois Lurette and those new blocks of apartments, what was once (so long ago now) Cathedral Lane. Suburbia at its best has charms. The streets are so well-paved. Children race along on bicycles, and there is a certain comfort in the knowledge that one is not quite so isolated as in the past, if the doctor needs to be called, or if one became a little less fit.

Besides, the truth must be told. The peasant is so full of wiles and tortuous, devious, circuitous, crooked (not straight-forward) ways. I must needs use up all the synonyms in the Oxford Dictionary to describe most inadequately the complexity of his crafty brain. Not that the present day farmer, at least in this part of the world, could be accurately termed a peasant. Until before the war of 1940–45 he was still so, hardly changed in centuries. But today he is only by antecedent peasant. There have been grafted upon him all the death-dealing marvels of modern science with which to kill the bees that hovered and sang over Miss Mitford's honey-scented violets, to destroy the honeysuckle and the wild rose, to gouge out the wood strawberry, to pollute the apple blossom.

For the second time that morning, the Austrian cow bell, tied to my garden gate, rang.

Had the Vietnamese returned for more water?

No, it was Albert – the Captain of the *Sarah Munro*.

'I've been in England,' he announced. 'I've brought you back a big chunk of boiling bacon.'

'How perfectly wonderful. You are just in time for lunch.'

'Alas, I can't. I'm busy varnishing the ship, and I want to get it done before it rains. Otherwise I shall have to start all over again.'

'Have you heard from Bud and Erni?'

'Yes, they are well. They'll motor up from Grindelwald as usual at the start of the summer.'

'It will be lovely to be all together again', I said. 'My grand-daughter is longing for you to tell her more stories.'

Albert looked sad.

'She will have to make haste,' he said. 'This will be my last summer with the ship. I've decided to retire.'

'Oh, no!' I cried. 'You mean that you are going back to England permanently? What will Bud and Erni do without you?'

'They won't,' he said. 'They intend to sell the ship!'

185

Just as I had been feeling more cheerful.

Bud had told me that this would be the *Sarah Munro*'s twenty-first year under his ownership. His houseflag, flying from the top of the mast, had seemed to me more permanent than any other landmark overlooking the Touques river and the hillside town of Trouville. This piece of England, this link with all we loved so much on the other side of the Channel.

'There are moments in life,' wrote Miss Mitford in *The Cowslip Ball*, 'when the spirits sink and fail, as it were, under the mere pressure of existence; moments of unaccountable depression, when one is weary of one's very thoughts, haunted by images that will not depart . . . with hopes disappointed; fruitless regrets, powerless wishes, doubt and fear, and self-distrust and self-disapprobation.'

'Look what I've found!' cried Dominique, rushing into the garden, breathless from having run all the way up from the 'Forest', 'A four-leaf clover!'

The red-brick house, in all its echoing emptiness, haunted me. Even the bell had gone. The bell right under the eaves which was rung by a heavy chain that reached all the way down to the pebbled path where the vine grew against the southern wall. I thought of all the dead people, milkmaids, farmhands, children, for whom it had rung so joyously to bring them home from the fields for the evening meal presided over by the farmer and his wife. Ghosts of long past when, more than a century ago, the house was first built. In my imagination I tell myself that the house in which Emma Bovary lived must have looked like this one. It was a house round which to weave strange tales.

I am not quite sure why I became so sentimental about it. Perhaps because the house looked as if it needed somebody to love it. It looked so desperately abandoned, with all this talk that it was going to be pulled down to make way for a housing estate.

I told myself that if ever while wandering through the empty stables, the deserted milking sheds, the once beautiful kitchen garden now run wild, where the lettuces grew and the strawberries under their straw became hot and gorged with sun,

– if ever I were to meet a witch with a burden of faggots on her bent back, disposed to give me three wishes, one of them would be – the gift of the red brick house!

But summer was not yet with us and the nights were long and cold. Our cats curled up near the Aga in the kitchen and only occasionally went off for moonlight adventures. But just in case they did and were hungry when all the rest of us were fast asleep, I used to put a plate of food for them on the big oak table on the terrace of the flower garden. The table had been made by a local carpenter from oak cut on the estate. Unfortunately he had made a mistake in his measurements and the table meant for the dining room (like a refectory table) was, when finished, too large to get through door or window. So it spent its life outside.

I began to notice that since the red-brick house was empty, a very elegant little cat with fur the colour of mink and emerald green eyes, as bright as precious stones, came to lap the milk – but at the first sight of me she would race away in a panic.

On opening the stable door one morning, a flash of mink fur darted out, brushing against my stockings. A small round basket on a table showed where my nocturnal visitor had curled up on a handful of hay. I must have locked her up without knowing it the previous night. At least she would have been snug and warm, away from the cold winds.

I knew her, of course, having seen her flashing across the forecourt of the red-brick house when the Levanniers were making ready to leave. They had already taken the two little bitch terriers and this kitten's mother to their new home but this one was altogether too wild, not at all the hearth cat petted by the children, but sleeping in secret, often inaccessible hideouts in hay lofts or milking sheds. Because she was obviously starving she had come to me. The problem was to make her understand that she was welcome.

I did everything I could to tame her. A new kitten is resented by cats in the house, and they spat at her, especially the black one, Petite Fille, who had suffered that expensive Caesarian, and who was spoilt. Tiggy, the New York cat, had also on first arrival been resented by whatever cats held sway at that time. It often took up to six months to get a new animal accepted. The same thing applied, of course, to any newcomer. The turkeys would grow red with anger if a carrier-pigeon came to rest for a few days or weeks on the slate roof. Intruders were savagely kept out.

Our visitor would crouch under the faggots in the cart shed, her green eyes shining, her poor, skinny body shivering with cold, but nothing would induce her to come into my arms, even if I brought her a saucer of warm milk. I would have to leave the saucer behind and hide myself. Then she would greedily lap up the sweet, warm milk.

What a great number of hours I wasted trying to tame her! I put a dish of something really excellent in the cart shed so that agreeable vapours should steal in her direction. Her green eyes were fixed upon me. She listened to my words of cautious endearment, and finally advanced, ears low, tail touching the ground but when I put a hand out to touch her, she mauled me so savagely that I let out a cry and went back to the house to bathe my wounds.

My weak, feminine arms have been mauled so many times. Viciously bitten by a rabbit while putting him out on the grass, deeply torn by claws when helping a cat to bring her kittens into the world, pecked at to the bone by turkeys whose strength and savagery are sometimes unbelievable. A farmyard is full of jealousies, of hatreds but also of love. These are sentiments severely repressed in those egg and fowl factories like the one on the road to St Vaast where the birds are scientifically fed, robbed of their freedom and never see the light of day.

In spite of my bandaged arm, I continued to woo my new friend. What I found hardest was the immobility and the cold. In the end I made progress as I knew I would. She would come within a yard of me, seize a morsel of food and even purr. Her body trembled with hunger and cold.

One evening while my grand-daughter and I were collecting the eggs, putting them in the big basket that we kept specially for this agreeable task, I leant forward to pick up a clutch from one of those inaccessible places where hens choose to lay. Something very light, light as handful of feathers but very warm, alighted on my bent shoulders and then ensconced itself round my neck like a beautiful fur collar. I guessed what it was but I was terrified because of my eyes. I knew that if I frightened the animal she might put out her claws and go for my face. I closed my eyes tight and remained perfectly still. Dominique gave a little cry of enchantment and stood waiting on tiptoes beside me. We had tamed the untamable! Our kindness was rewarded.

Soon like a witch with her back bent, I would wander about with my new love round my neck, purring herself silly. She was my cat – mine and Dominique's. Soon she was in the house, first in one room, then in the other, chasing the other cats away as if it had been they the strangers, not herself. Downstairs and upstairs. Before long when Dominique went up to bed (my bed) at 10 p.m. the new cat would accompany her and I would find them, cheek to cheek, their heads on their respective pillows, hands and paws on the white linen sheet, one smiling, the other purring, waiting for me to join them.

As my grand-daughter refused to curb her magnanimous ways, far too happy to see some fifty or sixty fowl following her like a female Piped Piper into the orchard, the two great bins, one of corn and one of wheat, became empty every few days. Never had a poultry yard cost such a fortune. I kept a secret reserve in the cottage for use in an emergency, like a sudden snow storm when we might not be able to get down with the car. All my secrets were known to Dominique who would often have to remind me of them.

'I remember hiding the key of that door,' I would say to her. 'But I can't recall where.'

'Don't worry, Grand'mère. I know where it is. Under the pink knitting wool.'

She called the grain reserve, the Hidden Treasure.

'Grand'mère, we need more corn, and the baby chicks want first month meal.'

'If you did not fill your apron with corn everytime you go out, it might last longer.'

'They are always hungry, Grand'mère, and I do really think they love me.'

Now that the corn merchant at Dozulé had closed his doors, and the one at Touques had done the same, not to mention the one at Dives near the old market place and the church from which William the Conqueror had set out, I had taken to buying what we needed from Mme Clérice's little shop in the harbour area of Deauville.

Soon there would be no more shops of this kind, so reminiscent of the horse-and-buggy age. Riding had become a nostalgic pastime amongst city folk who arrived in their secondary residences at weekends anxious to eat shrimps fresh from the sea and to ride horseback as in Victorian times. The family at the château ran a riding school and led their pupils single file along our lanes, which soon, by stronger forces, would be turned into cement. The sea gave forth only the tiniest shrimps, and most of the fish had scuttled away. The horse had disappeared from the farm, together with the violet and the wood strawberry. The problem with the riding schools was to know what to do with the horses in winter time. But to ride a horse from time to time was a prestige symbol, especially for parents proud of their offspring, just as going out with a gun in the first week of October was a rage with all the male population, though everybody knew that hardly a rabbit was left in the hedges – and never a hare. The trouble with the countryside was that most of the nation dreamed unreal dreams.

But Mme Clérice and her husband supplied many of the great stud-farms in the Deauville area. The French government did everything to facilitate the *tiercé*, one of its most sensational sources of revenue – gambling on the first three horses in a race. So Deauville with its stud-farms (the French called them *haras*), its yearling sales, its famous race course and Polo ground allowed Mme Clérice and her husband to continue their old trade.

Their shop from the outside did not look the least important. In a small, narrow street between the muddy bank of the Touques river and the yacht harbour it had some old placards of race meetings at Dieppe outside and a few old daffodil bulbs in the window, together with some dog food. It was almost as if the

Clérices didn't want to let people into the secret that they sold not only corn but every imaginable other sort of grain. When you pushed the white door open and the bell tinkled, the Clérices' marmalade cat, half asleep on Mme Clérice's account book in her small partioned-off bureau, would look up. If somebody brought in a dog, the cat would climb various impedimenta up to the ceiling and remain watchful. Otherwise it merely blinked.

Built all round and behind their little warehouse was a firm of timber merchants whose lathes were piled on the quays of the small harbour where ships came in from Norway, Sweden, Finland and Russia. Wood from distant forests smelt delicious under a warming spring sun. Seamen with beards spoke strange tongues as they unloaded the wood from their holds. A single-track railway line, from the top of the yacht harbour for a distance of some two hundred yards along the quay, crossed the high road leading to Trouville bridge and was used in the old days to take merchandise to the main railway station. I doubt if any locomotive any longer puffed its way along these rails which were half hidden by sawdust. It was said that the Harbour Master by virtue of his status as lord of the ground had a free pass over the French State Railways but that was the sort of tale that made men laugh on the yachts at evening drinking time. The quay was not only used for ships bringing timber from northern forests. Every November it was covered with cider apples which ships from Cardiff came to fetch for making English cider.

Inside Mme Clérice's shop jute bags with their mouths open contained sample grains and seeds, potatoes and all other things that a grain merchant sells. Mme Clérice would take my order and her husband would trundle the 50 lb bags out on a trolley to the back of my small car. As he put each one into the boot the entire car gasped like a winded man.

His wife told me that in his youth he had been chosen by a firm of millers to deliver bags of flour to bakers all over the province. As a result he was acquainted with most of the baker's shops between Honfleur and Cherbourg. When he fell in love with her – she was a Breton girl – they worked for a time for a corn-chandler who in those days had a small place facing the river Touques. Then they set up on their own.

Dominique and I now drove across this same river by the new bridge. I was determined to buy her a thimble. In Trouville, opposite to where the fishing fleet anchored, was a shop that sold everything for the housewife and the needlewoman. What we called a haberdasher. Soho, and indeed every quarter of London, had at least one in my youth. One would go there for a piece of ribbon, a packet of needles, a reel of cotton or some elastic. Gradually they have all disappeared.

The one in Trouville was called *Le Gagne Petit*. The very name was evocative of those beautifully produced French children's books of the last century in which lady authors taught children to be hard-working, honest and satisfied with a modest profit. This was not altogether bad advice but the sentiments are out of date.

Here at least I could be tolerably certain to find a thimble even for a little girl, and I must confess that to see a woman trying to sew without a thimble fills me with indignation. Such a sorry sight denotes in advance that her stitches will be clumsy and rude. My mother taught me to feel something akin to nakedness when holding a needle in a thimble-less hand. She also claimed that those guilty of this crime were *des ravaudeuses,* botchers, bunglers and menders of old clothes – but in no circumstances women who could sew!

The owner of the *Gagne Petit* was very dignified and stood by a desk behind the door. His father founded the business in 1903, the dawn of the English Edwardian era, and the son had something of the long disappeared Bond Street shopwalker.

The lady assistants were past middle age, somewhat severe but extremely expert. They did not need to be asked twice for what one needed, and one felt that they knew how to embroider and how to hem just as well as oneself. When Dominique held out her middle finger, one of these women inspected its diminutive size and opened a drawer. 'It is well that she should learn young,' she said, 'but I note that Mademoiselle is left-handed, and if you are not so yourself, Madame, you are going to find it very difficult to teach her.'

'I have already discovered that,' I said. 'Shall I not succeed?'

'Yes, you will succeed and it may even happen that if she likes to sew she may surpass you. We had an assistant once who was left-handed and we had a great admiration for her. She sewed beautifully but even so it is apt to create complications. For instance, she would leave her scissors on, what was for us, the wrong side.'

That evening back at home while Dominique and I were watching television by the log fire in the big room we were shown pictures of a man who had suffered a sensational accident, not so very far from our farm. In the course of a road smash he had lost an arm, completely severed from the body. It so happened that a qualified nurse arrived immediately afterwards in her car on the scene. The man was rushed to hospital – together with the severed arm and by a miracle of surgery it was grafted back to his body. This inspired a number of surgeons to show us on television the miracles of sewing that a surgeon can accomplish with the finest of needles – wearing his rubber gloves. This caused me to reflect that those misguided women who would be ashamed in this age of sex equality to be seen sewing properly with a thimble, for fear that they might be thought too feminine, would do well to ponder this matter. Good seamstress that I am I shall never be as nimble with a needle as those men in their rubber gloves! Perhaps it is a case of each in their station.

11

SUMMER CAME AT LAST and Bud and Erni resumed their residency on the *Sarah Munro*. Tran Ngoc and his wife and two fascinating children brought their oriental colour and the sound of their native tongue to the top of the neighbouring orchard. They ate their meals in the open air in front of the cowshed door, worked, played, hammered, dug, and even planted seeds and multicoloured flowers in a specially designed garden of the tiniest size. The bride, the bridegroom and all the guests arrived for the wedding feast, music of a new kind floated away over the tops of the apple trees to the stream meandering along its mossy, tortuous course at the bottom of the field. Tran Ngoc very ceremoniously nailed to the trunk of an apple tree the number of his building permit, his name, occupation and address, and the extent of the modifications envisaged. This was something that nobody passing along the lane could fail to see. It was a magnificent piece of handpainted work, impressive and noble in proportions. Later a machine arrived with a mechanical shovel for digging a trench for the electric cable. New openings were cut in the hedge of the lane to facilitate the access of motor cars, and Tran Ngoc put up a tall, narrow, wooden edifice like a guardsman's sentry box which he painted white. This, standing prominently at the far end of his compound, was the family closet.

It rained every day, and my kitchen garden was a sorry sight. The green peas should be sprouting by now but there was little in the ground except potatoes. The previous year's potato crop had failed throughout Europe, and they had reached such absurd prices that I had made a special effort to plan sufficient for our needs. Mme Clérice who had sold me a 50 lb sack when I went to buy the corn for the hens, being a native of Brittany, had taken these wild fluctuations in price much to heart. Her province depended on its potatoes, its cauliflowers and its oyster beds, these last having been cruelly hit by the wreckage of a giant tanker only a few miles from the coast.

My pride were the tender lettuces in rows of twenty-five which I tended with loving care. Every week Dominique and I had planted a new row so that they would reach maturity progressively. Some we had bought at Dozulé, others at Trouville, and we fought steadfastly to prevent the hens from flying over into the kitchen garden and gobbling them up.

We were both anxious for the kitchen garden to be a source of pleasure and utility when the family arrived to take her back to America. They would, we hoped, spend at least a fortnight in the cottage before returning home by way of England. Would the strawberries and the raspberries be at their best for Dominique to take her little brother by the hand and help him to plunder them under a hot sun? He was constantly in her thoughts, especially now that her long visit was nearing its end.

The sixteenth-century bakehouse in which four centuries earlier our predecessors must have baked their bread had three comfortable rooms, each with its door opening out on a small garden which was filled with roses, hollyhocks, and peonies. In these we kept mowing machines, spades, forks and other garden tools and a great quantity of those light wooden crates and hampers in which fruit was packed, and which we would collect empty on market days from behind the stalls.

My grand-daughter did more or less as she pleased on the estate. She would amuse herself alone for hours on end but as she always came at the ringing of one of the cow bells – a pre-arranged signal that I needed her – I was never anxious.

That summer she had cleared the central room of the bakehouse to turn it into her private drawing room, nailing postcards or coloured illustrations on the half-timbered walls, making deftly with her left hand tables and chairs for her dolls. Wild flowers picked in the orchard or down by the stream would be put about in old jam pots, and from time to time I would be invited to a meal at which I would be offered dishes of fruit gathered in the kitchen garden and served on tiny plates.

I treated these invitations as seriously as her pleadings to get me to play bézique, that card game that my father, Milou, had taught me to play when I was the same age as was my grand-daughter now. My father and Matilda played together on the kitchen table on Saturday nights, and I would follow every game eagerly, marking the score with a pencil on a sheet of paper pinned to the wall. Occasionally my mother would allow me to take over her hand but like herself I was invariably beaten. My father was a splendid card player which made my poor mother exclaim that it was about the only thing he did really well. This two-edged compliment put him in a good humour and he would say: 'When I was a young conscript in Nice we played cards in the Regiment for gold. Alas, you two females have none!' 'If you had the gold, we would have it also!' my mother would retort bitterly. Thus the evening which had begun with smiles and laughter, too often ended in recrimination.

In spite of this I had retained a certain fondness for this game that Sir Winston Churchill particularly favoured. Both my husband and my son disliked this mild recreation and it fell upon my grand-daughter to rekindle in me half-forgotten memories. With a piece of green baize laid over the table Dominique, with cries of joy, would deal the cards in front of the Aga stove and away we would go, a saucer of silver francs at our side.

The cat with the green eyes came up regularly now in Dominique's arms to bed and when, after locking up the house, I would join them, it was a joy to see their heavenly content.

Early one morning this cuckoo in the nest (she had displaced the black cat) began labour pains, and I just had time to carry her to a specially prepared basket at the bottom of a cupboard. When Dominique woke up, two kittens – one golden and the other grey – were being licked dry, and my grand-daughter's excitement was intense. We kept the golden one and called her Marmalade. Soon her eyes would open and she would prove one more treasure to surprise Edward.

Summer brought Andrée Pradeau and a number of her family to Bois Lurette, this great house that looked faintly Russian.

Two of Andrée's daughters, Laurence and Danièle, now had children of their own, little girls of Dominique's age who would introduce her into their circle of *petites filles modèles*, and thus bring back echoes of the famous books of the Comtesse de Ségur. The house and its park were much grander than our small farm, and much more compact so that for little girls it was ideal – hayfields and woods at hand, a rose garden, meadows with sheep and their lambs, hothouses, the farm, the pigs, the cattle. Andrée herself, only just recovered from a painful operation, invariably elegant, ready to welcome with a smile, mistress of a great domain, with virtually nobody to help her, accomplished every day a staggering amount of work. Her husband had been ill, and needed careful nursing back to health; there were her children, her grandchildren, a house that in the days when it was built would have at least four servants to run it, a farm with a bailiff and accounts to keep. Never, to paraphrase Sir Winston Churchill, was so much being accomplished by frail women in high positions. Andrée's aged mother, though she had somebody to look after her in the mornings, had at her own request been left virtually alone in Paris. Andrée's anxiety was great. We laughed over our separate ills and misfortunes, and our uncomfortable awareness that in this part of the world at any rate, the days of the townswoman trying to administer agricultural land to the benefit of everybody concerned were over for ever. We were a doomed race.

By temporarily deserting the heat, the glare, the noise and the fever of London, to what extent had I willingly cut myself off from the convulsions of the universe? Having read voraciously both in English and French all my life, plunging from the eighteenth to the nineteenth centuries, I no longer had at my disposal in the middle of a damp orchard the classical treasures of great libraries. At my elbow, beside where I write these words, are merely the vital books that can cling to the side of a wall. To these I find myself adding the latest outstanding feminine autobiographies – the thoughts and experiences of women who like myself are able to look back on the events of a century fast coming to a close. How rich in only these last few

197

years is the gift by contemporary women writers to the history of our time! The Garsington of Lady Ottoline Morrell, the 1915–18 diaries of Lady Cynthia Asquith, the pre-Nazi Germany seen by the Kaiser's daughter, Viktoria Luise, the India of the Maharani of Jaipur, the nightmare Berlin of Hildegard Knef, the war-scarred Italy of Susanna Agnelli, the brilliant memoirs of Tatiana Metternich and Countess Cecilia Sternberg, both memorable books, the posthumous letters of Sylvia Plath and the London of the 'thirties by women in such different milieus as Diana Mosley and Margaret Duchess of Argyll. Not to mention erudite feminine biographies such as the life of Louisa May Alcott by Martha Saxton, Elizabeth Wordsworth of Lady Margaret Hall by Georgina Battiscombe and yet two more of equal interest, Mary Shelley by Jane Dunn, and Mary Webb, the authoress of *Precious Bane*, by Gladys Coles.

Strange to think what whilst women's colleges at Oxford and Cambridge were foolishly racing towards co-education with its doubtful benefits, other colleges and universities in America no less important, like Wellesley and Smith, were determined to remain steadfastly feminine, allowing one hope that at least these and similar great women's universities throughout the world would be allowed to continue their autonomy. The child who was my grand-daughter, in spite of having seen so much, travelled so widely, from New York to Washington, from Washington to Singapore, was still sister in thought and behaviour to the little women of Louisa Alcott, and to the *Petites Filles Modèles* of the Comtesse de Ségur. She was by nature, and quite to my delight, a bundle of femininity from the moment she landed from a trans-Atlantic plane into my lap. See how brother and sister play together – she the future woman, he the man in embryo! My neighbour, Andrée Pradeau, does the work of four people, though she is no less feminine. What a dull world if there did not remain a vast difference between women and men!

On hot summer evenings we would go down to the sands. Dominique loved it and quickly discovered a club where she could join other children of her age who were drilled and amused by an athletic young instructor. Our bathing tents were in front of what used to be an elegant hotel but had become, in a changing world, a holiday house for employees of the State gas and electicity board. The sands in the height of summer became increasingly crowded, the sea a little more polluted but one could still find space to lie down and bronze. There was much less of the village atmosphere. To some extent the regulars were swamped out; in addition to this, customs had changed. People of all ages felt it necessary to their dignity and to the high opinion they held of themselves to visit Athens, tour the Greek islands, or even spend a fortnight in England where the exchange was so favourable. The girls came back with men's shirts to wear over their jeans, and a few words of the language which might prove useful to help them pass their *baccalaureat*.

Just now and again I would find bronzing in front of the bathing tent a young married woman I had known as a little girl. Most of them, because of long spells on the Mediterranean, were bronzed all over from the tips of their noses to the soles of their feet, including their firm, youthful breasts which at Juan les Pins, as in so many other places, they exposed openly to the burning rays of the sun. Though this was not yet tolerated in our Channel seaside resorts, it was not uncommon for me when calling upon young women friends in the secluded gardens of their villas to find them unconcernedly bare-breasted. At the beginning I felt slightly embarrassed but this feeling quickly wore off. One is so accustomed to see men in the hairy nudity of their chests that logically one should, I suppose, not be squeamish when members of one's own sex take the same sort of liberty. Especially when their bodies are evenly bronzed. Curiously enough the darker the tan the less one is shocked. Moreover I found many young women more elegant naked than when wearing a man's shirt and rather grubby jeans. At least, nudity made women of them again. They rediscovered their lost femininity. Martine, the youthful mother of two little girls, walking across her lawn to meet me, said of her second delivery in a Paris hospital: 'No, I had no problem at all with breast feeding. I had all the milk I needed – so much indeed that the nurses brought me a baby whose mother had died in giving birth to her. I fed both of them – one at each breast. It was perfectly marvellous!' Her eyes positively shone with remembered pleasure. 'I found it so wonderful to feed not only my own little girl but this innocent angel who had just lost her mother!'

She threw her head back and laughed happily. We were standing, believe it or not, under the overhanging boughs of a fig tree whose luscious green fruit, in spite of northen climes, was delicious to eat. Martine's story filled me with delight and looking at her breasts, as she threw back her head in merriment, I told myself that seldom had I seen breasts so firm, so youthful, so perfectly upheld. Nobody could have told that she was the mother of two little girls and the breast-milk provider of a third! She could have walked on to the stage of the Folies Bergère and made girls of eighteen jealous.

I had an idea that my grand-daughter was well informed on the matter of childbirth but it was not my business to enlighten her any further. Though her knowledge was, perhaps, veiled with mystery – the acceptance that there comes an end to life was an equal reality in her busy little mind.

'When you are dead, Grand'mère, we shall have your farm, won't we?'

'I hope so,' I agreed.

I felt that she was on the point of adding:

'How nice that will be!'

On the whole she was paying me a compliment – that of appreciating these endangered orchards sufficiently to want one day to own them.

Bud and Erni were back on the *Sarah Munro* and before long the Smeets arrived on their twin-screw ketch *San Lucar* from Antwerp after buffetting a storm and spending a night at Boulogne. Once again the two ships berthed side by side, the Blue Ensign next to the Belgian flag.

Things were not quite the same as before. The knowledge that it was for Bud and Erni their last summer on this beautiful ship, something just as tangible for them as their home in Grindewald, their glacier village at the foot of the Wetterhorn, took the edge off our happiness. For me so many things appeared to be coming to an end at the same time. I needed the promise of my grand-daughter's future to help me accept the inevitable.

Her parents, together with Edward, the little boy, would be flying over from Washington D.C. for a brief holiday after which they would take Dominique home in time to start school in America at the beginning of September. On and off she had spent the best part of eighteen months with me. In this time she had become perfectly bilingual and grown up into a little woman.

Though my son and daughter-in-law had not given me an exact date for their arrival, the knowledge that their sudden appearance at the top of the orchard was imminent produced a subtle change in my grand-daughter's behaviour. Part of the intellectual intensity that had been focussed on our life at the farm would be gradually withdrawn and remain hovering above us ready to be given back to where it belonged. She was no longer exclusively mine.

We cleaned out the cottage, aired the beds and prepared the blankets and the sheets. We checked the log stove, the electric heaters and even bought what was necessary to restore some wallpaper that was unstuck. When the water was boiling in the pipes and towels laid out in the bathroom, and a bowl of flowers set on the big oak table in the living room, we tried to continue as if nothing so important as the family's arrival was in the air.

From time to time my grand-daughter would be invited by her two little friends, Camille and Victoire, to lunch under Andrée's hospitable roof at Bois Lurette. Extremely pretty and sophisticated, they both showed her an affectionate respect filled with wonder at the thought that at little more than eight she had flown so many thousands of miles between New York and Singapore, Singapore and Europe, and spoke English as perfectly as if it were not her native tongue. Nevertheless I gave my grand-daughter strict injunctions concerning her table manners, to eat what was given her, declare it excellent and be careful not to stain the tablecloth. Little boys were often troublesome but grown-up girls were different! It behoved them to set a good example. At the end of her visit, she could in turn invite Victoire and Camille to lunch at the farm – and to make the acquaintance of Marmalade, the new baby cat whose eyes were not yet open.

Meanwhile I tried to fill a light case with what I felt that my daughter-in-law would be glad to have for Dominique during the coming winter in their new home in Washington. The weather could be very cold, and I knitted pullovers and vests, even gloves and bought her coloured tights in pure wool which were treasures that, even in France, were disappearing from the shops, so much wool being mixed with nylon thread. Curiously enough she had hardly shown any signs of asthma during the long stay so that I was tempted to believe that the damp orchards and sea air had done her, in this respect, more good than harm.

Camille and Victoire, invited some days later by my grand-daughter to lunch, were taken up to the bedroom to see the marmalade kitten, and then all three of them descended upon the poultry yard and struck terror into the chickens and turkeys by their cries of delight. Yet all the birds continued to follow Dominique about wherever she went and she in turn had a favourite chick of her own, who used to hide in her blouse or her pullover or sit on her shoulder while she went about her business. Lucie Delarue-Mardrus, with Guy de Maupassant, the writer who best described the Norman countryside, once wrote a book called *L'Enfant au Coq* which I read almost with disbelief as a young married woman in the early 'thirties. Only with my grand-daughter did I realise the quite extraordinary relation-ship that can exist between a chick only a few weeks old and a little girl. It makes one ashamed to reflect that nowadays these unfortunate birds are imprisoned without light or liberty in merciless batteries.

One lovely July morning, just after lunch, while Dominique and I were playing bézique, a white hired car came down the orchard and stopped between the tall blue cedar and the garden gate. Warned by some secret instinct the little girl rose from her chair and darted across the lawn to where her parents were getting out of the car they had hired at Roissy airport on their arrival from America earlier that morning. Her small brother, sturdy and powerful, threw himself into her arms. I had not expected such peals of laughter, such an explosion of joy. My grandson had grown into a fine little fellow but nothing could have better exemplified boy and girl, she so elegant and slim, he so full of roguish laughter and strength that small as he was he nearly knocked me over with exuberant, boyish assaults. A moment later the two children had run off to the old bakehouse to celebrate their reunion in an atmosphere all of their own.

Before many minutes had passed, a car came down the drive, and drew up beside the one that my son had rented at Roissy airport. A young man, arriving at the garden gate, enquired if he and his wife could camp in our orchard till morning. All the hotels were full. I asked him where he came from and he told me he and his wife were Belgians on their way to visit the Invasion beaches. The young woman had left her baby in the care of her mother at home.

My son accompanied the young man to the car, and I left them to their own devices. Before long our guests set up a very modern tent near the pear tree half way between the bake-house and the stables. Then, under the interested gaze of Dominique and her brother, they arranged beds and a table and chairs. The sight of this comfortable home intrigued the two children who doubtless would have been only too glad to spend a night under canvas. Our guests closed the door of their tent, went back to their car and announced their intention of going for a bathe, and having dinner at Deauville. We heard them return just before midnight.

My daughter-in-law meanwhile arranged everything in the cottage for her own family, coming over for sheets, blankets, pillow-cases and towels. The two houses were now throbbing with life, and the questions arose as to whether my grand-daughter wished to spend the night with me, or join her brother in the cottage. In fact, Lisette found herself short of beds, and Dominique stayed with me.

But the little girl's thoughts were already with her family, and in particular with her brother to whom she was anxious to show the cascades in the stream, and the wonders of what remained of her 'Forest'. She was up so early next morning that she had no time to brush her hair and secure it in the nape with a slide. I said:

'You have forgotten to be a little woman. You have suddenly become a baby again.'

Her femininity was taking on a different form. Busy mothering her four-year-old brother, she quite neglected to attend to her own appearance. She would put him to bed on a mossy bank, and make him pretend to go to sleep. When he was tired of this game, he would say: 'I want my real mother!' and dash off to Lisette, pounding her legs till she took him up in her arms.

Our young Belgian and his pretty wife were soon at the kitchen door asking for hot water and a jug of milk. They enquired if we were acquainted with their country, and my husband said:

'During the First World War I was at Eton with Prince Leopold who in 1934, on his father King Albert's death, became King of the Belgians.'

'Leopold?' said the young man thoughtfully. 'Yes, I suppose so, but the name means little to me. It's a long time since he abdicated in favour of his son.'

'All the same,' said my husband, 'he was your king during the whole of the Second World War.'

'Of course! Of course!' said the young man very politely. 'But that is even longer ago. I'm only in my early twenties. King Leopold! Fancy coming to this out-of-the-way orchard and talking to somebody who was at school in England with him. How very strange. It's like meeting somebody out of a history book. What could he have been like when he was young?'

'Extremely handsome, and very well-versed in the classics. A great reader of Racine, also. He used to spend his holidays with his father, King Albert, in the front line. He was brave as behoves a future king.'

'Didn't he marry first a Swedish princess called Astrid?'

'Yes, indeed, I used to visit them at their castle at Laeken, just outside Brussels. I drove round town with him once. It was a curious sensation driving round a capital city with its future young monarch at the wheel. The policemen always looked so surprised when he stopped behind their raised baton. They would jump to attention and let us pass. He would laugh happily. Sadness had not yet descended upon his youthful head.'

'I never thought about it before,' said the young man, 'but sure enough he must have known a lot of sorrow. Thanks for the hot water. Thanks for the jug of milk. I have learnt something I did not know before about my own country.'

'If you go to the Invasion beaches, see that you don't miss the American military cemetery overlooking Omaha Beach. I know few sights in the world more moving – especially at evening, looking out across the ocean. I'll lend you a map, and a book if you like.'

'We would like that,' said the young man. 'What is more, I promise to send them back.'

My grand-daughter had a great desire – to take her brother to Dozulé on market day so that she could show him the baby chicks, the ducklings and the young turkeys.

'Please, Grand'mère, take us both in your little car!'

Accordingly on Tuesday (which was market day) we set off, myself at the wheel, the two children behind. There is a law in France which forbids one from having a child beside one when one drives. Children are not allowed to occupy what is known as the 'death seat'. The road to Dozulé was still very beautiful, narrow and continually twisting and turning, up one hill, down the other, and then through a wood after which one came upon the single track railroad line that ran from Deauville to Cabourg, the honeysuckle in summer almost tumbling over the hedges on to the rails – and there was the prettiest little cottage beside the level crossing in which lived the lady who closed the gates when a train was due to pass, and then opened them again when everything was again safe. We used to smile at each other as she hung out her washing on the line in her pretty garden with the marigolds and the hollyhocks, the roses and the foxgloves. She was very stout, moved with a majestic slowness and often had a baby at her breast and some toddlers hanging on to her ample, old-fashioned skirts. In order to supplement her wage from the French National Railways she took in children from the towns who needed country air. If a train was due to pass, she would lean over her little white gate and talk about her charges. Everybody knew and loved her. Once when I was waiting beside a van for the gates to open and the train to pass, the vandriver, who was a commercial salesman for a biscuit firm, brought out samples of his wares and distributed them to the children – and even to me. It made us feel like members of a big family, gossiping happily as we ate our biscuits.

But the level crossing woman in her house and garden was being increasingly replaced by the impersonal, strident, automatic ringing of bells to warn the oncoming motorist. As I arrived with my two grandchildren I found that the cottage was still there but the stout woman and her children had gone. Fortunately the railroad track, with its steel rails gleaming in the August sun, its graceful curves as it wound its way through the countryside, was still there and this was just one of the marvels that my grand-daughter, remembering it from previous occasions, was anxious to show her brother.

'Grand'mère, just supposing a locomotive were to come round the bend before we had time to get to the other side? Wouldn't it be exciting !'

'The bell would have warned us of its coming!'

'Something might prevent it from ringing?'

'We shall close our eyes and cross quickly!' I said, unwilling to rob her of that exquisite moment of fear.

Now here we were once again driving through Dozulé on market day, hearing the hour strike from the church tower, watching the cattle turning in through a country road, admiring the flowers in their pots spread out on the pavements, turning sharply into the forecourt of the covered market where the chicks were already being set out in their cages on the trestled tables. Half a dozen countrywomen, in modern dress, no more bonnets and black skirts, mostly pullovers and jeans, sat on stools, as in the old days, silently, and rather gloomily gazing upon their sparse produce – a few slabs of home-made butter, a small jug of cream, half a dozen pots of crab apple jelly, some sprigs of rosemary and a tin of dried beans, an old hen with its feet tied up, a basket of eggs and small panniers of red-currants from their garden.

Taking her brother by the hand my grand-daughter led him to the trestled tables, too excited to speak, eyes gleaming, her slim, little-girl body shaking with emotion.

'Grand'mère, go and do your shopping. I want to stay here for a few moments alone with Edward.'

'Will you promise not to move?'

'Of course, Grand'mère. I just don't want to be hurried!'

A quarter of an hour later, on my return, the children had chosen four little white chicks. They had, of course, fallen in love with the ducklings which far from being ugly as in the Hans Andersen story, looked like a collection of live powder puffs, softer and more cuddly than the chicks, but I would have none of them. Not only do they foul the forecourt but they can play strange tricks in a farmyard. The previous year one of the those I bought to amuse Dominique had grown up to exhibit murderous tendencies, snapping the heads of my home-born baby chicks off as soon as I had my back turned. For a long time I was unable to discover how these poor little things had died until one day I caught Dominique's duck snapping off the head of an innocent little chick under the eyes of its affrighted mother. Presumably this vicious trait stemmed from the jealousy of a sterile mother in the duck world.

The woman with the bewitching eyes and long, pointed crimson finger nails to whom Dominique offered the note she had taken from the purse in her handbag, glanced at me suspiciously:

'You are not allowing the little girl to buy these four chicks to amuse herself and her brother?' she asked. 'Baby birds are not toys to be played with. They have lives of their own just like children.'

'Have no fear,' I said, 'they will, I hope, grow up normally in a farmyard.'

'That's different,' she said, putting the birds in a cardboard box which she began to stab with the point of her long knife. 'Otherwise I would not sell them to her.'

'Could we also have a couple of young turkeys?' asked Dominique, unwilling to tear herself away too quickly.

'Yes,' I agreed, 'this is the ideal time of year to buy them.'

The children were delighted. Seated at the back of the car with these chicks and the turkeys between them their laughter and young voices mingling with the cries and the screeches of the birds, we stopped at the baker's shop in the High Street, famous for its 4 lb loaves of golden bread and its great assortment of cakes and buns. Edward, who at the age of four was only just discovering the more picturesque angles of life in France, was in ecstasy over the bread, so crusty and hot and fresh from the oven.

The expedition to Dozulé thus ended as it had begun – an unforgettable adventure.

My grand-daughter, at her father's request, was being given a last dictation in French before her return to America. He and his pretty young wife would go down to the sands with Edward who was anxious to make sand castles and to paddle. So once again Dominique and I were alone together.

It was no longer fashionable to dictate to children in schools those short passages from the works of the great writers of the nineteenth-century, like de Musset, Anatole France, Alphonse Daudet, Victor Hugo, and so many others. Too many of them had a patriotic or sentimental undertones that were not considered appropriate by modern pedagogues for the education of the young. Apart from the feeling that patriotism had suffered too big a decline during the Occupation and was now an uncomfortable bedfellow to the ideals of the European common market, spelling, it was thought, and indeed literature itself, should not be forced down the throats of the modern child. Politically the classics could prove harmful to the trend which was, in the schools, progressively Leftist.

I cannot deny that on turning the yellowed pages of the pre-1914 dictation book with its line drawings from which I taught my son, Dominique's father, to spell correctly when he was her age, some of the chosen pieces make one smile. Even the words that the great)La Fontaine put into the mouth of his aged farm labourer to his children: 'Work hard, don't spare your pains, this is the greatest heritage a father can leave his children,' would seem slightly unreal if heard on the lips of our modern farmers on the plateau, accustomed to thinking in terms of more than one hundred pounds a week, and vast unemployment benefits. But that should not blind us to the continuing lesson to be learnt from Alphonse Daudet's goat who invariably had a feeling that the grass in the field next to his was better and more tender than his own. These, alas, are timeless sentiments.

So here we went. My grand-daughter with her pen firmly grasped in her wrong hand, her left hand, waited to spell out on a clean sheet of ruled paper the title of this most famous passage: 'La chèvre de M. Seguin'.

Are girls more gifted than boys? I would like to think so. At all events they are more painstaking, far better tempered. When at the age of eight my son was making that film *The Fallen Idol* with Sir Ralph Richardson, Sir Carol Reed had arranged for us to spend the evenings, sometimes the weekends, at the studios at Shepperton. After a long day's work with grown-ups my son would have his dinner, take a bath and start dictation. If night had not fallen all the robins from the park would come to our windows – and what hundreds of them there were! I was incredibly cruel with my son at dictation time. Determined that he should spell both in French and in English without a mistake and that in doing so he should get into his youthful ears the music of good prose, I had no pity for his tears. But with his daughter, my grand-daughter, the very thought of her tears melted my heart. After a while I would say:

'Very well. Let us pack up for the day. Shall we take the car and go to visit Erni and Bud on the ship?'

'Wait till I do my hair, and change my dress!' she exclaimed, already the little woman, anxious to make a good impression.

We parked the car on the quayside between that of Bud, with the Swiss number plate, and that of Albert, with the English one. then carefully down the narrow gangway, past the dipping Blue Ensign, and on to the shining deck of the *Sarah Munro*.

A fresh breeze was blowing from the west. We found Erni and Bud in the cabin, Erni delighted because the Smeets had arrived which meant that she had the feminine companionship of

Yolande and the two girls. Dominique, with her hair beautifully groomed and looking seductive, sat demurely beside me on the edge of the sofa. She knew that at any moment Bud would offer her a drink, and that she could choose from an incalculable number of alluring soft concoctions, none of which, on grounds of economy, I kept at home on the farm. But first, said Erni, she had a new camera that took coloured pictures with instantaneous development. She would take a photograph of my grand-daughter to show her family in Grindelwald.

The yacht basin was excited by the arrival of Sir Max Aitken on his sensational twin screw *Blue Max* with oil engines so powerful that Bud claimed he could cross the Channel in four hours against the eight or nine that he, Bud, habitually took in the *Sarah Munro*.

'He came on board for a drink last night,' said. 'Why weren't you here?'

'I meant to be,' I said, 'but the family has arrived from Washington, and my poor head is full of household cares. What to give them for lunch, for instance? Who likes what? Did he talk about what has been happening to his father's empire?'

'Not a word,' said Bud. 'He was just great fun as he always is. We are such old friends.' He poured out drinks. Then reverting to Sir Max. 'Yes, he was in great form.'

'May he continue so,' I said. 'He bears his blushing honours thick upon him.'

Yolande Smeets, climbing carefully over the low, sturdy rails of the two ships, arrived from the *San Lucar* with an anxious look.

'Erni!' she cried, framing her lithe figure in the entrance to the cabin. 'I promised the family fried potatoes and what do you think? I have run out of oil to fry them in.'

She looked round appealingly:

'We haven't had time to unpack our bicycles from the hold, and if I walk – well, you know where the supermarket is, just this side of the bridge over the Touques river – I shall never be back in time.'

Her explanation in a delightful Belgian accent made us all laugh.

'Wait!' said Erni. 'I'll go down to the galley and get you some.'

Here we were, I reflected, in a sort of millionaires' row of ocean yachts, and what do the wives worry about? Frying potatoes for the family lunch! Yes, indeed, while the men discuss 660 hp engines and what the Swiss franc has done to the mighty American dollar (English, French and Belgian newspapers were strewn about the cabin under a notice printed: THINK.) elegant Yolande Smeets is worried because she has no oil for her French fried. How many cooks had there been in the old days on the *Flying Cloud*? Erni, running down to the galley, and Yolande telling us how the Belgians fry French fried, might just as easily have been wives on a caravan site, instead of on these great vessels riding at anchor at Deauville!

'There!' cried Erni, returning in triumph with a bottle of oil. 'Will this do?'

'You're a real sweetie!' said Yolande clasping the bottle to her bosom. 'Now I must hurry back.'

'Can I come with you?' asked my grand-daughter. 'To watch you cooking?'

She followed Yolande to the side of the ship and then found herself being lifted bodily over the rails. A moment later they were both on the *San Lucar* where the Smeets sisters in their wide cotton frocks, their long hair gently undulating in the wind, were waiting for them, having just returned from a visit to other young women on another British ship.

On our return home, Dominique was clutching an enormous carrier bag, almost as big as herself, filled with all the different kinds of biscuits made in a biscuit factory that Yolande Smeets owned in Belgium. Packed in individual cartons, they exemplified the varied art of the biscuitmaker. This was the second time that Mme Smeets had thought of Dominique, phoning the factory before her departure from Antwerp. Perhaps because it was not part of a combine but still in private hands, the biscuits made in this Belgian factory had a delightful taste of their own. Few things today retain distinct national characteristics.

Our friends waved us goodbye as we turned into the timber

211

yard that skirts the inner harbour and along which ran that railway line on which, on this occasion, stood a single wagon. As there was no locomotive in sight one wondered how it had arrived – a phantom on a ghost railway. The track was scattered with pieces of wood from Scandinavia or from Russia jettisoned during the unloading of a ship. We picked up some odd ones to use as supports for the tomatoes in the garden.

The next day, inspired by Yolande, I dug some potatoes up and made French fried. They were a great success, and the children amused themselves by giving some to Julot. This was the only surviving chick from a total of twelve which one of my best hens had produced, and then allowed in some mysterious way to die, one by one, until only Julot remained. We kept him in the kitchen where he trotted happily round the Aga, occasionally making sorties into the front garden. The cats, though good hunters, never attacked the chicks who often chased them from the most comfortable chairs, and invariably waited for morsels of food. We named this sole survivor Julot because it was the nickname of those bad boys in the Paris of pre-1914 – the apaches with their red scarves, and caps pulled over their beady eyes. Nobody was afraid of Julot. Every morning when I came down to the kitchen I expected to find him dead, but he would dance round my bare ankles, chirping his happiness at the start of a new day.

12

MORE THAN HALF A YEAR had passed since the Levanniers had gone. But nothing yet pointed to the demolition of the red brick house. If it were true that Mme Bompain had sold the house, the stables and the orchard, why did nothing happen? One would have expected fast action. A speculator does not normally allow the grass to grow on a property he has purchased at high cost.

A farmer called Leblanc had permission to use the grass for his cattle, on a month – to – month basis. If nothing happened before the cider apples were ripe, he might have these also. Prices could be high this autumn.

Every time I heard a tractor in the distance I supposed it might be the vanguard of the demolishers. The kitchen garden was now a sorry sight, trampled by cattle who discovered that the gates were off their hinges. They ate what was left of the rhubarb plants and the green peas. Lisette, my daughter-in-law, discovered one morning a mysterious gap of some twenty yards in the hedge that divided the top of our home field from the former kitchen garden. Who had made it and why? There was a faint track on the dewy grass as if from the pack horses of smugglers. The children wove delightful stories round this phenomenon which we never solved.

But that afternoon, Mme Bompain knocked at the kitchen door.

She wanted to know who, by ancient custom, owned the hedge that separated my orchard from the piece she had sold to Tran Ngoc, the Vietnamese. I invited her into the low room and enlightened her. After a polite pause I asked:

'I am intrigued because the red brick house is still standing. Is the property sold?'

She appeared surprised at the directness of my question but

answered:

'There is a verbal agreement to sell under certain circumstances but no documents of a final nature have been exchanged.'

'Oh!' I said, puzzled. 'What is holding it up?'

'An unforeseen circumstance,' she said. 'There has been so much building in the neighbourhood that, according to the authorities, there just might not be enough water to supply the estimated needs of some fifty new houses.'

She smiled wanly.

'It is tiresome. I can only wait and see.'

I walked back with her as far as the gate.

'I noticed just now,' she said, 'that the shutters of the red brick house are flapping in the wind. I shall have to send a man along tomorrow to nail them back.'

Her voice was a trifle sad.

I too was unhappy – unhappy in the midst of my happiness. Soon the Smeets would sail back to Antwerp on the *San Lucar*. Soon Erni and Bud would drive off in their smart red car to Grindelwald at the foot of the Swiss Alps. Soon Albert would go back to England – and I might never see the *Sarah Munro* again.

The next morning something most unfortunate happened. The little cat I had saved from hunger and cold in the deserted brick house – the young mother of Marmalade – affectionate but still very wild, knocked over the huge porcelain rabbit with the flowers and four-leaf clover that I bought at Asprey in New Bond Street during the bombardments of 1940, and which I had kept preciously since.

With its beautiful wide ears and painted china nostrils, it stood on my make-up table, a reminder of the dangers that beset us in London during the nocturnal raids, the bombs, the incendiaries, the guided missiles. In falling down, it broke into half a dozen pieces, exploding the joy of having my family under my roof, awakening the inevitable sadness of their certain, inexorable departure, making me wonder if my sunny days were coming to an end.

The carpet at the foot of the make-up table was covered with fine sand which had fallen out of my china rabbit. It had been sealed in to give the animal weight. This surprised me. I had imagined it to be solid and I would never have guessed the secret. When bringing it from England in my hold-all many years earlier I had indeed been naïve. It might so well have been filled with opium or cocaine. What an excellent trafficker I would have made.

In truth, I had a great desire to weep, and in going through some balls of very special knitting wool, carefully hidden away, I found that moths had been at them. Then also the Irish linen sheets and table clothes that had served me so well for half a century urgently needed to be replaced, and so did the dish cloths with *Made in Ireland* embroidered into them and *Pure Irish Linen*! What an evocation of my young married days. That which I could now buy in France was so very inferior in quality, so superior in price.

Matilda, my mother, used to laugh at me for bringing over Irish sheets and dishcloths, tablecloths and napkins. She would watch me, exhausted after a terrible journey by Channel steamer and by coach from Le Havre, my poor back aching, drawing them laboriously out of an overstuffed travelling bag. She would then tell me the story of the genteel Mademoiselle X.

'When I was young,' my mother would say, 'there lived in the same block of apartments as ourselves a very old demoiselle. She lodged alone at the top of the house in a one-room flat. I used occasionally to meet her on the stairs at which moments she would greet me with exquisite politeness for she was educated and had obviously seen prosperous times. In winter she would keep warm by the childish pastime of a skipping rope, sometimes keeping it up for long periods, counting aloud each skip in a tremulous voice. She ate so little that she had become very thin. In spite of this her continual skipping shook the floor which happened to be our ceiling. Of this I never complained, quick to realise that her slender means did not allow her to buy wood or coal for the hearth.

'One day the noise of her skipping ceased. We were in mid-January and snow was falling. I immediately feared for her

215

health, and running up stairs found her door ajar. I tiptoed in: "Mademoiselle?" I cried. "Are you there, Mademoiselle?"

'I found her in bed wrapped up in countless shawls like an Egyptian mummy. What do you think she was doing? She was embroidering linen dish cloths with the most sumptuous designs like those on church vestments. She had a great pile at her elbow.'

Matilda would look up archly and enquire:

'Do you suppose that when you grow old you will take to embroidering these linen dish cloths that you bring from London?'

I used to laugh but were it not for the fact that all my dish cloths are threadbare, I might indeed start to embellish them like Matilda's Demoiselle.

Yolande and Robert Smeets were on the *San Lucar* making ready for their departure. They were always the first to go. Erni and Bud liked to remain till the last moment but whereas the Smeets sailed their ship back to Antwerp themselves, Erni and Bud motored back to Switzerland, leaving the *Sarah Munro* to Albert who would either take it to England or remain with it in France.

This year, of course, everything was different. Albert was to retire. Nothing could make him change his mind. As Bud refused to have another captain, the *Sarah Munro* really was going to be sold. Already offers were being tentatively made. Any day now Bud might exclaim: 'I've sold the *Sarah Munro*!' but even if this did not happen while he was on board with Erni, its fate appeared certain. They would drive back to Switzerland as planned and allow the ship to be sold in their absence.

Bud tried to pretend that he did not mind but there was a sadness I had never seen before in his eyes.

Yolande and Robert Smeets were just back from a lightning visit to Antwerp by way of Paris. During their absence, Albert had kept an eye on their ship. He merely needed to jump over the rail and there he was on board. But now the Smeets were back and Yolande wanted to give a small, intimate dinner party to mark the end of this decisive season. She had brought back a

216

consignment of Russian caviare – oh! not one of those diminutive tins but enough for her guests to serve themselves properly to their hearts' content – passing the dish round and round, as in Russian story books, till nobody could eat any more. The men would drink what they usually drank, together with vodka, but for us women there would be champagne.

Vodka, hot toast and butter, caviare and champagne. Nothing else. That would be the menu.

'Come early,' Yolande had said. 'About 6 p.m. We want to have a long night before a dawn departure.'

We were at the bottom of the gangway which, because it was low tide, was at an acute angle. Erni, whose *Grès* perfume was gently carried on the breeze, was extremely elegant in a most artful garment which consisted of a cashmere pullover into the front of which was incrusted the most beautifully designed Hermes silk squares. Thus the sleeves and the back kept one warm and snug from sudden squalls, the front remained as dressy and as sophisticated as any silk blouse. Over this she wore her necklace from which hung a golden Kruger coin.

Even while she talked, I planned to make myself a like garment, a blouse-pullover. For instance, did I not own amongst my treasures, put away in moth balls, a fine black cashmere that Paloma gave me? I would cut the front out and introduce in its place one of the many silk squares that had been given me and which I seldom had occassion to wear. Too often I would spend the day in a blouse, a pullover and a tartan skirt. This made me think of the song that Juliette Gréco sang:

> *T'es toute nue*
> *Sous ton pull!*

and it always struck me that it would be difficult to invent more sexy an image than being naked in such circumstances.

Driving home through Deauville, I passed the Armenian's shop and with the smell of Erni's perfume still in my nostrils, I parked the car along the kerb and inspected the shop door closed and over the glass panels of which a blind had been drawn. A notice said that the Armenian was dead and that his funeral had just taken place.

The last time I came to talk to him in this shop he was celebrating his ninetieth birthday but he never looked old to me, and he was full of picturesque malice. His tiny shop was packed from floor to ceiling with expensive French perfumes. There were so many of them in their beautiful boxes and satin-lined caskets that one simply did not know where to look. But none of them was in any sort of order. Or at least in the order that would make sense to anybody trying to sort them out. The *Balmain* elbowed the *Grès* and the *Dior* tumbled over the *Lanvin*, and the whole place smelt simply delicious as if all these precious essences like spirits in the *Boutique Fantasque* had come out at night to dance some mad tarantella. In this amazing cavern the Armenian moved cautiously like a human spider climbing a wall, delving down into the depths of yet unopened cardboard cases. He, of course, knew where everything was – on the condition you gave him time to remember!

Because I have a fondness for the strange and the picturesque, I loved his shop, and because he himself had the unreality of a gnome in an enchanted forest, I would spend hours seated on a broken kitchen chair listening to his tales. Somewhere along our different lives we found a streak in common. As a child in Clichy my mother would send me to a haberdasher's shop kept by a lovely young girl who stood, like a fairy with a wand, in the middle of her tumbling array of silk skeins, cotton reels, ribbons and lace. There were yards upon yards of broderie anglaise with which we used to hem our petticoats, even after the First World War. For the little female that I was this shop was more exciting than any cavern of the Arabian Nights. My mother would give me a piece of material and say:

'Run along to Mademoiselle Fouillis, and find me the right coloured thread to match this material. You will surely find just what I need.'

Mademoiselle Fouillis, who was so pretty that she might have been waiting for the fairy prince, wore a bandeau like those of the tennis star Suzanne Lenglen, but Mademoiselle Fouillis changed the colour of her bandeau every day so that it was a delight to guess what colour it would be today.

The strange thing was that noboby had ever seen Mademoiselle Fouillis talking to a young man so that she had the reputation of being some sort of ethereal goddess – pure and virginal. Had she once been in love? Was her fiancé killed in the trenches as so many others were?

My Armenian who also sufficed unto himself emerged when one entered his shop from a cloud of this heavenly perfume, the essences of all one's favourite perfumes mixed together! He was the Enchanter, ready to touch one with his wand.

But he was very touchy and rudely turned his back on any customer whom he did not like the look of. One had to be very careful not to hurt his acute sensitivity.

One day while I was listening to his tales of Armenia and that persecuted race, a young woman came into the shop, and looking round imperiously, asked for a certain perfumed hair lacquer, expensive and made by a very famous name. The Armenian disappeared into what he liked to call his office, and the young woman, believing us to be alone, explained (woman to woman) that she was going to a gala at the Casino that evening, a very important affair, but that she would not have time to go first to the hairdresser. We conversed on this subject for a few moments and then I saw her inspecting with something like disbelief the incredible tumble of precious perfumes and ointments that occasionally overbalanced from their ceiling level, tobogganing down the side.

'What a prodigious *fouillis*!' she exclaimed.

This description of the Armenian's shop, so, perfectly fitting, brought back to my mind the sound of my mother's voice: 'Run along to Mademoiselle Fouillis, and find me the right coloured thread to match this material.'

'Yes,' I laughed 'but I rather like it.'

At this moment my Armenian reappeared.

'I haven't what you ask for!' he said. There was a strange intonation in his voice.

'But surely,' she insisted. 'Aren't you holding it in your hand?'

'I regret, Madame, I have not what you ask for – and, indeed, I have nothing in my stock that would suit you.'

His words had a terrible finality. The young woman blushed slightly and walked out into the sunlit street.

When she had gone, my Armenian said, very dignified:

'That young woman had the audacity to criticise the manner in which I keep my shop. Did you hear me seek her opinion? Then why should she give it gratuitously? This is my domain, my Eastern palace. It is a shop, and it is not a shop. I sell to those who please me, and I turn away those whom I do not consider worthy of these costly essences. It is a great satisfaction, Madame, to be rich enough to do what one wants in this world.'

Now he was dead, and I wondered what would happen to his shop. What inexpert hands would fumble through his wares?

But, of course, my Armenian was very old – and who pities an old man when he dies?

> Green leaves hang, but the brown must fly;
> When he's foresaken,
> Wither'd and shaken,
> What can an old man do but die?

What was the matter with me? Why did so much that I loved appear to be slipping away? Was it my fault if the primrose ceased to bloom, the bee to suck, my Armenian to inhabit his secret world of perfume? Youth also has its tragedies.

Yolande Smeets had told me that afternoon on the San Lucar that their trip to Belgium had been darkened by the death of a young cousin killed outright in his car while driving home from the Ardennes. He was not quite twenty-six and his mother had been waiting for him to start dinner.

'My elder daughter Carole,' said Yolande, 'wept during the whole trip. It was very distressing.'

Her story made me think of Patrice de Rochambeau, so young, who bore lightly on his shoulders one of the greatest names in France.

My son woke up the next morning with a sudden attack of

lumbago. He looked tired and overworked, and I suggested that Lisette and he should spend the day at Caen, and amuse themselves while I kept the two children. They could wander through the town hand in hand and visit the tomb of William the Conqueror.

'Don't hurry,' I said, 'Find yourselves the best restaurant and forget for one entire day that you have an exacting family.'

In the old days such moments might have been less rare. They would doubtless have had an English nanny. Today my son and daughter-in-law might perhaps make more money but they enjoyed fewer privileges.

The children left to themselves behaved like grown-ups, the boy much easier to feed than his exacting sister. He ate everything and once more sang the praises of French bread. After lunch we drove down to the beach and played a game with pins and a pincushion that my mother had played when she was a little girl in her convent at Blois. Expensive toys did not figure in her Spartan childhood. Imagination replaced them. Before we had been playing long, a dozen other children joined us, and I was able to note that, as far as the pin game was concerned, children appeared to be no different in their tastes from what they were in my mother's time.

My husband and I had our birthdays on successive days in mid–August which was a matter of surprise, if not disbelief, in the minds of our friends. Mine was the 13th, and his the 14th. They gave rise to no particular rejoicing, and on this particular occasion they foreshadowed the imminent departure not only of my family but of my grand-daughter who had been lent to us by her mother and father for such a wonderful, long spell. Would I ever see them again?

Nevertheless on the eve of my birthday when combing my hair, as I invariably did very meticulously, I must admit that within a few hours of being seventy-two, my hair was long enough and thick enough to have allowed me, like the woman who was a sinner, to have washed the feet of Jesus, and wiped them with it – were I to be given the joy of finding myself in His presence. And indeed why not? My friend Paloma was quite convinced, when walking through the narrow, tortuous streets of her native Saulieu, that Jesus had trodden those same uneven paving stones.

Not one white hair! Perhaps because in twenty years I had not gone to a hairdresser. The lines on my face? That, alas, was another matter. One evening at the Courtehaie when Hélène Leonard and I were exchanging feminine gossip, she told me about a friend who achieved wonders in hiding these tell-tale lines by wearing yards of billowing chiffon – over her graceful shoulders, round her neck. Then one morning she examined herself closely in the mirror – and committed suicide.

Dismissing these unhealthy thoughts from my mind, I joined my grand-daughter in the big double bed, and for a while we sat very demurely together, our heads against a heap of white pillows. Shortly before midnight my husband arrived with some boxes tied up in pink ribbon.

For my grand-daughter this moment was one to be fully shared with me. Her fingers quivered as she helped me untie the ribbon, break the seals, peer into the contents. A different Guerlain perfume for all my handbags – in their beautiful enamel cases, so that according to my mood, I could spray myself with *Heure Bleue*, *Mitsouko* and *Parure* . . .

'Grand'mère, which are you going to try first . . .?'

The next morning – Sunday – all of us, including Edward, went to 8 a.m. Mass – three generations. Surely this was something to be remembered! Afterwards we bought *croissants* just out of the oven, piping hot from the baker's, and after driving home merrily, we breakfasted in front of the Aga. Dominique proudly brought me a new basket for my knitting in which she had put, wrapped in tissue paper, a breakfast cup and saucer in Limoges china. My son came with a bottle of Champagne which he and Lisette had acquired during their visit to Caen. It was for the birthday lunch.

These were things that, as the poet said, do often lie too deep for tears.

Monday 14 August – we wished my husband a happy birthday. The children, joyful at the prospect of their flight to England,

222

ran excitedly in and out of the house and garden. Dominique's travelling bag, the one she carried slung over one shoulder, was so full that when she was not looking, I peeped inside. Under some coloured pencils what should I come upon but a bundle of turkey feathers lovingly tied up with a piece of ribbon. They were taken from her favourite turkey, the one sitting so diligently on half a dozen hens' eggs in the hope of becoming a mother after all! Would these precious reminders of the farm-yard eventually find their way to America? Lisette, who had watched me with a smile that was tantamount to admitting she would never herself have dared such an indiscretion, now gathered her two children under her wing. It was time to get everybody into the one small car and drive to the airport of St Gatien above Deauville.

The countryside on this August morning was radiant, the rising sun painting the hedges with fingers of gold.

This small but modern aerodrome with its shiny floors and glass walls, its plastic tables and contemporary armchairs, not yet fully awake to the traffic of a new day, was set in a clearing where only a short time ago the wild boar still roamed. What majestic trees had been cut down to allow aeroplanes, after banking over the port of Le Havre and the estuary of the Seine, to come to rest in safety. On a lovely summer evening after the war, before the erection of these airport buildings of glass and chrome, before the bulldozer had matched its mechanical strength against giant oaks and beech, my husband was coming in from London on a plane that was to land on the relatively small hayfields on which then stood a control tower and landing strip. Visibility over Le Havre was only sufficient for him to look down uncertainly on the great ships tied up at the quays, on the dirty little coasters making their way down the Seine to Rouen, but over the forest it lay dense.

My husband, perhaps even more attuned to the journey than the pilot, peered down, expecting the worst. Now suddenly it came! The trees of the forest came up to meet them, and a great tearing sound of metal against wood as half a tree was beheaded and caught up in a wing. The pilot reacting in this emergency brought the nose of his machine up so precipitously that there was a vibration of metal as it gained height and safety. At Le Bourget the aeroplane and the top of an oak tree came down safely together.

My grand-daughter sat demurely at my side. Charwomen were cleaning the shiny floor with complicated machines. It really did not need cleaning at all and no wonder that after a while they stopped and trooped off together, leaving their machines in a corner. 'Can I go and have a look at the Ladies?' asked Dominique. 'Just to see what it's like. We could go together?' She was always a little afraid of finding herself locked in – as indeed once happened to my friend Paloma in a Paris railroad terminal. A locksmith had to be sent for and to make her shame complete – the locksmith was a fierce looking man with a black beard!

My son and daughter-in-law returned with their son who had caught a glimpse of the small plane which was to take them to England. They were to spend three weeks with Lisette's mother – their maternal grandmother. There might be ponies for the children to ride. The idea filled them with new happiness. The flight was announced on a loudspeaker. I felt chilled. My feet were cold, like slabs of ice, but I must smile, try to appear as happy as they were themselves.

We kissed goodbye and they passed beyond the barrier to the waiting plane. It might have been their own machine. They were more or less the only passengers.

We drove away in the little car – but only to the side of the road where on a grassy verge we waited for the plane to take off. The wait appeared interminable. What were they doing? Occasionally a car would come along the road at great speed – perhaps 60 m.p.h. or more, leaving a trail of white dust in its wake. I wondered if I had seen my family for the last time. Would there even be another birthday for me? I was broken-hearted to be without my little grand-daughter, my constant companion for so long.

Now suddenly the small plane taxied to its starting position on the far fringe of the forest, waited a few moments, then took off. Seconds later it was over our heads making for Le Havre and the English Channel. We waved frantically. Doubtless inside the cabin, unseen by us, they were waving too. Now the aeroplane was a mere silvery dot above the limitless blue of the ocean.

The black cat was waiting for us in the courtyard and there was a great pile of sheets twisting and turning in the German washing machine. Soon I would hang them out to dry on the long lines. The sun was so warm that we would be able to lunch out in the garden, finishing the last drops of champagne left over from my birthday celebration. Edward had forgotten one of his toys, a small yellow truck, on the kitchen floor. The cats appeared to sense that the house was quieter than it should be. I went up into the bedroom where Marmalade, still a mere baby, lay curled up on my pillow, and burying my face in her warm, golden fur I wept.

At the market the next day, while buying a pound of butter from Rémy, the young farmer who had taken over the old man Déliquaire's farm on the far side of the stream, I enquired about his wife and the children, and if the cider apples on his land were coming along nicely.

'Not too badly,' he said. 'The older trees should give a little fruit.'

'Are there any young trees?' I asked.

'Yes,' he said. 'I plant a dozen or so every winter.'

'Well done,' I said. 'I wish more tenant farmers followed your example.'

Rémy with his hand poised over the beautifully packed slabs of butter ranged one beside the other on a tray and a clean napkin, looked round to see that nobody was listening.

'If you are looking for somebody to buy your grass next year, Mme Henrey, I might well be interested.'

'I hardly think that likely,' I said light heartedly. 'I'm quite happy with the Roberts. They are a delightful couple.'

Rémy dismissed my airy remark.

'I just thought . . .' he said. 'I wanted to be the first to ask.'

'What do you mean?' I asked suddenly, fear pounding at my breast.

I knew now that he was hiding important news. 'Has something happened that I'm not aware of?'

'Well . . .' said Rémy, noncommital.

'Please tell me?' I asked.

'Rumour has it that the Roberts will not be renewing their arrangement with you next spring.'

'Did they tell you so?'

'No,' he said. 'It's just a rumour.'

He waited for the news to produce its full impact.

'Well, think about it, Mme Henrey.'

This was the kind of experience to plunge me into dark unhappiness. I hated things to happen behind my back, to be told in a crafty, cunning way, something that everybody except myself knew about.

What could possibly want to make the Roberts, for whom I had quite a real affection, take such a decision without telling me?

Somebody else's birthday was in mid-August, and every year when I was in France I would go down to convey him my good wishes. He was the doyen, the wisest, the richest, and most respected of our citizens – Maître Vincent, the notary. Here at the corner of the Rue Pasteur was his house, now his eldest son Jean's house – the offices very airy and modern, forming part of it. A small empire of its own.

I saw him first just before the Second World War when he drew up the documents by which Victor Duprez sold me the farm. The notary lived with his family at that time in a large house facing the sea. The sound of the waves beating against the foreshore at high water rolled through the northern windows of his study and lost themselves in the stillness of the park into which the southern windows led by a short flight of steps. He was a little man with a neat moustache, mocking blue eyes, and an impeccably cut suit. There was a heavy oak desk in the middle of his study which he used for the signing of documents. Another, much smaller, at which he sat when alone, stood under a gilt mirror, into which it was his habit to look up quickly as the clerk opened the big double doors. This trick allowed him to size up his clients in a split unsuspected second before he turned to greet them. By that time he had a shrewd idea of what the peasant mind would shortly try so hard to conceal.

He had fought bravely through the First World War, especially at Verdun, of which photographs hung on the wall. His smile was delicious, and he had a gift of expressing himself with devastating clarity. His voice attacked an enemy sardonically and stopped dead when it had finished saying what it wanted to say, so that those farmers who feared him most declared that he stabbed them with a smile.

During the Occupation the villa by the sea was abandoned because the Germans requisitioned most of the promenade for fortifications. The Vincents therefore moved to their present house at the corner of the Rue Pasteur. In addition Mme Vincent, the notary's wife, owned a house at Caen. Towards the end of the war, Jean, the eldest son, joined the maquis and Mme Vincent, believing Caen to be safer than the seaside, took their little girl and their youngest boy there. Then came the sudden landings and the aerial bombardment of the city. Nobody ever heard of Mme Vincent and the two youngest children after that. They completely disappeared, perhaps under the devastation of what was once their beautiful house, buried under those English and American bombs for which Maître Vincent, the one really patriotic man in the village, had so often prayed. What irony!

My husband was the first to see him again after this tragedy. He had flown over from London, and was talking to Jean, the eldest son, when the door opened and Maître Vincent appeared, looking very small and wan. My husband hurried forward. The door closed, and the notary, without a word, buried his head in the bend of my husband's outstretched arm. He remained thus, a moment, sobbing. Then he drew himself up and turned his features to the wall to hide his tears. My husband could do nothing to lessen the grief of this broken heart. He saw again the arid desolation of Caen stretching away to infinity, beyond the ruined church of St Sauveur. There perhaps, under the rubble, lay the notary's wife and two children.

Time probably helped to heal these wounds but if tragedy was to be his lot over the death of his wife and two children under aerial bombardment in an agony presumed though never proved, which only after long months had to be accepted, other influences at his birth did their best to compensate. Everything he touched, as if in a fairy story, turned to gold.

Land, which when he was a young man nobody wanted, for a few francs and tenaciously held, added to, rounded off, became as the notary grew into old age of prodigious value. The years sat lightly on his frail shoulders, and with a mind attuned to every subtle change, he saw himself approaching the age of ninety, crowned with wisdom and with gold. People considered him like some local Croesus, last king of Lydia. He became a legend.

His birthday fell on the same day as Napoleon's, and this was very important for him. It gave him confidence in his ability to achieve his particular line of greatness. He fell ill some six weeks before his ninetieth birthday, and on a lovely, warm, July afternoon Dominique and I went to see him at the clinic at Deauville. My little grand-daughter brought with her a great bunch of roses from the garden and advanced timidly towards him – a slight pathetic figure in the narrow, high hospital bed, his intelligent features wan against the white pillows. The little girl of eight, and the sage of eighty-nine considered each other and smiled. They made together a span of close on one hundred years.

'I've brought you roses from the garden,' she said.

It was, after all, through him that we had bought the house and the garden.

The sun shone through the huge plate glass window of this very modern clinic. But the room was cold and bare – not even a vase for the roses.

Some days later they brought him back to the house at the corner of the Rue Pasteur. The Abbé Thiron went to see him. 'How was it?' I asked him later. 'Towards the end?'

'You mean what did he say?' asked the good parish priest. 'He said to me: "Please, Monsieur l'Abbé, *aidez-moi à mourir*. Help me to die!"'

Balzac would have known how to tell the story of Maître Vincent, no ordinary man. About the youthful warrior at Verdun, and how a young man's carefully saved-up coppers, – his *sous* – were to be turned by the good fairy into gold. Much can be achieved – and a great deal suffered – in so very many years. It would be a man's story. These few lines are quite inadequate. Martha Saxton, in an admirable life of Louisa May Alcott I was then reading, quoted Nathaniel Hawthorne as saying to his publisher, James Fields:

'All women as authors are feeble and tiresome. I wish they were forbidden to write!'

Our arrival on board the *San Lucar*, – without my grand-daughter (now with her other grandmother in Gloucestershire) – was like entering into a Belgian home. The big table with its damask cloth and beautiful silver was little different from a comfortable dining room in the home of a Flemish burgher. The scene was terribly reminiscent of the great painters. Through long windows one saw the *Sarah Munro* against the sunlit background of a summer tide, the two ships gently riding at anchor, breathing slowly and deeply like living things.

Erni and Bud came visiting, looking their very best. Bud's round features were rosy and scrubbed. Erni wore a yellow rose above one ear, pinned into her hair which was built up like a beehive. Her necklace and bracelets sang with warm, red gold. Both almost exaggerated their happiness, their fleeting moments of joy.

Yolande Smeets bent over the electric toaster with a huge pile of ready–cut bread. There had been a fuse and her husband and Albert had been putting it right. It was useful to have two such able men about the place. The caviare in its big Russian tin reposed on ice. The vodka was open, the glasses set, the Champagne ready to be uncorked. Toasts fell joyously out of the electric toaster, mountains of hot toast ready to be buttered and covered with caviare. Yolande took her seat at the head of the table, with me on her right. We kept up a long, enthralling exchange of female chatter while the rest of the table carried on. She wore a black bandeau round her head and smoked a long, narrow Belgian cigar which sent a delicious aroma through the evening air. She looked like a pirate on board her trusted vessel. One expected her at any moment to intone:

> *Fifteen men on the Dead Man's Chest –*
> *Yo-ho-ho-, and a bottle of rum!*
> *Drink and the devil had done for the rest –*
> *Yo-ho-ho, and a bottle of rum!*

It was not the skull and cross bones but the Belgian flag that hung from the stern of the ship. I never saw this flag without memories of 'Brave Little Belgium' of 1914.

'But,' said Yolande when I mentioned this, 'you would be surprised how few people in France recognize it. It happens that we are on occasion even taken for East or West Germans. One sometimes has the impression that our flag carries greater weight in England than in France.'

She laughed. Such problems notwithstanding, she was determined to be happy on this last evening of the season before they all returned to Antwerp. Her husband had engaged a man to help with the two engines and the navigation. This year he was beginning to feel that running so large a ship all by himself (except, of course, for the help he received from herself and the two girls!) was a big responsibility. Depending on the weather they might take three, even four days, to complete the journey. Often they would set out at dawn in the calmest sea, only to run into the teeth of a gale before night. The English Channel was treacherous even at this time of year. It was sad to think that when they came back to Deauville next summer they might not find the *Sarah Munro* at its usual berth. Would Erni and Bud desert Deauville or perhaps come and stay for a short while in an hotel? But suppose another owner sat on the deck of the *Sarah Munro*. Another flag but the Blue Ensign flew from the stern? How could a man bear a sight like that?

But now they must open another bottle of champagne and keep their thoughts exclusively happy. For Yolande Smeets this season at Deauville had again been memorable because her lovely daughter, Carole, had danced with Prince Charles when he came over for the polo. That was something that could not fail to remain bright and fresh in the mind of any young girl! Moreover this was the second summer that it had happened. 'These,' said Yolande, 'are great satisfactions for a mother!' She smiled at the memory of her tall, lovely daughter back like Cinderella from the ball, having danced with the heir to the British throne!

Erni also was smiling.

'How I loved dancing at her age,' she said. 'I think I could have danced half my life away!'

Some days passed before I drove back to the yacht basin. The *San Lucar* had gone. Its berth was empty. Bud's red car with the Swiss number plate was parked on the quay by the stern of the *Sarah Munro*, and as we came nearer we saw Erni and Bud packing luggage into the boot.

'You are not going yet?' I called.

We had not expected them to leave for at least another ten days.

'The weather is breaking,' said Erni, kissing me on both cheeks. 'We must return to Grindelwald.'

'Albert will stay for a while,' said Bud. 'Then he goes back to his own family in England.'

'Oh!' I sighed, 'and I've brought you the last roses of the summer.'

'Let's go back to the saloon,' said Bud. 'We have time for a final drink.'

The saloon looked just as it always did – warm and cosy. Winston Churchill was still in his frame, the armchairs and sofa inviting. Bud poured me the usual tonic water.

Erni appeared restless. She put the roses in water and then paced up and down the room, picking up various small objects. There was a Swiss calf bell, smaller than a cow bell but with an equally beautiful sound reminiscent of spring in the mountain passes. She held it up, caught Bud's eye and asked:

'Can I?'

'Of course,' said Bud.

Erni put the bell in my basket, and added a multitude of other small objects to it as if anxious to keep the memory of our friendship long and deep.

'We could perhaps stay a little longer on board,' said Bud, reflectively. 'I mean until it grows dark – or even till morning.'

'It would be better to go now.' said Erni.

We walked up the gangway. There, on the quay, I bade them farewell. I did not feel inclined to watch them driving off in their little red car.

Back on the farm, Mme Robert was driving the cattle out of the home field.

'The cider apples are beginning to drop into the grass,' she said. 'Soon we shall come to gather the early ones.'

She was pretty in the evening light and had the most endearing smile.

I would have to ask her if there was any truth in what Remy had said but not for the moment. I would wait. So many other problems loomed ahead now that another winter was on the way.